ONTOLOGY MADE EASY

ONTOLOGY MADE EASY

Amie L. Thomasson

OXFORD
UNIVERSITY PRESS

OXFORD

UNIVERSITY PRESS

Oxford University Press is a department of the University of Oxford.
It furthers the University's objective of excellence in research, scholarship,
and education by publishing worldwide.

Oxford   New York
Auckland   Cape Town   Dar es Salaam   Hong Kong   Karachi
Kuala Lumpur   Madrid   Melbourne   Mexico City   Nairobi
New Delhi   Shanghai   Taipei   Toronto

With offices in
Argentina   Austria   Brazil   Chile   Czech Republic   France   Greece
Guatemala   Hungary   Italy   Japan   Poland   Portugal   Singapore
South Korea   Switzerland   Thailand   Turkey   Ukraine   Vietnam

Oxford is a registered trademark of Oxford University Press
in the UK and certain other countries.

Published in the United States of America by
Oxford University Press
198 Madison Avenue, New York, NY 10016

© Oxford University Press 2015

Library of Congress Cataloging-in-Publication Data
Thomasson, Amie L. (Amie Lynn), 1968–
Ontology made easy / Amie L. Thomasson.
pages cm
ISBN 978–0–19–938511–9 (hardcover : alk. paper)   1. Ontology.   I. Title.
BD311.T45 2015
111—dc23
2014008982

3 5 7 9 8 6 4 2
Printed in the United States of America
on acid-free paper

To my parents, Clarissa Camfield Thomasson
and Walter Neill Thomasson

CONTENTS

PART I
DEVELOPING EASY ONTOLOGY

PART II
DEFENDING EASY ONTOLOGY

CONTENTS

ACKNOWLEDGMENTS

I am extremely grateful for support that granted me the time to write this book. A semester of support from the University of Miami Center for the Humanities enabled me to start the project in 2011, and a fellowship for academic year 2013–14 from the National Endowment for the Humanities enabled me to finish it. My enduring thanks go to both the Humanities Center and the National Endowment for the Humanities for this crucial support.

I have been presenting work related to this book for some time, and am so thankful for all of the helpful comments and constructive criticisms that have been made during my various presentations. I only wish I could remember all the names to list here, though that would no doubt put the manuscript over its word limit. At any rate, you know who you are, and please know that you are appreciated. I would also like to thank my students, Nurbay Irmak, Sarah Beth Lesson, and Kyle Driggers, who worked through an early draft of the manuscript with me during an independent study and offered many valuable insights. My greatest thanks go to Uriah Kriegel and Simon Evnine, whose detailed and helpful comments on complete drafts helped me restructure the project at different crucial stages; I am so fortunate to have philosopher friends like them to give such insightful assistance. I also wish to express my deep gratitude to a number of philosophers who were so generous as to read and comment on the whole manuscript, including Huw Price, Paul Livingston, Alan Thomas, Mark Moyer, David Kovacs, and David Ripley. For comments on individual chapters, I wish to thank Thomas Hofweber, Stephen Yablo, and Richard Creath. For multiple insightful discussions, I also would like to thank Tim Button, Ted Sider, Stephen Schiffer, and Eli Hirsch. I have also been very lucky to have Amanda McMullen as my excellent research assistant, who helped with two phases of editing as well as with philosophical comments and discussion. Thanks to Peter Ohlin for being an awesome and supportive editor. My greatest debt, always, is to my husband, Peter Lewis, for philosophical support (particularly whenever I edged incautiously into territory bordering on philosophy of science), and endless moral and logistical support. My thanks and love also go to Natalie, for her boundless confidence in me and also for putting up with me being away to present this work on many occasions, and to May, for occasionally sleeping while I write, and for always cheering me up when I'm not writing. The book is dedicated with love and gratitude to my parents, Clarissa Camfield Thomasson and Walter Neill Thomasson. Ontology may be easy, but life is not. The further I go on the more I come to appreciate all the love and guidance they gave me, and still give me, to help deal with all of its difficulties.

Earlier versions of parts of the material published here have appeared in article form. Chapter 1 overlaps with my paper "Carnap and the Prospects for Easy Ontology", forthcoming in *Ontology after Carnap* (ed. Stephan Blatti and Sandra LaPointe, Oxford: Oxford University Press); thanks to Oxford University Press for permission to use this material here. Parts of chapter 2 (now heavily revised) were first published by Springer in *Philosophical Studies*, vol. 141 (2008), pp. 63–78, as "Existence Questions", and appear here with kind permission from Springer Science and Business Media. Portions of chapter 3 appear in "Easy Ontology and its Consequences", in Gary Ostertag, ed., *Meanings and Other Things* (essays on the work of Stephen Schiffer), Oxford: Oxford University Press, forthcoming, and I thank Oxford University Press for permission to use this material here. An earlier version of chapter 5 was published as "Fictionalism versus Deflationism", *Mind*, 2013, doi:10.1093/mind/fzt055, and appears here by permission of Oxford University Press. Finally, earlier drafts of parts of chapter 6 were first published by Springer in *Axiomathes*, vol.19 (2009), pp. 1–15, as "The Easy Approach to Ontology", and appear here with kind permission from Springer Science and Business Media B.V.

INTRODUCTION

The Forgotten Easy Approach

Ontology, the discipline now considered to lie at the center of metaphysics, is concerned to answer existence questions. In recent metaphysics, many of the most vigorous and contested debates focus on existence questions such as "Do numbers exist?", "Do ordinary objects, such as tables and chairs, exist?", "Do people exist?", "Do mereological sums exist?", and "Do temporal parts exist?".

Beyond answering these individual existence questions, metaphysicians strive to formulate 'an ontology'—a total view of what exists. In recent work we see defenses of an ever-widening array of ontologies. Some accept the existence of ordinary objects, microscopica, and mereological sums of any arbitrary combination of entities. Others accept the existence only of simples. Others accept only one single great 'blobject'. Others accept the existence of simples and organisms but deny the existence of artifacts, and so on, seemingly ad infinitum.

Most of the existence questions that fill the pages of current journals hardly arose until the mid to late twentieth century, and existence questions have only really proliferated in the last few decades. Of course some existence questions have always played a central role in metaphysics, for example, "Does God exist?", "Does free will exist?", and even "Do universals exist?" But many of the currently contested ontological questions, e.g. "Do tables, chairs, and persons exist?" would have been thought far too obvious to be worth contesting. Even where similar existence questions appear to have surfaced in classical debates, they were generally about the *natures* of familiar things rather than their *existence*. So, for example, Berkeley did not deny the existence of everyday objects such as tables and chairs, but rather held the view that they were collections of ideas rather than objects made of 'matter' (an idea he thought confused and even contradictory). Other debates, about recondite philosophical entities such as mereological sums and temporal parts, had not even been dreamed of. Indeed the sorts of debates about existence that have made ontology into the core of metaphysics have really only taken center stage in the last sixty years or so, after the ascendency of a neo-Quinean approach to metaphysics.

The neo-Quinean approach to ontology treats ontological questions as continuous with the questions of the natural sciences. The idea, roughly, is that the enterprise of ontology is that of developing the best 'total theory', where that involves choosing the theory with the most theoretic virtues, including (prominently) simplicity. In Quine's familiar words:

> Our acceptance of an ontology is, I think, similar in principle to our acceptance of a scientific theory, say a system of physics: we adopt, at least insofar as we are reasonable, the simplest conceptual scheme into which the disordered fragments of raw experience can be fitted and arranged. Our ontology is determined once we have fixed upon the over-all conceptual scheme which is to accommodate science in the broadest sense.
>
> (Quine 1948/1953, 16–17)

It is this approach that has led to the prominence of 'ontological' questions over the past sixty years, and to the seriousness with which metaphysicians take them. The neo-Quinean approach has also created a whole industry within philosophy that had no equal before: the industry of 'formulating an ontology', defending detailed views about which things exist (and which purported things should be 'eliminated'), on grounds largely of the ability of the 'theory' to preserve such theoretic virtues as simplicity of ontology and ideology, explanatory power, and empirical adequacy better than its rivals. The theories formulated are presented as being like scientific theories, only deeper and more general.[1]

The neo-Quinean approach has become so dominant as to become almost invisible as a methodological choice. As Ted Sider puts it, "Recent work on ontology nearly always relies on the Quinean methodology" (2011, 169). The new metaphysics, dominated by ontology, is, from a methodological point of view, a neo-Quinean metaphysics—so much so that David Manley simply refers to this approach as "mainstream metaphysics" (2009). To those brought up on analytic philosophy over the past sixty years, the neo-Quinean conception of ontology has come to seem natural, even inevitable. Indeed it seems to be such a natural view that it is hard to see any other way of viewing debates about existence; either you happily jump in, trying to formulate a novel 'ontology' or provide a novel defense of or attack on someone else's, or you wander off in perplexity to work on other philosophical topics.

One thing that I hope to make clear in this book, however, is that the neo-Quinean approach is not as inevitable as it has come

1. As may be clear from the above, here I will use the term 'neo-Quinean' quite broadly, to include all those approaches to ontological questions that engage in a quasi-scientific attempt to develop the best 'total theory', where these questions are supposed to not be resolvable by conceptual or straightforward empirical means. Thus in this sense even some of those who reject Quine's particular criterion of ontological commitment in favor of some other (which they take to play the proper role in theory choice) may in this sense be classified as 'neo-Quinean'. For discussion of problems with that criterion see, e.g. Cameron (2008), Dyke (2008) and my (2007a, chapter 9).

to seem. I hope to show, first, that it is not inevitable in a historical sense. On the contrary, seen in the broader historical context it is quite a newcomer, diverging from ways of seeing philosophy, its proper roles and methods, that were dominant in the decades and centuries that preceded Quine. I will begin to make that point next. In the remainder of the book, I aim to show that it is not inevitable in a philosophical sense either, for there is a viable and indeed in many ways preferable alternative. That alternative is what I shall call the 'easy' approach to ontology. The approach (I will argue) may be traced back to Carnap's approach to handling what he called 'internal' existence questions, and has occasionally surfaced in isolated pockets since then, despite the dominance of neo-Quinean methodology. But it has seldom been seen as a unified movement, so that the commonalities among the views can be seen and their prospects and consequences assessed.

I hope in this book to do just that: to unearth the roots of a more modest, easy approach to existence questions. I aim to explicate how the view works and how it compares to some more familiar options, and to provide a unified defense of it against the variety of arguments that have been, and could be, wielded against it— all with a view to presenting it as an attractive alternative to the neo-Quinean mainstream.

I.1. THE HISTORICAL BACKSTORY

Looked at in the broader context of the history of philosophy, the neo-Quinean approach that has turned into 'mainstream meta-physics' does not seem at all inevitable. Instead, it is quite an outlier.[2] Indeed if it were looked at from around a hundred years ago, it would seem bizarre.

2. In fact, as I shall discuss below, it is unclear that this neo-Quinean approach that has come to characterize serious metaphysics is truly *Quinean*, in the historical sense.

After the diverse scientific disciplines began to peel themselves away from the general heading of 'natural philosophy', beginning with physics in the seventeenth century and ending with psychology at the end of the nineteenth century, perhaps the most pressing and recurrent question for philosophers became: what is the proper role, and what are the proper methods of philosophy, given the successes of the natural sciences? By the early decades of the twentieth century, such concerns had taken a central role, becoming a core obsession for many philosophers, from Husserl to Ryle to Wittgenstein. Thus, Ryle says of philosophers of his generation: "We philosophers were in for a near-lifetime of enquiry into our own title to be enquirers" (1970, 10).

The question was all the more pressing, as natural scientists seemed capable of converging in their results and theories, while philosophers seemed able only to prolong disputes and provide an ever-diverging range of answers to philosophical questions— a divergence that has exploded in post-Quinean metaphysics.

An answer that tempted certain empiricists was that the natural sciences were concerned with external, physical phenomena, whereas philosophy was concerned with internal, mental phenomena—a view that culminated in the psychologism Jakob Fries and Friedrich Beneke developed in the early to mid-nineteenth century. Brentano held that the concepts of mental phenomena must be acquired empirically through inner perception (a kind of simultaneous secondary awareness that Brentano held accompanies all our intentional states) (1874/1995). But Brentano saw that there are two ways in which one can go on to study mental phenomena (once those concepts are in hand): the first way is to study them

See Price for detailed arguments that "it turns out to be simply an illusion to think that Quine offers a recipe for any more substantial kind of metaphysics" (2009, 344).

empirically, seeking to understand their cause-effect relations (this he called 'genetic' or 'physiological' psychology). The second way is to study them in a 'pure' or a priori manner, analyzing the fundamental types of mental phenomena to determine, for example, what in general distinguishes judgments from mere presentations (this he called 'psychognosy' or 'descriptive psychology'), or in what ways different mental phenomena may be combined (Brentano 1995).

The latter sort of study, he often emphasized, is independent of the results of natural sciences like chemistry and physics, and does not have *explanatory* aims; instead it works through the concepts themselves to give us truths of reason, not truths of fact. Those doing this kind of work "must intuitively grasp the general laws wherever the necessity or impossibility of unifying certain elements becomes clear *through the concepts themselves*" (1995, 75, italics mine). The first of these approaches to the mental was to develop into empirical psychology; the second into phenomenology.

In developing phenomenology—which he considered the same as philosophy in general—Husserl would preserve the same distinction, writing:

> *Pure* phenomenology . . . is, on the one hand, an ancillary to *psychology* conceived as an *empirical science*. Proceeding in purely intuitive fashion, it analyses and describes in their essential generality . . . the experiences of presentation, judgment and knowledge, experiences which, treated as classes of real events in the natural context of zoological reality, receive a scientific probing at the hands of empirical psychology.
>
> *(1970, 249)*

On this view, then, the difference between the natural sciences and philosophy is not to be understood in terms of the phenomena studied (internal mental phenomena versus external physical phenomena), but rather in the method of study: the work of the natural sciences involves *empirical* work; that of philosophy involves *conceptual* work. This carries over to the famous and devastating criticisms Husserl (1900/2000) and Frege (1884/1974) both leveled against psychologism—taken as the view that the laws of philosophy, logic, or mathematics are psychological laws. For these attacks on psychologism were further aimed to clearly distinguish the role and methods of philosophy, logic, and mathematics from those of the empirical sciences. We might empirically study our minds, patterns of inference, or acts of mathematical reasoning all we like, but empirically investigating our actual thoughts *about* these subjects will not amount to doing philosophy, logic, or mathematics. In contrast with empirical psychology, the disciplines of philosophy, logic, and mathematics are not concerned with empirical psychological occurrences at all, and do not proceed empirically.

By the early twentieth century, a fairly uniform answer emerged to the question of respective roles of philosophy and the natural sciences:[3] philosophy and the natural sciences were seen as distinct and complementary. Roughly, the view was that philosophy is undertaken by *conceptual* methods (e.g., involved in linguistic or conceptual analysis); the sciences are undertaken by *empirical* methods and concerned with matters of fact. This is a view we see developed in Husserlian phenomenology, which also (via Husserl) would influence Gilbert Ryle and the development of ordinary language philosophy (cf. my 2002). Thus, Ryle, echoing Husserl, would write of his own *The Concept of Mind*: "The book could be described as a sustained essay in phenomenology, if you are at home with that label . . . . The book does not profess to be a contribution to any science, not even to psychology. If any factual

---

3. For a bit of background on prior answers and the emergence of this answer, see my (2002).

assertions are made in it, they are there through the author's confusion of mind" (1962/1971, 188). Ryle of course went on to defend
the view that the primary work of philosophy lay in conceptual
analysis (1970, 10–11), a task clearly distinguished from empirical
work. He took conceptual analysis to be involved in uncovering
the 'logical grammar' of expressions of various types, distinguishing sense from nonsense, and drawing attention to category distinctions (1971b, 170).

The idea that the philosopher is engaged in the conceptual work
of analysis, distinguishing sense from nonsense, and the like, rather
than in any empirical study of matters of fact also famously surfaces in the work of Wittgenstein. Even at the stage of the *Tractatus*,
Wittgenstein took a central goal of his philosophical work to be simply distinguishing sense from nonsense: "The book will . . . draw
a limit to thinking, or rather—not to thinking, but to the expression of thoughts . . . . The limit can . . . only be drawn in language
and what lies on the other side of the limit will be simply nonsense"
(1922/1933, Preface); "most of the propositions and questions
to be found in philosophical works are not false but nonsensical"
(1922/1933, 4.003). His later work developed the idea that philosophy is largely a battle against bewitchment of our understanding by
means of language (1953/2001, §109), and that the philosopher's
job is thus to reveal nonsense that is concealed: "For philosophical
problems arise when language *goes on holiday*" (1953/2001, §38).
This again involves a clear distinction between the roles of the
empirical sciences and philosophy. On this view, philosophy is not
concerned with constructing explanations or developing theories
as the natural sciences do. Instead (in words that echo Brentano's
original distinction between genetic and descriptive psychology) Wittgenstein insists: "We must do away with all *explanation,*
and description alone must take its place" (1953/2001, §109).
The tendency to think that philosophy should seek theories and

explanations like those in the empirical sciences, Wittgenstein held, "is the real source of metaphysics, and leads the philosopher into complete darkness" (1958, 18; cf. Hacker 1996, 117).[4]

In short, the basic idea that the fundamental roles of philosophy and the sciences are distinct and that the philosopher's primary work is conceptual rather than empirical work persisted across thinkers with otherwise very diverse presuppositions and interests—thinkers as diverse as Husserl, Wittgenstein, Carnap, and Ryle.[5] Differences abounded among philosophers about how we should understand 'conceptual analysis', and regarding whether one aimed largely to provide a positive analysis of meanings or the corresponding essences, to highlight category distinctions, or to distinguish sense from nonsense (the meaningful from the meaningless).[6] Nonetheless, the commonalities among these philosophers who took the role of philosophy to be distinct from that of the natural sciences, and concerned in some sense with conceptual matters (or perhaps better, the corresponding essences, studied using conceptual analysis), not matters of fact, make them far more like each other in their conception of the role and methods of philosophy than any of them resembles the Quinean naturalism that follows.

From this earlier point of view, the idea that metaphysicians were engaged in discovering deep truths about what exists or about the most basic constituents of the world, doing something like the natural sciences, only more deep and general, would have sounded

---

4. Related to this, I argue in chapter 3 that the easy approach to existence questions gives us a kind of simple realism (asserting that the disputed entities exist) but not a form of realism that is explanatory in the way Platonist views often purport to be.

5. For further discussion of the view that philosophy is concerned with matters of meaning, science with matters of fact, and of how it developed in phenomenology and ordinary language philosophy see my (2007c) and (2002).

6. For an excellent discussion of the different sorts of analysis, see Beaney (2007, 1–30 and 196–216).

bizarre, misguided. Indeed it would have seemed like a throwback to days before Hume's admonition to "commit to the flames" any writing that neither engages in abstract reasoning concerning quantity or number or "experimental reasoning concerning matter of fact and existence" (1777/1977, 114). In fact, looked at in the context of the broader history of philosophy for the last 150 years or so, it is the neo-Quinean approach that is the outlier, built as it is on the denial that there is any division of labor between philosophy and the empirical sciences.

The tradition of thinking of philosophy and the natural sciences as engaged in separate projects found one of its strongest and clearest formulations in the work of the logical empiricists of the Vienna Circle. On their view, philosophy and science were seen as having distinct roles and distinct methods: philosophy is concerned with a kind of linguistic or meaning analysis, which reveals analytic/necessary truths that are independent of any empirical assumptions; science, by contrast, is engaged in empirical enquiry aiming to discover matters of fact (Ayer 1936/1952, 57). 'Metaphysics' was often used as a term of abuse, and was considered acceptable only to the extent that it could be seen not as attempting to state truths about the world, but as concerned only with *analytic* questions. (Ayer argues at length, however, that a great deal of historical work in metaphysics—especially that of empiricists such as Locke, Berkeley and Hume—is really undertaking in analysis in this sense (1936/1952, 51–55)). Analytic statements, as Ayer understood them, are tautologies that make no factual claims about the world. They are knowable a priori, express necessary truths, and are true just given the meanings of the terms involved. Empirical statements, by contrast, are true or false in virtue of both the meanings of the terms involved and the way the world is; they are attempts to describe the world.

Philosophy is a diverse discipline, and here I do not aim to discuss the roles and methods of philosophy generally. Instead, the focus is limited to metaphysics—indeed to that part of metaphysics which is concerned with existence questions. The present work is part of a more global project of returning to a more modest and clear conception of the methods, roles, and epistemology of metaphysics than may be found in most recent work on and in the subject. It is a project in line with the goal of relying on nothing more than conceptual and(/or) empirical investigations as methods of acquiring knowledge, and on which there is a division of labor, with the metaphysician's share of work lying on the conceptual side and the natural sciences on the empirical. (This of course does not preclude the idea that they may, and often must, work together in answering existence questions or constructing and reconstructing conceptual systems.) It is thus a project firmly in the tradition of Husserl, Ryle, and others listed above—while breaking with the more recent neo-Quinean tradition. Nonetheless, I will not undertake the whole of that project here. For the focus here will be squarely on existence questions, though these form only a part (though a central part) of metaphysics.

Metaphysics of course is concerned with many other sorts of questions as well: modal questions about the natures or essences of things of various sorts, their identity and persistence conditions, and so on[7], as well as other (in some cases (re)-emerging) questions about what is fundamental, what grounds what, and so on. Those and other topics in metaphysics must be treated separately. The aim of this book is not to provide a death blow to metaphysics, but rather to develop an alternative way of looking at that particular corner of metaphysics which deals with existence questions. Primarily,

---

7. I have discussed modal questions elsewhere (2007b and 2013), and plan to treat them at greater length in the future. Indeed this book was originally planned with two halves: one on existence questions, the other on modal questions. Due to length constraints, however, the parts have separated, and a more thorough treatment of modal questions will appear separately.

I hope to clarify and revive a view that has been little considered in the last few decades—but that just may make more sense all things considered, and may be seen as preferable by those who approach these debates from a neutral starting point. I will return in the conclusion to assess how the work of metaphysics may change if we do adopt this view of existence questions: what questions remain to be investigated, and which inquiries may need to be undertaken in a new key. One might hope, however, that if we can escape the morass of neo-Quinean metaphysics we may find related work that can be done in a more epistemically transparent way and that may turn out to be far more productive.

Given the historical view outlined above about the relative roles of philosophy and the natural sciences, what sense can be made of existence questions? The best-developed historical answer along these lines comes in the work of Rudolf Carnap. On Carnap's view, those existence questions that may be seen as questions about matters of fact ('internal questions') can be answered straightforwardly, using conceptual and/or empirical methods. So, for example, questions about the existence of ivory-billed woodpeckers may be answered using the empirical methods of the biological sciences; questions about the existence of prime numbers between twenty and thirty may be resolved by mathematical reasoning. From these we may also make easy inferences to answer more general questions. For if there are ivory-billed woodpeckers there are organisms, and if there are primes between twenty and thirty, then there are numbers. Any other attempted existence questions ('external questions'), he argued, can be understood as sensible only if we take them to be implicitly pragmatic questions about whether or not to accept the relevant linguistic framework. I will have far more to say in interpretation and defense of this view below. For now it is simply worth noting that this is a view on which those questions about what exists that are well formulated (and are, as they purport to be, questions about matters of fact: about what exists) may be straightforwardly answered through empirical and/or conceptual means, in line with the modest approach to philosophy that dominated the pre-Quinean landscape.

I.2. THE RISE OF NEO-QUINEANISM

Quine is widely thought to have rejected Carnap's approach, and made the world once again safe for metaphysics, inaugurating a view of metaphysics as continuous with science, and engaged in theory choice by considering which theory has the greatest theoretic virtues.[8] Sider describes the approach as follows:

> We employ many of the same criteria—whatever those are—
> for theory choice within metaphysics that we employ outside of
> metaphysics. Admittedly, those criteria give less clear guidance
> in metaphysics than elsewhere; but there's no harm in follow-
> ing this argument where it leads: metaphysical inquiry is by its
> nature comparatively speculative and uncertain.
>
> *(2011, 12)*

The appeal of the neo-Quinean approach is obvious. After decades of dominance of ordinary language philosophy, and with it the idea that the philosopher's proper work lay in a form of conceptual analysis—not in discovering deep truths about the world—the thought that philosophers could return to their grander ambitions of discovering fundamental features of reality—and distinguishing what does and does not *really* exist—was appealing indeed. As

---

8. But again see Price (2009) for arguments that this is a misinterpretation and misappropriation of Quine.

Sider puts it, "Who would prefer exploring our perhaps parochial conceptual scheme to exploring the fundamental features of reality?" (2001, xxiv). Better still, one could adopt those old ambitions while clothing metaphysics in the modern respectable garb of science, borrowing its terminology and approach to theory choice, and insisting that there is no line to be drawn between them. But, unlike much work in the sciences, one need not work piecemeal on small focused questions to be resolved only given decades of cautious laboratory work, but instead may from one's armchair (perhaps equipped with recent journals on a nearby coffee table) pronounce directly on the total contents and structure of the world. To the intellectually ambitious metaphysician, what could seem more appealing? I will call this neo-Quinean approach to metaphysics, which takes questions about existence to be resolvable by serious philosophical argumentation, but not merely by empirical or conceptual means, 'hard ontology' in the sense that the neo-Quinean takes ontological questions to be deep and difficult philosophical questions requiring metaphysical inquiry and dispute, not as questions easily resolved by simple observations made utilizing conceptual and linguistic competence or by trivial inferences from uncontested truths.

Yet despite its appeal and widespread adoption, neo-Quinean metaphysics has proven to be, if not a dead end, certainly a morass. For although ontologists tend to appropriate the vocabulary of science and speak of themselves as formulating competing 'theories', unlike the sciences, we have nothing like convergence on the truth to show for our labors. Instead, every conference, every volume, seems to propagate more diverse and competing 'ontologies', with little agreement and little progress. Indeed there is little agreement not only about what the 'right' ontology is, but even about how we should go about deciding among them which is right, and which is wrong—apart from a vague appeal to a litany of theoretic virtues that seem to offer little help in narrowing down the choice of theories. This problem is compounded as loss of one theoretical virtue, such as ontological simplicity, is often compensated for by gain in another, such as ideological simplicity (see Bennett 2009, Kriegel 2013), and as competing metaphysical theories often accommodate the empirical data equally well (Kriegel 2013). On these grounds some have suggested that if we adopt the hard approach to ontology, we may have to simply resign ourselves to withholding judgment on many core ontological issues, where there are few or no grounds for choosing one theory over another (Bennett 2009, Kriegel 2013).

The neo-Quinean approach makes the epistemology of metaphysics obscure. First are familiar worries about the legitimacy of appeal to theoretic virtues even in deciding among scientific theories, worries that multiply when we ask whether these same virtues are relevant for choice among metaphysical theories. More directly to the point, although the neo-Quinean attempts to use the same criteria for 'theory choice' employed in the sciences, in the sciences empirical adequacy plays a prominent role in narrowing down our theory choices—yet there is seldom an empirical difference between competing metaphysical theories that would enable this criterion to play a selective role. Sider, perhaps the most explicit defender of the neo-Quinean approach, describes these worries for his approach as follows:

> The main ontological positions seem internally consistent and empirically adequate, so all the weight of theory-choice falls on the criteria; but are the criteria up to the task? What justifies the alleged theoretical insights? Are criteria that are commonly used in scientific theory choice (for example, simplicity and theoretical integration) applicable in metaphysics? How can these criteria be articulated clearly? And what hope is there

that the criteria will yield a determinate verdict, given the pau-
city of empirical input?

(2009, 385)

Moreover, when choices must be made among empirically equivalent scientific theories, appeals may be made to pragmatic advantages in simplifying our calculations and predictions—but those
doing hard ontology typically shun any merely pragmatic arguments in favor of adopting one proposal over another. Perhaps most
revealingly, simple appeal to theoretic virtues has proven woefully
inadequate in metaphysics to even narrowing down our choice of
theories—the menu of options seems ever widening, each justified
by appeal to best preserving theoretic virtues.

Other worries arise about what exactly the relation is supposed to
be between scientific and metaphysical inquiry on the neo-Quinean
model. While Quine does say the two are 'continuous', it is not clear
that this is to endow metaphysics with the respectability of science
rather than suggesting that the pragmatic element in metaphysics
affects scientific theorizing as well (Price 2009, 326–27). Moreover,
it is not at all clear that Quine himself meant to give—or has room
(given his other commitments) to give—any role to philosophers
at all in theory choice. Instead, he is insisting that if science reaches
the stage of accepting, say, that quantification over mathematical
entities is indispensible, "then there is no philosophical standpoint
from which it makes sense to doubt that there are mathematical
entities" (Price 2009, 338). The point is not to give the philosopher
a special role in assessing what ontology we should adopt (given
what science says), but rather to deflate or disallow "a certain sort
of ontological debate: a debate taking place outside science, about
whether there are things of the kind science quantifies over" (Price
2009, 338–9). Yet those metaphysicians who follow what they take
to be a neo-Quinean methodology clearly assume that there is a

role for metaphysics in answering existence questions, in selecting among the best metaphysical theories. Neo-Quinean metaphysicians do not merely wait on and reiterate the results of the sciences; instead they seem to assume that the work of metaphysicians may overturn the declarations of the sciences—for a great many, perhaps most, metaphysical theories plainly reject a number of entities one or more of the natural sciences quantify over (organisms, composite objects, etc.).

Neo-Quineans seldom clarify the exact relation supposed to hold between science and metaphysics, but one point that is clearly assumed is that, on this model, existence questions are to be resolved at least largely by philosophical debates about which 'total theory' exhibits the most theoretic virtues. A further assumption is that ontological questions about existence turn out to be hard in that they not only require protracted debate, but also can be answered neither by direct empirical methods nor by conceptual analysis: that they are (in Sider's phrase) "epistemically metaphysical" (2011, 187), giving metaphysical work a distinctive and important role in theory choice.

It is worth noting that neither of these difficulties arises for the older, division-of-labor, view. On that view, the epistemology is relatively clear and unproblematic: answers to ontological questions may be given by conceptual or empirical methods or (most usually) a combination of these two.[9] There is no reliance on the idea that any question can be answered by methods that are 'epistemically metaphysical' in the above sense; instead we may make

---

9. I say 'relatively' clear and unproblematic, since issues linger about how to understand the possibilities of acquiring knowledge through conceptual means. This is of course a much larger issue that I have touched on elsewhere (2007b) and to which I will return. But it is an issue that arises for anyone who thinks there is conceptually based knowledge, say in logic, mathematics or elsewhere. It is not a problem unique to those who take this meta-ontological approach.

use of familiar and pedestrian conceptual and empirical work to answer existence questions. And the relation between the natural sciences and philosophy is kept clear as well: the sciences investigate empirical questions, while philosophers are distinctively concerned with conceptual issues (though obviously their work may intersect and interact in a variety of ways, and working scientists may also have to revise and choose among conceptual frameworks). We have here a clear division of labor—and one in which philosophy is not entitled to overturn the empirical results of the natural sciences.

I certainly do not mean to present any of these worries as decisive arguments against the neo-Quinean approach to ontology. Instead, I mean to simply provide a reminder of the difficulties into which this view, and this approach, has led us. These are difficulties that will, I hope, motivate us to look again at the arguments that brought us there, and to consider an alternative way of looking at existence questions.

The epistemic and methodological perplexities neo-Quinean metaphysics leaves us with—and, perhaps more prominently, the evident lack of convergence of ontological theories—have recently led new questions to be raised about the legitimacy of ontological debates, bringing meta-ontological questions back to the fore for the first time in sixty years or more. And so we now see intensive discussions about whether or not ontological disputes are 'merely verbal', whether the quantifier does or could vary in the mouths of disputants, and whether we can understand the quantifier (or a special Ontologese quantifier) as having a fixed meaning in virtue of 'carving the world at its logical joints'.

It is safe to say that the neo-Quinean approach to ontology has been far more often simply assumed and utilized in defending one or another ontological position than it has been explicitly laid out and defended in its own right. Some important defenses have been offered, however, by van Inwagen (2009) and Sider (2009, 2011) among others. But van Inwagen's defense takes largely the form of an attack on Heidegger, and asserting five Quinean theses, the first four of which are also accepted by defenders of the easy approach to ontology. The fifth, that ontological issues should be addressed using Quine's criterion of ontological commitment, van Inwagen explicates but does not defend against objections (for objections see Alston 1957, Searle 1969, 107, and my 2007a, 158–68). Sider's defenses of the neo-Quinean approach consist largely in showing how to respond to the threat of quantifier variance—the claim that there are multiple equally good candidate meanings for quantifiers, leading to the deflationary position that apparent ontological debates often are mere cases of disputants talking past each other by using the quantifier in different senses. Indeed he takes quantifier variance to be *the* threat facing neo-Quinean metaphysics, and the route deflationists must take: "the central question of metaontology is that of whether there are many equally good quantifier meanings, or whether there is a single best quantifier meaning" (Sider 2009, 397).

I will argue in chapter 1, however, that this is mistaken—that there is an alternative to neo-Quinean methodology that does not rely on quantifier variance. And so, as I will argue, even as meta-ontological issues have been raised once again, in most of the recent discussion, there is a deflationary position—and a deflationary threat to the neo-Quinean approach—that has largely been missed. The missed position is not some obscure newcomer, but rather a view along the lines of Carnap's original form of ontological deflationism—that very deflationism which was thought to have been defeated by Quine as he inaugurated a renaissance for hard metaphysics. That is the view I will defend below: the 'easy approach' to ontology.

I.3. THE EASY APPROACH TO ONTOLOGY: A PRELIMINARY SKETCH

On the view I shall argue for here, existence questions are not deep questions of metaphysics requiring some special philosophical insight or formulation of a total 'best theory' to answer. I will argue that existence questions that are fully meaningful and well specified[10] are straightforwardly answerable by making use of our conceptual competence and (often) conducting straightforward empirical enquiries. (The philosopher's share of the work, I will argue, lies on the conceptual side.) I call this the 'easy' approach to existence questions, since it entails that those existence questions that are meaningful are not deep and difficult subjects for metaphysical dispute, but rather questions to be resolved straightforwardly by employing our conceptual competence, often combining this with empirical investigations.

Despite the dominance of neo-Quineanism, a small stream of the more modest approach has survived underground, surfacing occasionally in particular debates, as it was brought to light again by Crispin Wright (1983) and Bob Hale (with Crispin Wright 2001, 2009) in their neo-Fregean defense of numbers; by Stephen Schiffer (1996, 2003) in defense of a 'pleonastic' view of propositions, properties, fictional characters, and certain other sorts of entities; and by myself in defense of ordinary objects (2007a). But these approaches have seldom been seen as part of a unified approach to existence questions, nor have the relations among these views been made clear (this is a task I undertake in chapter 3).

---

10. Other existence questions that play a key role in motivating ontological debates (e.g., 'Is there some object here?', 'How many things are in this place and time?'), as understood by those practicing hard ontology, are (as I have argued elsewhere: 2007a, 2009a) badly formulated, unanswerable questions.

One thing all easy ontologists agree on is that answers to certain disputed ontological questions can be reached easily by starting from an uncontroversial truth (e.g., 'the cups and saucers are equinumerous' or 'snow is white') and reasoning by what seem like trivial steps (to 'the number of cups equals the number of saucers' or 'the proposition that snow is white is true') to reach ontological conclusions ('there are numbers'; 'there are propositions'). The uncontroversial truth may be an empirical truth ('snow is white'), or a conceptual truth ('snow is white or it is not the case that snow is white'). Thus some existence questions may be resolved conceptually (starting from a conceptual truth and engaging in easy inferences), while others also make use of empirical work to gain knowledge of the uncontroversial truth fed into the easy inference. Treating existence questions as resolvable by way of easy inferences like these is thus entirely in line with the older, more modest approach to philosophy outlined above, for it requires of us nothing more than conceptual and empirical work to resolve ontological questions. Moreover, the philosopher's contribution (where there is one to make) lies on the conceptual side: whether in analyzing the concepts in ways that can make explicit the conceptual truths that license the inferences, in addressing objections that would treat the concept as confused, in suggesting conceptual revisions, or removing doubts that rely on conceptual confusions.

The idea that answers to some of the most hotly disputed questions of ontology may be acquired easily runs so much against the grain of the neo-Quinean approach to metaphysics that views along these lines have attracted a great deal of criticism. So it is only now, as the criticisms accumulate after different attempts at deflationary approaches have resurfaced, that a thoroughgoing examination of the approach becomes appropriate. That is what I aim to provide here: an explicit articulation and defense of the easy approach to existence questions and of the deflationary attitude towards ontological debates that results from it.

The result of the easy approach, as we will see, is typically a simple realism about philosophically disputed entities, giving us the answers that yes, there are such disputed entities as numbers, tables and chairs, properties and propositions. However (as I discuss at greater length in chapter 3) it does not entail that there are witches, phlogiston, or other empirically dubious entities—indeed it seems to give us the intuitively 'right' answers to existence questions as they are asked as part of the ordinary business of life. Thus it seems to give us all we wanted and needed an approach to existence questions to do, outside of the business of philosophy.

But the easy approach to existence questions does not merely give us answers to first-order ontological questions. It also has meta-ontological bearing. For if these existence questions may be so straightforwardly answered, it seems that there is something wrong with the drawn-out disputes about whether entities of these types *really* exist (where those questions are supposed to not be answerable by straightforward empirical and/or conceptual means). Thus it leads to a kind of meta-ontological deflationism, holding that something is wrong with typical ontological disputes about what really exists, and arguments among those who defend competing 'ontologies'. It is because of these deflationary meta-ontological consequences more than the first-order positions that the easy approach has (where it has been noticed at all) attracted a great deal of hostility from warring metaphysicians on all sides of the first-order debates. It is particularly in that context that an extended articulation and defense of the easy approach comes to make sense.

I.4. THE PLAN OF THIS BOOK

In chapter 1 I explicate Carnap's approach to existence questions and argue that it is often misinterpreted in ways that have kept the real Carnapian position largely off the radar even in recent discussions in meta-ontology (despite the frequency with which Carnap's name is invoked). I also discuss why Carnap's view was left behind: a turn owing largely to the influence of Quine, and the widespread perception that he defeated Carnap's deflationary approach in their now famous debate. Despite this perception, however, I will argue that it is grossly premature to declare Quine the victor. As a result, despite the sea change in metaphysics that has followed, the earlier deflationary approach is not dead. Room remains for reviving and reexamining a more modest metaphysics. An interesting feature of the truly Carnapian approach is that it gives us a form of deflationism that does not rely on the idea that ontological disputes are merely verbal, or that the quantifier does or could vary in meaning. Thus it is also an option relatively untouched by recent defenses of hard ontology. This opens up room to reconsider an approach along these lines as a viable and underexplored alternative to neo-Quinean 'mainstream metaphysics'.

Having cleared the way historically, in chapter 2 I aim to develop a deflationary approach to existence questions in contemporary terms. (There may be more than one way to do this, of course; I aim to at least make one such path clear.) I show how to develop a deflationary view of existence, basing the latter in turn on a plausible view about the rules of use for 'exists'. I also show how this approach enables existence questions to be easily—often trivially and always straightforwardly—answerable. I will also show how this approach may be used to undermine a variety of proposals for substantive 'criteria of existence'. In chapter 3 I discuss the relations among various contemporary views that are thought of as providing easy approaches to different existence questions, including the work of neo-Fregeans in philosophy of mathematics, Stephen Schiffer's work on propositions, properties, and other entities, and my own work on ordinary objects. I also discuss the two key results of the easy approach: a first-order simple realism about most philosophically disputed entities, and a form of deflationism about ontological debates (quite distinct, however, from more familiar deflationary views based on claims that the quantifier varies in meaning). Chapter 4 undertakes a broader comparison of the sort of meta-ontological deflationism that results from the easy approach with other ways of articulating the suspicion that something has gone wrong somewhere in 'hard' ontological debates. I begin by comparing the approach to those that deny that we could ever *know* ontological facts, deny that there are such facts to be known, or deny that ontological disputes are genuine (not merely verbal) disputes, and close by discussing ways in which the skeptics may understand what is going on in hard ontological debates. The focus of chapter 5 is weighing up the relative advantages of deflationism versus another prominent skeptical view: fictionalism. Fictionalism has long presented an alternative view for those who think both heavyweight realists and eliminativists in a given debate are taking things too seriously. But although fictionalism tends to appeal to the same sort of philosopher as the easy approach does, the two are rivals. Indeed fictionalists raise a key objection against easy ontology, holding that the conclusions of easy ontological arguments should be taken as not making genuine assertions of existence but rather as in the context of a pretense, metaphor, or make-believe. I argue, however, that this objection is misguided and that fictionalism faces a serious problem of its own. Overall, I make the case that the form of deflationism we get from adopting the easy approach to ontology is a preferable and less problematic view that serves the motivations for fictionalism as well as or better than fictionalism itself.

In chapters 6 through 10 I provide an extended defense of the easy approach, addressing the many objections that have been raised against it or against related approaches. In chapter 6 I consider objections to the resulting ontology: that either there is no guarantee that there will be all the objects the easy approach says there are, or that it is not clear these will be the *right* objects. In chapter 7 I discuss objections to the inferences that the easy ontologist uses to reach ontological conclusions that arise from general suspicions of the very idea that there may be analytic or conceptual truths. Chapter 8 considers objections based on the idea that the particular existence-entailments keep 'bad company' with principles known to be problematic. In chapter 9 I evaluate Thomas Hofweber's arguments that the easy ontological inferences don't give us ontological conclusions on grounds that the quantifier used in the conclusions of easy arguments does not make a genuine existence claim. Finally, in chapter 10 I consider the increasingly popular idea that even if existence questions asked in ordinary English may be answered easily, we may shift to a special language of Ontologese and thereby revive hard metaphysical debates. I also examine Sider's related argument that if the easy ontologist wishes to reject this view, she becomes engaged in just as much hard metaphysics as her rivals. In the conclusion, I review how one may consistently argue for the deflationary meta-ontological approach solely on empirical, conceptual and pragmatic grounds—and thereby consistently arrive at an approach that has considerable advantages over approaches that take ontological questions to be far harder to answer. I end with some suggestions about what work remains to be done in metaphysics, if we are convinced that earnest debates about existence are out of place. The answer shall be 'plenty', though it may involve addressing new questions and working in a new key. But by making these changes we may be able to make our methods far less mysterious, and to make progress on more tractable issues than those that have dominated ontology for the last half century.

PART I

DEVELOPING EASY ONTOLOGY

[1]

WHATEVER HAPPENED TO CARNAPIAN DEFLATIONISM?

After more than a half-century of dominance of neo-Quinean ontology, metaontology has come back in fashion. We now see intensive discussions about whether or not ontological disputes are 'merely verbal', whether the quantifier does or could vary in the mouths of disputants, and whether we can understand the quantifier (or a quantifier in a special language of 'Ontologese') as having a fixed meaning in virtue of 'carving the world at its logical joints'.

Yet in most of the recent discussion, there is a deflationary position that has been missed. The missed position is not some obscure newcomer, but rather a view along the lines of Carnap's original form of deflationism—that very deflationism which was thought to have been defeated by Quine as he inaugurated a renaissance for hard metaphysics.

But how could a Carnapian form of deflationism—probably the most prominent historical form of metaontological deflationism—have been missed? And what difference would rediscovering it make to contemporary discussions in metaontology? Those are the questions I aim to answer in this chapter.

I'll argue, first, that Carnap's original position was often dismissed because it was wrongly associated with verificationism and antirealism. But I will argue that there is a way to interpret Carnap on which his view neither relies on verificationism nor leads to antirealism. Carnap's approach was then put aside and forgotten given the common assumption that Quine had won the Carnap-Quine debate and made the world safe for hard metaphysics. Some later attempts were made to revive a deflationary position: Hilary Putnam's deflationism linked the view to antirealism, and while Eli Hirsch rescued it from that association, he linked deflationism to the idea that the debating ontologists may use the quantifier with different meanings (or use quantified statements with different truth-conditions), leading them to simply talk past each other. Since then, quantifier variance has come to be considered *the* route deflationists must take. Putnam, Carnap, and Hirsch and other deflationists have all been lumped together as defenders of quantifier variance, and metaphysicians have set their sights on defending hard metaphysics by attacking quantifier variance or defending the idea that the quantifier is (or can be) univocal.

I will argue, however, that Carnap in fact is not committed to quantifier variance in the way it is commonly understood, and that he does not rely on it in his ways of deflating metaphysical debates. As a result, the contemporary focus in metametaphysics on quantifier variance is the product of a historical wrong turn, and is irrelevant to the prospects for evaluating a truly Carnapian approach. The upshot will be that the original and most promising deflationary position has been largely overlooked, leaving room to investigate the prospects for a neo-Carnapian metaontology—a project I will go on to undertake in the rest of this book.

1.1. CARNAP'S APPROACH TO EXISTENCE QUESTIONS

In "Empiricism, Semantics and Ontology" (1950/1956), Carnap addresses an old worry for empiricisms of every stripe: in science, semantics, and elsewhere we make use of terms that seem to refer to abstract entities such as numbers, propositions, and properties. Yet, as Carnap puts it: "Empiricists are in general rather suspicious with respect to any kind of abstract entities" (1950/1956, 205), for it seems hard to know how one can offer any empirical account of our knowledge of such entities. Indeed earlier empiricists such as the Warsaw logicians Lesniewski and Kotarbinski had, given such qualms, pursued a form of nominalism, and Quine and Goodman had recently published their (1947) "Steps towards a Constructive Nominalism". Carnap, however, aims to show that empiricists may employ these terms for abstract entities with a clear conscience, for "using such a language does not imply embracing a Platonic ontology but is perfectly compatible with empiricism and strictly scientific thinking" (1950/1956, 206). The compatibility arises not because the claims may be rephrased into a nominalistically accept-able language, but rather because the apparent commitments to abstract entities should not be taken in a serious, Platonic fashion to begin with.

This resolution to the problem of referring to abstracta is made possible by Carnap's approach to existence questions. Carnap famously argues that there are two "kinds of question concerning the existence or reality of entities" (1950/1956, 206): internal ques-tions and external questions. To be able to speak about a kind of entity at all, or inquire about its existence, we must introduce terms (governed by rules) for the relevant entity in our language or 'lin-guistic framework'. Carnap initially characterizes internal ques-tions as "questions of the existence of certain entities of the new kind [asked] *within the framework*"; they include questions (asked within the framework of everyday language) such as "Did King Arthur actually live?", or "Are there (still) any ivory-billed wood-peckers?" (1950/1956, 207). The answers to internal existence questions, Carnap holds, "may be found either by purely logical methods or by empirical methods, depending upon whether the framework is a logical or a factual one" (1950/1956, 206). So, for example, the questions "Did King Arthur actually live?" or "Are there any ivory-billed woodpeckers?" are to be answered by empirical methods (of history or biology), while questions like "Are there any prime numbers between 780 and 790?" are to be answered by the logical methods of mathematical reasoning and proof. In each case, internal questions may be answered by employing the rules of use for the terms in question, whether rules for our number terms (and terms like 'prime') introduced in the language of arithmetic or rules for using historical and biological terms. In either case, internal existence questions may be answered straightforwardly, either using analytic means (as in the prime number case) or empirical means (as in the woodpecker case)—there is no special mystery here, and no special role for philosophy. These are existence questions even Hume could love.

By contrast, external questions are raised "neither by the man in the street nor by scientists, but only by philosophers" (1950/1956, 207). They are typically formulated as highly general questions, such as 'are there numbers?', or 'is the thing-world real?'. Carnap argues that if we take external existence questions literally (as attempted theoretical or factual questions), they are ill-formed pseudo-questions. As a result, neither the nominalist's nor the Platonist's answer to the question 'do numbers exist?', taken as an external question, should be embraced. Instead, the best we can do with them is to reinterpret them as implicitly practical questions regarding whether or not to accept the relevant linguistic framework: "we have to make the choice whether or not to accept and use the forms of expression in the framework in question" (1950/1956, 207). Reconstrued as practical questions about the advisability of adopting a certain linguistic framework, there is here again no special philosophical or ontological insight into reality involved;

instead, the philosopher's work lies in constructing linguistic frameworks and making practical decisions about which framework to adopt for which purposes.

The existence questions asked in metaphysics are expressed as highly general questions such as "Do numbers exist?", "Do material objects exist?", "Do properties exist", and in that respect seem most like external questions. But although Carnap uses specific questions as his examples of internal existence questions and highly general questions as his examples of external questions, that is not to say that general existence questions could not be asked—and answered—as internal questions. They certainly can be answered that way, as we can get trivial entailments from positive answers to the specific questions to positive answers to the general questions, construed internally: from 'there is a prime number greater than 100' we may infer 'there is a number'; or from 'there are ivory-billed woodpeckers' we may infer 'there are material objects'.[1]

Carnap mentions this option for the numbers case (1950/1956, 209), but quickly goes on to say that this can't be the sense of the question meant by philosophers who dispute the existence of numbers, for

> nobody who meant the question 'Are there numbers' in the internal sense would either assert or even seriously consider a negative answer. This makes it plausible to assume that those philosophers who treat the question of the existence of numbers as a serious philosophical problem and offer lengthy arguments on either side, do not have in mind the internal question.
>
> (1950/1956, 209)

---

1. It is this side of Carnap's approach, treating general existential questions as *internal* questions that may be trivially answered by undertaking inferences like these, that surfaces in the neo-Fregean approach to the philosophy of mathematics. I discuss this more extensively in chapter 3 below.

Thus, he concludes, the sense in which these general existence questions are raised and seriously debated by philosophers must be the external sense. But if they are really external questions, on Carnap's view, they are not 'factual' questions at all.

So we get from Carnap a division: internal existence questions (whether specific or general) are perfectly (indeed often trivially or at least easily) answerable by analytic or empirical means. External existence questions are ill-formed pseudo-questions that can only be understood as doing something sensible if we understand them not to be theoretical questions about matters of fact (about what really exists), but rather to be practical questions about whether it is advisable to adopt a certain linguistic framework. To the extent that the metaphysician's existence questions are treated as subjects for difficult debates, not resolvable by trivial analytic or easy empirical means, they must be considered as external questions. But then, if they are to be thought of as sensible at all, they must be understood as implicitly *pragmatic* questions.

Defenders of hard metaphysics generally respond to this division of existence questions with two skeptical responses: First, how can internal existence questions be answered so easily, even trivially, and why should we care about answers to internal questions if they are only describing what exists 'internal to some linguistic framework' when what the metaphysician cares about is what *really* exists? Second, why must we think of external questions (if interpreted theoretically) as mere 'pseudo-questions'? Why can't we think of them as perfectly good questions: those debated by metaphysicians?

It is sometimes thought that the idea that internal questions must be answered 'internal to a linguistic framework' relies on some form of antirealism (an interpretation encouraged by some of Putnam's formulations, as we will see below). This line of worry can come up in one of two ways: either the view is thought to entail that what there is (or that certain disputed items: properties, numbers, etc.) depends on what linguistic framework we accept, leading to an unacceptable idealist thesis.[2] Or, secondly, the view is thought to entail that we can't answer the metaphysician's real question: 'what really exists, outside of all frameworks?'—but only uninteresting questions about what exists according to this or that framework. In addition to these worries about antirealism, it is sometimes thought that the point that external questions are pseudo-questions relies on a form of verificationism, dismissing the metaphysician's existence questions on grounds that they cannot be empirically verified and are therefore meaningless. Thoughts like these have been largely behind the dismissal of the Carnapian deflationary approach to existence questions.[3] Even Hirsch, who has done perhaps more than anyone to revive what is thought of as a neo-Carnapian approach, begins by distancing himself from the antirealist and verificationist associations with Carnap's view (2009, 231). More recently Hirsch writes, "I have a problem ... in calling Carnap a quantifier variantist, insofar as he is often viewed as a verificationist anti-realist" (2011, xvi).[4]

But these worries are misguided. There is a simple, straightforward way of understanding the internal/external distinction that can make sense of the why internal questions are easily answerable, and external questions (theoretically understood) are pseudo-questions, without appeal to anything like antirealism or verificationism.

2. Sider implies this when he writes, "What is incredible is the claim that *what there is,* rather than what we select for attention, depends on human activity. (Recall the rejection of Carnapian ontological relativity in the Introduction to this book.)" (2001,157).

3. Along similar lines, John Hawthorne (2009) argues that contemporary deflationists (he has in mind mainly Hirsch-style quantifier variance views) have trouble distancing themselves from verificationism.

4. Hirsch doesn't exactly endorse the idea that Carnap was antirealist or verificationist, only that his formulation 'sometimes seems to suggest an antirealist or verificationist perspective' (2009, 231). Nonetheless, he also does not reject this interpretation of Carnap.

One very good way of understanding the internal/external distinction is in terms of the use-mention distinction. Huw Price suggests this idea as follows:

> In my view, it is helpful to frame Carnap's point in terms of the use-mention distinction. Legitimate *uses* of the terms such as 'number' and 'material object' are necessarily internal, for it is conformity (more or less) to the rules of the framework in question that constitutes use. But as internal questions, as Carnap notes, these questions could not have the significance that traditional metaphysics takes them to have. Metaphysics tries to locate them somewhere else, but thereby commits a use-mention fallacy. The only legitimate external questions simply *mention* the terms in question.
>
> *(2009, 324)*

This is the reading I shall develop here, demonstrating also that (if we can understand the Carnapian deflationary view in this way) such a view is invulnerable to certain worries that have led metaontological deflationism to be dismissed.

Internal questions, questions asked *within*, or *using* the framework, are questions that make use of the relevant terms (property terms, number terms, material object terms) governed by certain rules that introduce them to the language. To introduce a linguistic framework requires introducing "a system of new ways of speaking, subject to new rules" (1950/1956, 206). The framework of number language "is constructed by introducing into the language new expressions with suitable rules": rules that take us from attributive uses like 'there are five books on the table', to introduce noun terms like 'number' and sentence forms like 'five is a number', and eventually to introduce new terms for properties of those entities (e.g. 'odd' and 'prime'), and variables that take numbers as values in sentences quantifying over numbers (1950/1956, 208).

Once those rules for introducing the new terms are in place we can *use* the relevant terms in accord with those rules and straightforwardly evaluate the truth of existential sentences containing those terms. Making use of those rules, we are able to evaluate the truth of 'There is a white piece of paper on my desk' by engaging in the usual straightforward kind of empirical checks (we look, touch, etc.), and of 'There is a prime number between one and five' by engaging in mathematical reasoning and proof. We can also answer *general* internal questions in this way. By making use of not only the rules of use for the terms but also 'customary deductive rules' (1950/1956, 208), we can make simple inferences from specific truths like these to general truths such as 'there is at least one material object' and 'there is at least one number'. As Carnap puts it, the statement 'There is an n such that n is a number' "follows from the analytic statement 'five is a number'" (1950/1956, 209). Linguistic frameworks for introducing talk of propositions and properties are introduced similarly: in the case of properties, for example, we may begin from the 'thing' language that contains predicates such as 'red', 'hard', and the like, and then introduce noun terms for properties, and variables for which the property terms are substitutable. Finally, "new rules are laid down which admit sentences like 'Red is a property' and 'Red is a color'" (1950/1956, 211).

So understood, we can easily see why questions asked within— or better, *using*—a linguistic framework are straightforward to answer. For example, the very rules for introducing property language (combined with 'customary deductive rules') license us to infer from an ordinary truth like 'the house is red' that 'the house has the property of being red' and so to provide an easy affirmative answer to the general question (asked internally) 'Are there properties?' (cf. Schiffer 2003, 61–71). But that is not to say that what there is depends on what linguistic framework we accept. In fact, Carnap himself clearly insists that although *talk*, for example of propositions, is introduced by introducing noun terms for propositions and variables that range over them, that does *not* entail that propositions are linguistic entities or in any way subjective. On the contrary, the rules of use for proposition talk (which do not demand that there be a language, a subject, or an observer in order for there to be propositions) show that propositions themselves are *not* linguistic, mental, or subjective entities (1950/1956, 210–11)—or, one might add, mind-dependent.

Nor does Carnap, on this interpretation, leave us with a kind of antirealism on which we can only answer questions of the form "what exists, *according to* this or that framework"[5]—or, as André Gallois puts it, according to which "whatever ontologically committing discourse we consider, sentences in it will be true only in a framework-relative sense" (1998, 273). On the interpretation I am defending, when Carnap says that internal existence questions are questions of the existence of entities of a certain kind asked "within the framework" (1950/1956, 206), the point is not that claims about what exists are 'internal to' a framework, where that is like saying what exists *in the story* in a work of fiction. Existence questions asked within a framework are not questions of what exists *according to the story*, or according to someone's theory or set of beliefs, or in the content of a game of make-believe. The view is commonly presented in this way—for example, Yablo suggests that we should treat internal truths as statements that pertinent rules of make-believe tell us to imagine-true (1998, 244). This common sort of misinterpretation seems to be in part behind the common resistance to Carnap's view. Instead, the point is the simple, almost trivial observation that for

---

5. Price likewise (2009, 342) argues that it is a mistake to think of Carnapians as putting existence claims in the context of a 'disowning preface' such as 'according to the story'.

a question to be asked meaningfully the terms in it must be governed by rules of use: we must be *using* a linguistic framework to ask an (internal) existence question. For example, if we are to ask 'Are there properties?' in a way that has sense, then the crucial term 'property' must be introduced with some rules of use. On Carnap's view, once those rules are mastered (rules that license inferences like those above), then specific questions about whether certain properties exist (or whether two red houses 'have something in common') may be simply answered, and the answer to the general existence question (construed as internal) follows trivially from the answers to these specific questions. We can answer direct questions about whether this or that sort of thing exists—not just about whether they exist *according to* this or that theory or framework. But to ask them we must be *using* language—using a framework that establishes the rules of use for the terms used in asking and answering the question. And the answers we get may be true. Even though they may only be *expressed* using language that is no reason to think they are true merely in some 'framework-relative sense', or anything less than simply true.

What then of external existence questions? Why must we think of them as pseudo-questions, if they are construed as factual/theoretical questions? The answer now becomes equally simple. In raising an existence question, we must use a term ('number', 'property', 'proposition', . . .) to ask "are there numbers/properties/propositions?" But if we are using those terms according to the rules of use by which they come to be introduced to the language, then those rules enable us to resolve the questions straightforwardly (through analytic or empirical means), as above: the question is an internal question. So, if the external question is *not* supposed to be so straightforwardly answerable (so it is *not* an internal question), then it must be aiming to use the terms in question *without* their being governed by the standard rules of use. But if they attempt to use the terms while severing them from these rules of use, they make the terms meaningless, and the questions pseudo-questions. A question like "Are there huasadoes?" cannot be answered, as 'huasadoe' is a meaningless term, without rules of use that would determine under what conditions 'husasdoe' is to be applied or refused. So similarly, if we take a familiar term but strip it of its rules of use (not using it in a way governed by those rules), the term is left meaningless, and the existence question unanswerable. That (and not any sort of verificationism) is what makes external questions (theoretically construed) unanswerable pseudo-questions.[6]

This also explains why external questions can be given a pragmatic construal according to which they are really asking about the advisability of adopting the new linguistic framework.[7] For what else is left to do with the terms, apart from using them? Mentioning them, of course. So if we are charitable, we may interpret external questions not as *using* the disputed terms (governed by their associated rules of use) nor as attempting to use them while severing them from their meanings, but rather as *mentioning* the terms and raising the pragmatic question of whether we should adopt (or retain) the terms (of the number-language, property-language, proposition-language) with the associated rules of use. Such pragmatic questions *mentioning* the terms in question can indeed be meaningfully formulated and debated, and so if we want to make some sense of the debates in hard ontology, one may see the

---

6. Though Carnap does occasionally appeal to verificationism, the point here is that his deflationary position may be understood in a way that does not rely on it.

7. Contemporary hard ontologists have a new option. They may accept that external questions are (at least in part) questions about what language we should adopt to do ontology, but deny that this is a merely *pragmatic* matter. Instead, they may say, there is a single objective answer to what [whether] language has quantifiers that best carve the world at its logical joints. (Thanks to Uriah Kriegel for raising this point so clearly.) In chapter 10 I return to examine that suggestion, as we find it in Sider's work. For now I will stick to the historical story.

disputants as engaged in that sort of dispute.[8] Thus on this view the nominalist in philosophy of mathematics would be best seen as suggesting that we do away with the noun-use of number terms, and instead make do with a nominalistic language. This still is an interpretation most of those committed to hard ontology would find unappealing, as they want to see themselves as addressing deep theoretical questions about the world, not practical questions about what language to adopt. But it is no doubt less hostile than treating them as either making pseudo-statements or engaging in drawn-out disputes about internal questions that can straightforwardly be answered. Seen in that light the interpretation is charitable, as it does provide some sense and point to their debates.

On this interpretation, then, we do get something like an easy approach to those existence questions *that can be meaningfully stated and asked.* If we ask a general existence question such as 'are there numbers?', 'are there properties?', 'are there propositions?', using those terms *in the only sense they have—using the rules by which they are introduced into the language,* the answer is a straightforward, easy 'yes'.[9] If we are spoiling for a debate (if it is to be meaningful), we must undertake it on other territory: regarding whether we should use these terms, along with their customary rules of use, at all.

Some who go this far with Carnap nonetheless resist at this stage on the grounds that it seems to make it totally *arbitrary* which

8. I return to discuss how we may interpret the debates and claims of hard ontology in section 4.4 below. John Bickle (2003, 31–40) explicitly endorses this sort of Carnapian reading of his psychoneural reductionist position about the mental.

9. Some readers will be suspicious of the idea that these terms are introduced to the language by such rules. Most often, this suspicion will come from sympathy with causal or direct reference theories: but of course (given their abstract, noncausal status) one cannot hold that terms for numbers or propositions are introduced via causal contact with their referents; something else must be said about how these terms acquire their meaning. Others will hold doubts on grounds of general worries about there being conceptual or analytic truths. I address these doubts in chapter 7 below.

linguistic framework we use, and so also makes it arbitrary which assertions of existence we make. But this is a needless worry, for Carnap himself acknowledges that some languages may be better than others for various purposes, and that there may be theoretical issues involved in determining which language is best for a given purpose (or set of purposes). The acceptance of a linguistic framework can "be judged as being more or less expedient, fruitful, conducive to the aim for which the language is intended" (1950/1956, 214). The decision to accept a language, such as the thing language,

> will nevertheless usually be influenced by theoretical knowledge, just like any other deliberate decision concerning the acceptance of linguistic or other rules. The purposes for which the language is intended to be used . . . will determine which factors are relevant for the decision. The efficiency, fruitfulness, and simplicity of the use of the thing language may be among the decisive factors. And the questions concerning these qualities are indeed of a theoretical nature.
>
> *(1950/1956, 208)*

The question of what rules we should adopt for NCAA basketball is a practical question (not a theoretic question), but may be made on the basis of theoretic considerations about which sets of rules (e.g., jump ball or alternate possession, shot clock or no shot clock) will best facilitate the relevant goals (providing a reasonably safe and engaging form of exercise for the players and exciting competition for viewers). So similarly the question of which linguistic frameworks we should adopt is a practical question, but may be influenced by theoretic considerations (e.g., about the usefulness of introducing terms for propositions to aid us in formulating our semantic theories in a clear and concise way, or about the cumbersomeness of scientific explanation and prediction if we attempt to eliminate number terms from scientific discourse). The rules we adopt need not be arbitrary, given our purposes, since some rules may serve the purposes better than others.

Another line of reply to the arbitrariness worry may also be available (see my 2013a), though it is not (to my knowledge) one Carnap himself considers. Some recent work in cognitive psychology suggests that a handful of basic concepts (including object in a sortal sense, agent, and number) have evolved in humans and other mammals (Carey 2009). If so, then it is certainly not arbitrary that we employ these basic concepts (themselves governed by certain fixed rules) and, ultimately, terms to express them. Nor do we have to say they evolved because they are the most metaphysically apt set of concepts—only that possessing these concepts in the relevant environments aided our survival and reproduction. A different story, of course, would still have to be told for terms that express nonbasic concepts.

In any case, theoretic debates about what linguistic framework will best serve our purposes, and practical debates about what purposes we should adopt or how we should prioritize among them, may all legitimately be engaged in, but none is perspicuously framed as a debate about whether or not there *really are* the entities in question. And once we adopt a set of rule-governed terms to use in framing the question of whether things of a certain kind exist, the answer will not be arbitrary.

I have argued that we can understand Carnap's deflationary approach to existence questions in use-mention terms: internal questions *use* the relevant terms, and external questions attempt to employ them in a way that strips them of their meaning—but can be reformulated as questions that *mention* the terms and ask whether we *should* adopt and use them according to the relevant system of rules. This interpretation provides a clear way of understanding the distinction and why it is supposed to render internal questions easily answerable, and external questions (theoretically construed) as pseudo-questions. It is also an interpretation that easily sidesteps accusations that the position leads to antirealism (either in the sense that it takes what exists to depend on our minds or language or in the sense that it holds that we can only ask what exists *according to* a linguistic framework or theory) or that it relies on verificationism.

A position along these lines will provide the basis for the easy approach to ontological questions to be defended in the remainder of this book. Of course, there will be some differences, and the goal here is simply to revisit the history to find room for developing a view along these lines, rather than to engage in interpretation of the historical Carnap. One important difference between Carnap's actual historical work and the work of this book is that Carnap's primary interest lay in formal, technical languages, while I will be more concerned with existence questions that are (at least apparently) asked in ordinary English.[10] This does lead to certain differences, for where existence questions are asked using the terms of ordinary language it may not always be clear exactly what the rules of use are that govern those terms. As a result, it may sometimes be less clear whether a certain question should be understood as internal (and so answerable making use of the customary rules) or external. For our ordinary terms, conceptual analysis often plays a crucial role in attempting to elucidate the rules of use for these terms (whereas, for technical terms, they may be simply stipulated).[11] Nonetheless, in most of the existence questions to be considered

---

10. Thanks to Paul Livingston for raising this issue.
11. See my (2007a, chapter 11) for further discussion of the role of conceptual analysis in metaphysics, and my (2012) for discussion of the methods involved in such conceptual analysis.

below, a compelling case can be made that there are conceptual rules that enable the relevant questions to be answered easily.[12]

But before moving to develop a contemporary approach along these lines, it is worth finishing the historical story. Why was the Carnapian deflationary approach to existence questions discarded, left behind in the history of philosophy, with Quine's brand of ontology soon to take over and dominate for the next sixty years or more? Only if we examine that can we be reassured that we are not wasting our time in attempting to resurrect an approach to existence questions along the original Carnapian lines that has become unpopular and nearly forgotten.

1.2. QUINE AND THE ASCENDENCY OF ONTOLOGY

If we ask why Carnap's deflationary approach fell by the wayside and hard metaphysics made a comeback in the wake of positivism, the answer usually begins with the Quine-Carnap debate. Around the same time as "Empiricism, Semantics and Ontology" (1950/1956) came out, Quine was laying out his own vision for 'ontology'— most famously in "On What There Is" (1948/1953). Immediately after Carnap's paper was published, Quine directly criticized his teacher's position in "On Carnap's Views on Ontology" (presented at a colloquium with Carnap in 1951, and published later that year).

---

12. In other cases, it might not be so easy; more difficult questions may arise about what it would take (given the standard conceptual rules) for there to be free will, or moral right and wrong, etc., making it difficult in turn to determine whether the required conditions are fulfilled. I will leave such cases to the side below. For the general point remains that a great many of currently disputed existence questions can be straightforwardly answered; and where difficulties arise, these are to be resolved by conceptual methods (difficult though those may be) rather than by any epistemically metaphysical procedure.

After a review of his own approach to ontological commitment, the core of the latter paper is devoted to criticizing Carnap's distinction between internal and external questions. Carnap describes the method of introducing a framework for the new forms of expression as follows. First, we introduce "a general term, a predicate of higher level, for the new kind of entities, permitting us to say of any particular entity that it belongs to this kind (e.g., "Red is a *property*", "Five is a *number*")" (Carnap 1950/1956, 213). Second, we introduce "variables of the new type", with the new entities capable of serving as the values of the variables. It is after introducing a framework in this way that we may formulate and answer internal existence questions.

Quine recasts Carnap's internal/external distinction as 'derivative' from another more basic distinction: the distinction between *category* questions and *subclass* questions. Category questions, as Quine defines them, are "questions of the form 'Are there so-and-so's?' where the so-and-so's purport to exhaust the range of a particular style of bound variables"; subclass questions are questions of the same form "where the so-and-so's do not purport to exhaust the range of a particular style of bound variables" (1951/1976, 207).

Carnap's internal questions then, on Quine's view, are by and large *subclass* questions: they ask, of a general kind of entities (say numbers), whether there are any that have certain other features (say, are prime)—where the entities enquired about would not include *all* of the numbers, but only a subclass of them. That is why internal questions, as I mentioned above, are most often specific existence questions. Quine acknowledges, however, that internal questions may also take the form of category questions "when these are construed as treated within an adopted language as questions having trivially analytic or contradictory answers" (1951/1976, 207). That is, we may also ask general existence questions about *all* of the entities of a given category (which would exhaust the range of the introduced style of bound variable) in an internal way, and we do so if we treat them as being answerable trivially, by moves such as going from 'five is a number' to 'there is a number'. Carnap's external questions Quine describes as *category* questions asked "before the adoption of a given language" (1951/1976, 207). This seems to be compatible with the understanding I have suggested above of external questions as not *using* the terms (once a language has been adopted), but rather implicitly *mentioning* them as we consider "the desirability of a given language form" (Quine 1951/1976, 207).

However, Quine argues, the distinction between category and subclass questions depends on a "rather trivial consideration" (1951, 208) of whether we use different styles of variables for different sorts of thing. For we may choose to adopt a single style of variable for several sorts of thing, and if we do, then even general questions of existence, for example of numbers, abstracta, physical objects, can be phrased as *subclass* questions. Informally, they may be thought of as asking, say, of all the *things* there are, whether any are numbers (and thus as parallel to asking, of all the *numbers,* whether any are prime). Since such purported external existence questions may be turned into internal (subclass) questions by simply adopting a style of variable to range over a more inclusive domain, Quine concludes, the distinction between category questions and subclass questions is of little concern, since it varies given 'logically irrelevant changes of typography' (1951/1976, 210).[13]

But although it occupies the vast majority of this influential article, the discussion about styles of variables, and category versus

13. It is interesting to note that if Quine means to adopt the stronger view implied here—that *any* purported external question can be turned into a subclass question by adopting a style of variable to range over a broader domain—then he must be implicitly rejecting the idea that we can engage in absolutely general quantification over *everything*. For if we could, then existence questions so framed (is there something?) could not be turned into subclass questions.

subclass questions, is a technical sideshow distracting from the real metaontological issues. For if I am right above, the real issue is not (and never was) the distinction between category and subclass questions: that was Quine's own imposition. Carnap's internal/external distinction is not the same as Quine's subclass/category distinction—as can be readily seen by the fact that category questions may be asked either as internal questions (answerable trivially) or as external questions.

The real distinction instead is between existence questions asked *using* a linguistic framework—which, Carnap held, may be answered through straightforward empirical or analytic means (these are the internal questions: whether subclass or category)—and existence questions that are supposed to be asked somehow without being subject to those rules—asked, as Quine puts it, "before the adoption of the given language". As I have suggested, this makes them either meaningless (because attempting to employ terms without rules of use) or construes them as implicitly *mentioning* rather than using the terms and inquiring about whether we should adopt them. That distinction is not in the least undermined by Quine's arguments that the distinction between category and subclass questions rests on trivial typographical decisions.

Moreover, as Huw Price has pointed out (2009), Quine's argument here does nothing to revive the idea that there are general existence questions that can be construed as meaningful questions *not* answerable by trivial (or straightforward empirical) means: external questions. Instead it shows how anything we might have considered to be an external question can instead be turned into an internal question—but internal questions are, on Carnap's view, easily answered. So (as Price 2009 again points out) it is quite bizarre to think of Quine, in this paper, as serving as the champion of hard metaphysics, making way for a new discipline of 'hard' ontology. Quine himself makes this evident, declaring himself at the outset of the paper "no champion of traditional metaphysics" (1951/1976, 204), and acknowledging at the end that the category/ subclass distinction "is a distinction which he [Carnap] can perfectly well discard compatibly with the philosophical purpose of the paper under discussion", namely, the deflation of metaphysical debates (1951/1976, 210).

In short, neither Quine nor Carnap seems to be in the business of reviving external questions, or showing them to have a sense that is other than pragmatic. Quine only arrives at what he himself calls the 'basic point of contention' between himself and Carnap in the penultimate paragraph of "On Carnap's Views on Ontology". The real point of contention is only whether to accept Carnap's view that *internal* questions may be easily answered by analytic or empirical means, while *external* questions can only be sensibly understood as purely *pragmatic* questions of whether to adopt a certain linguistic framework. This three-way division of questions (into the analytic, empirical, and pragmatic) relies on the analytic/synthetic distinction, and that is what the real core of disagreement between Carnap and Quine comes down to. That distinction is required to distinguish the empirical nature of existence questions such as 'are there black swans?' from the analytic nature of existence questions such as 'are there prime numbers between 5 and 10?' More crucially, we need a notion of analyticity (or something along those lines, such as analytic or trivial entailment or conceptual truth) to maintain the idea that many of the metaphysician's most general existence questions can (taken internally) be answered trivially by analytic means (as we can answer 'are there numbers/properties/propositions?'). Most importantly, Carnap needed to be able to distinguish between questions that are analytic or empirical on the one hand, and questions that are pragmatic on the other in order to keep the pragmatic issue of which linguistic framework to choose (a pragmatic issue that nonetheless, as I have emphasized above, may be empirically influenced and informed) separate from the empirical issues about what true statements (including what existence claims) may be made using that linguistic framework.

Quine, of course, had by this stage already rejected the analytic/synthetic distinction in "Two Dogmas of Empiricism" (1951/1953). Without the analytic/synthetic distinction, Quine can't (with Carnap) accept a division of labor between constructing and pragmatically selecting among linguistic or conceptual frameworks on the one hand, and empirically determining the truth of statements made using that framework on the other hand. Nor can we say that (given the rules of the linguistic framework we use) questions about the existence of numbers, propositions, properties and the like may be answered through trivial analytic means.

Quine also, of course, develops an alternative approach to existence questions that does not rely on the analytic/synthetic distinction. Rather than speaking in terms of linguistic frameworks and (empirical or analytic) statements made using those frameworks, Quine speaks in terms of 'theories'. Famously, to decide which ontology to accept we must decide which theories to accept, and we are then committed to all and only those entities we must accept in order to render the statements of the theory true:

> Our acceptance of an ontology is . . . similar in principle to our acceptance of a scientific theory, say a system of physics: we adopt, at least insofar as we are reasonable, the simplest conceptual scheme into which the disordered fragments of raw experience can be fitted and arranged. Our ontology is determined once we have fixed upon the over-all conceptual scheme which is to accommodate science in the broadest sense.
>
> *(1948/1953, 16–17)*

And how do we choose among those scientific theories, and ways of translating their claims to determine their ontology? By such familiar criteria as explanatory power, explanatory simplicity, ontological simplicity (parsimony), etc.

There are several things to notice here, making clear the differences between Quine and Carnap. One: for Quine, we have no separate pragmatic choice of a linguistic framework; rather, our language comes along part and parcel with *theory* choice, which is empirically loaded (though it is also not *merely* empirical, but rather empirical-cum-pragmatic in an inextricable mixture). Two: only one goal remains in view here as a guiding purpose in choosing a 'theory' (now, not a linguistic/conceptual framework)—accommodating 'science in the broadest sense', not regulating our social conduct, managing our institutions, entertaining, evaluating actions or works of art, or any of the other purposes to which language is daily put (and apparently involving linguistic frameworks that aren't so naturally called 'theories').[14] This of course is part of Quine's scientism. It is by repudiating Carnap's distinctions of analytic versus synthetic statements, pragmatic choices of linguistic frameworks versus empirical truths stateable using the framework, that Quine ends up with the radical conclusion at odds with the prior hundred years or so of philosophical thought: that there is no division of labor between philosophy and the natural sciences. In opposition to the generally received view of the early twentieth century (held by such figures as Brentano, Husserl, Carnap, Wittgenstein, and Ryle), Quine maintains that philosophy and the sciences are engaged in the same project of seeking the best 'total theory', which comes as a package deal in which we can't separate the choice of language from the choice of theory. It is in that sense

---

14. Price (2009) likewise interprets Quine as implicitly—and unwarrantedly—rejecting a kind of pluralism about the functions of language.

that "Ontological questions . . . end up on a par with questions of natural science" (1951/1976, 211).

The points to emphasize here, however, are, first, that Quine does not aim to revive traditional metaphysics or inaugurate an era of 'hard' metaphysics, but merely to undermine the borders between the conceptual, empirical, and pragmatic questions Carnap separated. Second, Quine's reasons for rejecting Carnap's particular form of deflationism (and the basis for his own positive alternative) lie firmly in his rejection of the analytic/synthetic distinction. But, as I (2007a, chapter 2) and others (Strawson/Grice 1956; McGinn 2011; Russell 2008; Chalmers 2011) have argued elsewhere, Quine's arguments against the analytic/synthetic distinction are far from decisive, notwithstanding the extraordinary influence they have had on the profession. Even Quine himself backpedals substantially in his later work, allowing that analyticity "undeniably has a place at the commonsense level" (1991, 270). Moreover, as Richard Creath has argued (2004, 49), Quine's arguments against the analytic/synthetic distinction ultimately rest on his behaviorism: it is the failure to find a behavioral criterion for applying the terms that ultimately leads him to reject the distinction (see also my 2007a, 34–37).[15]

It thus becomes a sociological curiosity that Quine has been so broadly taken to open room for hard ontology, and that what is taken to be his approach to ontology has been nearly universally taken on board. For it relies on his rejection of the analytic/synthetic distinction—a point less universally agreed on—and that in turn relies on his behaviorism, which most contemporary philosophers would reject.[16]

---

15. Of course others have also raised more recent arguments against analyticity; e.g. Harman (1999) raises arguments based on Quine's, while Williamson (2007) raises independent arguments against the notion. I discuss Williamson's more recent objections in chapter 7 below, but for the present will keep the focus historical.

16. Though imperfect for this purpose, it is worth noting the results from the Phil Papers survey of philosopher's views: nearly half (49.8%) declare themselves to be 'naturalists'

Why is the Quinean approach to ontology so universally adopted, and interpreted as making room for hard metaphysics, despite greater skepticism about the doctrines on which it is founded? Here mainly sociological explanations come to mind: there was, perhaps, a longing to return to metaphysics (in the wake of positivism and ordinary language philosophy). Moreover, it was attractive indeed to think of metaphysics as 'on a par with natural science', and thus borrowing its respectability without the annoyances of tending the lab on weekends and holidays, or of being compelled to address mainly small detailed questions rather than directly inquiring after the 'ultimate structures of reality'.

I will not undertake here again to defend the analytic/synthetic distinction against Quine's (early) attacks.[17] But the important thing to note here is that without good reason for rejecting the analytic/synthetic distinction, Quine's famous criticisms give us no reason to reject Carnap's form of deflationism about metaphysics. As long as room remains for something like Carnap's analytic/synthetic distinction and room remains for the use/mention distinction, room remains for Carnapian deflationary metaphysics.[18]

More broadly, it is important to remember that although he had reservations about Carnap's particular form of deflationism, Quine's criticisms were never intended to revive anything like hard metaphysics. As Price (2009) argues, Quine certainly develops

about metaphilosophy, a term at least standardly allied with neo-Quinean metaphysics (though its meaning of course varies in the literature, and was not specified in the survey), while just over a quarter (27%) reject the analytic/synthetic distinction. Views on behaviorism were not surveyed, presumably because the doctrine is so overwhelmingly unpopular.

17. I have done this elsewhere, in (2007a, chapter 2). I defend the distinction against Timothy Williamson's more recent attacks in chapter 7 below.

18. Uriah Kriegel has similarly pointed out (correspondence) that one doesn't need a hard and fast analytic/synthetic distinction to preserve a broadly Carnapian approach to metametaphysics. For that would also be compatible with the idea that there is a spectrum, with the relevant conceptual principles at issue in these ontological debates on the 'quite analytic' end of the spectrum.

an alternative to Carnapian deflationism, but it is not an approach designed to revive a form of hard metaphysics lost with positivism, or to give a special role to philosophers in discovering the deep structure of reality. Instead, he simply treats ontological questions as answerable *internal* to our best scientific theories. If the analytic/synthetic distinction goes, the boundary between questions that are purely conceptual, empirical, and pragmatic may become more fluid—but that does not mean making room for hard metaphysical questions that cannot be addressed by these methods.

As we have seen, the crucial differences between Carnap and Quine lie in the fact that Carnap accepts (while Quine rejects) a three-way distinction between questions that are analytic, empirical, and pragmatic, and in the fact that Quine implicitly limits our focus to one use of language: its usefulness in scientific theorizing (while Carnap shared this interest in usefulness to science, he would have explicitly rejected the idea that this is the *only* legitimate use of language: the principle of tolerance extended quite widely [Creath 2009, 213]). Passages of Carnap's *Meaning and Necessity* make evident another difference between them, though interestingly, at this stage in the history, Carnap himself saw it as perhaps a merely terminological difference:

> Quine has repeatedly pointed out the important fact that, if we wish to find out what kind of entities somebody recognizes, we have to look more at the variables he uses than at the constants and closed expressions . . . I am essentially in agreement with the view, as I shall presently explain. But, first, I wish to indicate a doubt concerning Quine's *formulation*; I am not quite clear whether the point raised is not perhaps of a merely terminological nature. I should prefer not to use the word '*ontology*' for the recognition of entities by the admission of variables. This use seems to me to be at least misleading; it might be understood

as implying that the decision to use certain kinds of variables must be based on ontological, metaphysical convictions. In my view, however, the choice of a certain language structure and, in particular, the decision to use certain types of variables is a practical decision like the choice of an instrument; it depends chiefly upon the purposes for which the instrument—here the language—is intended to be used and upon the properties of the instrument. I admit that the choice of a language suitable for the purposes of physics and mathematics involves problems quite different from those involved in the choice of a suitable motor for a freight airplane; but, in a sense, both are engineering problems, and I fail to see why metaphysics should enter into the first any more than into the second.

(1947/1956, 43; italics original; compare Quine 1951/1976, 203).

Thus while Carnap accepts something like Quine's quantificational criterion for determining what entities an individual is committed to, he—quite legitimately, it seems in retrospect—worries that Quine's use of the term 'ontology' makes the issue sound too metaphysical. For on Carnap's view, to say that one is committed to the existence of those entities that must serve as values of one's bound variables is *not* to say that one has anything like a *deep ontological* commitment to a metaphysical view that could be seen as a competitor in traditional debates, for example, between Platonic Realists and nominalists about numbers, and that would be used to *justify* including certain terms in our language (1947/1956, 43). Instead, its point is much simpler: if a language contains certain variables "then we can define in it a designator for the values of those variables" (1947/1956, 44). From a language with variables to range over numbers, for example, we can define 'number'. And so, "once you admit certain variables, you are bound to admit the corresponding universal concept" (1947/1956, 44). So admitting variables that range over entities of a certain type commits you to employing the *concept* of number. Once we employ, that is, *use* that concept, however, its associated rules of use entitle us to make trivial inferences, for example, from 'five is a number' to 'there is a number', and thus to make inferences to claims such as 'there are numbers'. Given the rules of use for the concept *number*, once we admit the concept, we accept claims like 'there are numbers' or 'numbers exist'. But in doing so we are not committing ourselves to a deep Platonistic metaphysics and cannot be accused of 'illegitimate hypostatizations'; we are simply making the trivial, internal existence claim.

In short, on Carnap's view, admitting variables of the relevant type does not evince a deep 'ontological commitment' that places one on the realist side of a traditional metaphysical debate. (And Carnap seems to have been quite right in his fear that many would interpret Quine's 'criterion of ontological commitment' in that way.) Instead, it simply shows that one admits the general concept. But given the rules of use for a concept like 'number' or 'proposition', Carnap holds, those who make use of such concepts are committed to the legitimacy of trivial inferences that lead to true existence claims concerning entities of that type—construed as *internal* claims made *using* the relevant concept.

1.3. PUTNAM TAKES DEFLATIONISM ON AN UNFORTUNATE TURN

The history of the Quine/Carnap debate is of course only part of the story—though a crucial part. There is more to be said about why the Carnapian approach remained underground for so long, and this part of the story may have more to do with the friends than the enemies of deflationary metaontology.

The next prominent appearance of something like a Carnapian deflationism about metaphysical issues writ large (rather than as applied to particular debates) was in the work of Hilary Putnam (1987, 1990). Putnam of course famously argues for what he calls 'internal realism': "the insistence that realism is *not* incompatible with conceptual relativity" (1987, 17). Conceptual relativity, in turn, he considers to be the idea that the question 'what exists?' can only be answered in terms of a particular 'version', that is, in terms of a particular conceptual/representational system. Put in Carnapian terms, that sounds like the claim that existence questions can only be answered *internal* to a particular framework, that is (if our earlier interpretation was correct), *using* a linguistic framework which provides rules of use for the terms and thus for answering such questions. Questions asked outside of all 'versions', or external to a linguistic framework, are rejected (at least as long as they are supposed to be 'factual' metaphysical questions). So far, so Carnapian.

But there are two ways in which Putnam's deflationism takes importantly different turns than Carnap's, both of which have had unfortunate consequences. For these differences have deflected the main metaontological dispute away from the central issues and have contributed to making the deflationary project distasteful and keeping it largely underground.

First, Putnam ties the idea of conceptual relativity to the idea that certain core terms used in metaphysical debates—"exists" and "object"—have different meanings in different 'versions'. As he writes:

> . . . it is no accident that metaphysical realism cannot really recognize the phenomenon of conceptual relativity—for that phenomenon turns on the fact that *the logical primitives themselves, and in particular the notions of object and existence, have a multitude of different uses rather than one absolute 'meaning'.*
>
> *(1987, 19, italics original)*

And elsewhere:

> . . . the idea that there is an Archimedean point, or a use of 'exist' inherent in the world itself, from which the question 'How many objects *really* exist?' makes sense, is an illusion.
>
> *(1987, 20)*

Second, Putnam uses this observation in the service of a general denial of 'Realism',[19] for from the fact that a question like 'how many objects are there' can only be answered within a version, Putnam concludes that we must reject the idea that there are objects that exist independently of our conceptual scheme:

> What is wrong with the notion of objects existing 'independently' of conceptual schemes is that there are no standards for the use of even the logical notions apart from conceptual choices
>
> *(1987, 35–36).*

These two features of Putnam's view have been very influential. The first, the idea that 'exists' and 'object' vary in meaning, turned metaontological debates to focus heavily on the idea of 'quantifier variance'. Indeed most of the focus of metaontological debates for about the next twenty-five years centered on the question of whether the quantifier varies in meaning or not (see, e.g., Hirsch 2002a, 2002b, 2007, 2009; van Inwagen 1998, 2009; Sider 2007, 2009).

19. Where the capital 'R' signifies this is realism on Putnam's reading of it as committed to three theses:

1. The world consists in a fixed totality of mind-independent objects.
2. There is exactly one true and complete description of the way the world is.
3. Truth involves correspondence between our description and the way the world is.

Quantifier variance has come to be strongly associated with Carnapian deflationism. Thus, for example, Matti Eklund writes:

> ... it is common to take Carnap to be what I will call an *onto-logical pluralist*: to hold a view not unlike that today defended by Eli Hirsch (under the name *quantifier variance*) and Hilary Putnam (under the name *conceptual relativity*). (Sometimes Hirsch and Putnam are even described as 'neo-Carnapians').
>
> *(2009b, 137)*

Kit Fine explicitly attributes quantifier variance to both Carnap and Hirsch (2009, 164 n. 2). Ross Cameron labels Hirsch's quantifier variance view 'neo-Carnapianism' (2008, 2), and Ted Sider writes: "Carnap's challenge to ontology is that there are many possible linguistic frameworks containing different rules of use for the symbol '∃'" (2001, xxii).[20] The second feature, the association between ontological deflationism and antirealism, has often been encouraged by fans of hard metaphysics. Sider, for example, explicitly associates "Carnapian ontological relativity" with the claim that "what there is ... depends on human activity" (2001, 157). And this association with antirealism has led many to reject deflationism, keeping it very much a minority position among metaphysicians until quite recently.[21]

But both of these features are separable from Carnapian deflationism: the first (quantifier variance) is a mistake to attribute

20. He does go on to note that different frameworks may, despite their variations, "agree on a core inferential role" for the quantifier (2001, xxii), but clearly holds that the key feature of the Carnapian view is accepting quantifier variance.

21. Although, anecdotally, there seems to be far more sympathy for some form of deflationism among philosophers at large than among metaphysicians. (This would not be surprising, for it seems plausible that most people self-select as metaphysicians only if they think the debates are interesting and substantive).

to Carnap; the second (the thesis that on this view there are no objects independent of conceptual schemes) is a flat-out philosophical mistake. That the second is a mistake should by now be well known: the idea that from the fact that the meanings of terms like 'object' or 'exists' vary it follows that objects don't exist independently of conceptual schemes has been quite fully and properly demolished (Hilpinen 1996; Hirsch 2002a).[22] In brief, the mistake is a use-mention mistake (Hirsch 2002a, 52). The *meaning* of a term like 'object' or 'exists', or of the existential quantifier, may vary according to our conceptual scheme.[23] And it is surely the case that unless such terms have meaning (as part of a conceptual scheme or linguistic framework) a question framed using the following symbols: "how many objects exist?" cannot be answered (since one or more of the terms would lack meaning). So, without some meaning attached, the question "how many objects exist?" would be meaningless. That observation of course, while true, is trivial.

But to say that the meaning of the term "object" or "exists"—or the meanings of sentences using those terms—depends on our conceptual scheme is not at all to say that *objects* (the term now being *used* in accord with the rules of an established language, say English) depend on our conceptual scheme. The meaning of 'planet' similarly depends on our choice of conceptual scheme, but *planets* (now using, not mentioning, the term) don't depend on there being any conceptual scheme whatsoever (cf. Hilpinen 1996). On the contrary, according to the very rules of the linguistic framework, there may have been (and were) planets even before there were thinkers, and so even in the absence of all conceptual schemes. So despite Putnam's ill-advised ways of talking, it should by now be

---

22. I have also addressed a related point extensively elsewhere (2007a, chapter 3).
23. I say *may* here because I don't want to say that the deflationist must be committed to that—more on that below.

well known that accepting the idea that we cannot evaluate existence claims except internally to a conceptual scheme (i.e., while having a rule-governed linguistic framework to *use* in expressing and answering the questions) does not mean that we must reject the idea that there are mind-independent objects, planets, alligators, or whatever. Yet I suspect that the association of deflationism and anti-realism set up by Putnam has persisted in turning off many people from being sympathetic to and further considering deflationism.

Let us go back, then, to the first point: that key terms used in metaphysical debates, such as 'objects', 'exists', or the existential quantifier, do (actually) vary, or (if we are to interpret the disputants charitably) may be interpreted as varying in meaning. Putnam developed the Carnapian idea of conceptual relativity in this way, arguing for *actual* quantifier variance, that is, the idea that there is no single absolute meaning for the quantifier and allied notions (1987, 19). Eli Hirsch, inspired by Putnam, developed the idea of quantifier variance, and showed that it did not lead to any conflict with realism. Unlike Putnam, however, he argues only for *possible* quantifier variance: he thinks that there is a unified meaning of the quantifier in standard English, so that if we interpret the disputants as speaking English literally, at least one is saying something plainly false. Nonetheless, he holds that if we are charitable we may interpret each disputant as saying something true in her own language (or a different possible language), where each uses the quantifier in a different way. Most crucially, in defending the idea of strong quantifier variance, Hirsch holds that no such use of the quantifier is metaphysically privileged.

For a long time the focus of newly re-emerging metaontological debates came to be on the question of whether the quantifier does or could vary in meaning, with deflationists like Hirsch embracing, and defenders of hard metaphysics like Peter van Inwagen and Ted Sider arguing against, quantifier variance. Both sides agreed in treating the possibility of quantifier variance as the main threat to hard metaphysics. Indeed Sider writes:

> The deflationist *must* claim that the participants in ontological debates mean different things by the quantifiers. And so, the deflationist must accept that quantifiers *can* mean different things, that there are multiple candidate meanings for quantifiers. In Hirsch's phrase, deflationists must accept *quantifier variance*.
>
> *(2009, 391)*

In arguing against quantifier variance as an attempt to defend hard ontology against deflationism, Van Inwagen argues that 'existence' is univocal. He does so by arguing that it is interdefinable with expressions that clearly apply in the same way to objects of different types. First, he argues, following Frege, that "existence is closely allied to number":

> To say that unicorns do not exist is to say something very much like this: the number of unicorns is 0; to say that horses exist is to say essentially this: the number of horses is 1 or more . . . . The univocacy of number and the intimate connection between number and existence should convince us that there is at least very good reason to think that existence is univocal.
>
> *(2009, 482)*

Second, apparently following Carnap (!),[24] van Inwagen argues that 'exists' may also be defined in terms of disjunction and 'all', as "we may replace the statement that there exists a prime number between 16 and 20 with the statement that 17 is a prime or 18 is a

---

24. He attributes the argument to Carnap but says he hasn't been able to locate it in his writings (2009, 484).

prime or 19 is a prime," and (van Inwagen adds) that those are *all* the numbers between 16 and 20. But 'or' and 'all' van Inwagen takes to be 'obviously univocal' (2009, 484).

There is an interesting point to this line of argument that may be put succinctly: 'exists' and the existential quantifier are (like number terms, 'or', and 'all') topic-neutral. They are *formal* terms that may be conjoined with *material* terms of different categories while retaining their same sense—at least in the sense of retaining the same core rule of use. This seems right. But notice the lineage of the idea: van Inwagen attributes these observations to Carnap, the father of deflationism, and Frege, the grandfather of deflationism (as both teacher of Carnap and inspiration for the deflationary neo-Fregean position in the philosophy of mathematics).

This should give us a clue already that something has gone awry, and that the metaontological deflationist position may not really be in tension with the idea that expressions like the quantifier and 'exists' are formal expressions that may be used univocally by disputants in ontological debates. To track down what happened and whether we've gone wrong here, it will be useful to pause to look at the history of treatments of 'exists', and see where this notion of 'exists' as a univocal formal notion—which van Inwagen takes to be the key to defending hard metaphysics—really comes from.

1.4. 'EXISTS' AS A FORMAL NOTION: A BRIEF HISTORY

The idea that 'exists' is a formal (topic-neutral) term has quite a long history.[25] The goal here is not to argue for this claim (which

---

25. For an excellent history of the idea that various logical notions are formal, see McFarlane (2000).

would require a long detour through the history of debates about existence) but rather to show that it can be developed in a way that is consistent with and leads readily to a sort of neo-Carnapian deflationary approach to existence questions.

Though 'exists' can function in the predicate position ('Jen runs' and 'Jen exists' having the same grammatical structure), it has been a common and recurring view that 'exists' does not name a property of objects. An early version of the view is expressed by Gassendi, who argued that existence is not a property, but rather a prerequisite for having any properties. In this sense, 'exists' may be seen not as a material term (that names a property or activity of an object) but instead as playing the formal, topic-neutral role of enabling application of any (material) predicate. Hume famously held that the idea of existence 'makes no addition' to the idea of any object (1739/1985, Bk. I, Part II, sec. vi). For there is no distinct impression from which the idea of 'existence' could be derived. The idea of an existing cow, in short, is no more than the idea of a cow. The idea that existence makes 'no addition' to the idea of an object again may be read as suggesting that the term has no *material* content (it is not saying anything about what sort of object an object is, or what it is like). By contrast, the idea of a *white* cow does add something to the idea of a cow. Kant followed Hume in denying that 'exists' is a predicate. Austin similarly noted the lack of any added descriptive content, in his memorable claim, "The word ['exist'] is a verb, but it does not describe something that things do all the time, like breathing, only quieter—ticking over, as it were, in a metaphysical sort of way" (1962, 68).

The view that 'exists' does not name a property or activity of objects (or that it is not a first-order predicate) is an attractive one. For while it seems natural to think that property terms enable discriminations among objects that do and do not have the property (as we can distinguish the white from the nonwhite cows), it seems absurd to think that we can do the same, in distinguishing the cows that do and do not exist (this is perhaps another way of expressing Hume's point that 'existence' adds nothing to the idea of an object).[26] But this so far is just to say what 'exists' *isn't*: it isn't a first-order predicate, predicating some property of objects. The very idea that 'exists' adds nothing to the idea of an object, however, makes it difficult to see what the role is of positive claims of the form 'Ks exist'.

We find a more positive view in this direction in Frege, who argues that 'exists' is a second-order concept "analogous to number" (1884/1974, sec. 53, p. 65e). Numbers, Frege argues, are second-order concepts, and so statements of quantity are covertly making assertions not about *things* but rather about the instantiation of the *concept:*

> . . . the content of a statement of number is an assertion about a concept. This is perhaps clearest with the number 0. If I say 'Venus has 0 moons', there simply does not exist any moon or agglomeration of moons for anything to be asserted of; but what happens is that a property is assigned to the *concept* 'moon of Venus', namely that of including nothing under it.
>
> *(1884/1974, sec. 46, p.59e)*

Since number terms appear as first-order predicates applied to objects, but really function as second-order predicates of concepts, quantity statements may be misleading. If I give a statement of quantity:

---

26. Following David Londey, who considers 'the absurdity of a farmer who daily inspected his flock with the aim of sorting the existing from the non-existent ones—searching for the stigmata of existence', as cited in Miller (2002).

... on the face of it we are talking about objects, whereas really we are intending to assert something of a concept. This usage is confusing. The construction in 'four thoroughbred horses' fosters the illusion that 'four' modifies the concept 'thoroughbred horse' in just the same way as 'thoroughbred' modifies the concept 'horse'. Whereas in fact only 'thoroughbred' is a characteristic used in this way; the word 'four' is used to assert something of a concept.

(1884/1974, sec. 52, p. 64e).

The term "existence", on Frege's view, works like a number term: "Affirmation of existence is in fact nothing but denial of the number nought" (1884, sec. 53, p. 65e). Denial of the number 0, in turn, Frege understands quantificationally:

It is tempting to define 0 by saying that the number 0 belongs to a concept if no object falls under it. But this seems to amount to replacing 0 by 'no', which means the same. The following formulation is therefore preferable: the number 0 belongs to a concept, if the proposition that *a* does not fall under that concept is true universally, whatever *a* may be.

(1884/1974, sec. 55, p. 67e).

So we have here a three-way equivalence setting up 'exists' as a formal notion interchangeable with the (clearly formal) concepts of number and quantification. To say "Ps don't exist" is equivalent to saying "the number of Ps is zero", which is equivalent to saying "there are no Ps", or "for everything whatsoever, it is not a P". In each case, on Frege's view what is really asserted is something about a *concept*, not about an object—namely, that the concept is uninstantiated.

Frege's view that 'exists' is not a first-order predicate of objects, but rather a second-order predicate of concepts, adds an additional attraction to the original, negative view. For it enables us to resolve the old riddle of nonexistence: if 'exists' is a predicate that applies to everything, then it seems that it would be plainly contradictory to assert, for example, 'Unicorns don't exist'. For to assert anything of them, they must exist, contradicting the claim that they don't exist. Frege's treatment of 'exists' provides a simple way of showing how nonexistence claims may be both meaningful and true: to say 'Unicorns don't exist' is only to say that the concept *unicorn* is uninstantiated (the number of unicorns is zero)—which clearly may be both meaningful and true.

Frege of course was Carnap's teacher, and a major influence on Carnap's approach to philosophy throughout his life, so it should be no surprise if Carnap assumes something like Frege's view of existence: not as a material notion that may be associated with different standards by different disputants to ontological debates, but rather as a formal notion that says of a concept that it is instantiated. Carnap indeed follows Frege in treating number expressions as second-level predicates (Gabriel 2007, 69; Carnap 1947/1956, 116–17).[27]

Carnap also, like Frege before him and Quine after him, tends to treat claims of existence (to the extent that they are using a meaningful notion at all), claims about what 'there is', and existentially quantified claims, as interchangeable. Thus, as we have seen, Carnap expresses agreement with the letter of Quine's view that "to be is to be the value of a variable", though he warns against interpreting this in an *ontological* sense. The person who introduces

---

27. Though he treats numbers as *properties* of second-level rather than *classes* of second-level (1947/1956, 117).

variables for which all and only expressions for natural numbers are substitutable is willing to speak about numbers in general, and

> will, for example, make statements like: 'for every m and n, $m + n = n + m$' and 'there is an m between 7 and 13 which is prime'. The latter sentence speaks of the existence of a prime number. *However, the concept of existence here has nothing to do with the ontological concept of existence or reality.* The sentence mentioned means just the same as 'it is not the case that for every m between 7 and 13, m is not prime'. By the same token, we see, furthermore, that the user of the language is willing to recognize the concept Number.
>
> (*Carnap 1947/1956, 43–44; emphasis mine*)

Here we see Carnap embrace, for that (nonontological) concept of existence that he accepts as having sense and as employable, that to speak of the existence of, say, a prime number between 7 and 13 is just to deny that all such numbers are nonprime. Claims of existence, to the extent that they are employing a legitimate concept of 'existence', are interchangeable with quantificational claims.

Immediately following that, we see Carnap argue that an existentially quantified claim employing a term like 'Human' ('H'), for example, "$(Ex)\ (Hx)$", may be translated in any of the following ways:

  (i)   'There is an x such that x is human'
 (ii)   'There is an individual x such that x belongs to the class Human'
(iii)   'There is an individual concept x such that x is subsumable under the property Human'
(iv)   'There is an individual x such that x has the property Human' (1947/1956, 46)

So again here we see Carnap claim that there is an equivalence between existence claims, existentially quantified claims, and claims that a certain class is occupied or a certain property is instantiated. What we have here in short are rules of use articulated for the quantifier, treating it as a formal concept and showing its relation to other expressions—not any claim of the form that the quantifier varies in meaning. One can argue about exactly what view we should take of the meaning of 'exists' and of its role (I will discuss some options in chapter 2 below). Nonetheless, we clearly see here already the important idea of functional pluralism: that the term 'exists' does not serve a function of describing a feature of objects (as many first-order predicates do), and that it instead plays something like a formal role. I will return to discuss this idea, ways of developing it, and its significance in chapters 2 and 10 below. We can also see that it would be a mistake to think of this view as one committed to quantifier variance in anything like the contemporary sense attacked by those who aim to defend hard metaphysics. I turn to make that point next.

1.5. IS CARNAP COMMITTED TO QUANTIFIER VARIANCE?

The answer to this, of course, depends on what one means by 'quantifier variance'. I will argue, however, that Carnap clearly accepts a view of the quantifier like van Inwagen's insofar as he considers it as a formal term with fixed core rule(s) of use, and that his way of dissolving ontological debates does not rely on anything like quantifier variance as it is commonly understood in the contemporary literature.

First, however, I should mention a sense in which one might take Carnap to accept quantifier variance. Carnap famously accepts the 'principle of tolerance': "It is not our business to set up prohibitions, but to arrive at conventions", thus giving up the search for a single, correct logic, and instead permitting everyone "to build up his own logic, i.e., his own form of language, as he wishes. All that is required of him is that if he wishes to discuss it, he must state his methods clearly, and give syntactical rules instead of philosophical arguments" (1937/2002, 51–52). Given this principle of tolerance, of course, Carnap would not deny that philosophers *may* associate the letters 'exist' or the symbol '∃' with any number of different meanings or rules of use, provided only that their proposal comes with sufficient clarity. But we do not see Carnap making any such proposal himself. Instead, as we have seen, he uses the quantifier as a formal term with certain fixed core rules of use that make it interchangeable with claims of existence, and treats assertions of existence as equivalent to the second-order assertion that the property is instantiated or the class nonempty.

Hirsch himself holds that even in the varied meanings that may be attached to the quantifier, it may retain the same role in language, and the same syntactic and formal logical properties (2002a, 53; 2011, xiv). The changes that come with the changes in meaning, however, he argues, are changes in the 'concept of the existence of something' that lead to a difference in truth-conditions for quantified sentences, for example, a difference between whether or not one takes it to be a sufficient condition for the truth of 'there is a mereological sum of F and G' that the expressions 'the F thing' and 'the G thing' both refer to something (2002a, 53–54). But Carnap is not committed to the idea that the 'concept of existence' may vary in ways that seem to implicitly shift the standards for existence and the truth-conditions for quantified claims.

More importantly and revealingly, in "Empiricism, Semantics and Ontology" Carnap does not appeal to the idea that disputants use the quantifier in different senses as part of his way of dissolving apparent ontological debates. Instead, the differences he points to among the distinct 'frameworks' that lead to diverse ontological claims are differences in what *material* terms the adherents of different frameworks accept, that is, whether or not each accepts nominal terms like 'proposition', 'property', 'number', along with predicates that take them as values and variables to range over them. A Carnapian way of deflating ontological debates need not rely on saying that the ontological debates turn out to be merely verbal debates or pseudo-debates *because the disputants are using the quantifier in different senses*.

But how *does* Carnap diagnose the problem with ontological debates, if not by treating them as merely verbal disputes arising from each using the quantifier in a different way? As we have seen above, Carnap's crucial point is that existence questions can only be asked within, or *using the terms of*, a framework. But frameworks that differ, in Carnap's terms, for example, as the property-framework or the number-framework differ from linguistic frameworks that have not introduced these new singular terms, need not differ in *every* respect, or with respect to the rules of use of *all* the terms employed. Instead, one framework may be built on top of another, employing shared terms in the same sense. So the Carnapian may perfectly well accept that there is a single formal rule of use for the quantifier and 'exists' that is shared by the nominalist and the Platonist.[28]

The difference may instead lie in what *material* terms they have introduced and continue to accept (with what rules of use). The

---

28. Sider acknowledges that Carnap allows that frameworks may agree on a core inferential role of the quantifier, but holds that (on Carnap's view) the quantifier differs 'in other respects' in these frameworks: "for example, over whether '$\exists x$ x is a keyboard' follows from 'there are some things arranged keyboard-wise" (2001, xxii). What I am suggesting is that this difference is ultimately due to not to a variation in the meaning of the quantifier but in whether one accepts the material term 'keyboard' along with this constitutive rule for its use, which entitle us to introduce the relevant noun term and variables to range over keyboards (and other artifacts).

nominalist must be understood as implicitly refusing to admit noun terms for numbers (and refusing to quantify over numbers), or refusing to accept or make use of the general predicate *number* (though she will use number terms in their role as determiners— i.e., she will allow 'there are four books on the table' but not 'four is an even number') or for properties (she will say 'the phone is red and the shirt is red' but not 'there is some property that the phone and shirt have in common'). Put more formally, those who accept the relevant extended linguistic framework accept a predicate of higher level that we can apply to the terms, now used as nouns (e.g., the predicate *property*, enabling us to say not merely "this shirt is red" but also "red [noun form] is *a* property"). Once we have accepted noun terms, we can also introduce variables for which these nouns may be substituted (1947/1956, 213–14). Once the new noun terms (and predicates and variables) are introduced governed by the relevant rules, we can formulate internal existence questions *using* those terms, and those will be either "empirical or logical" questions (1947/1956, 214).

The nominalist employs a different framework from the Platonist about numbers or properties, and will not accept sentences such as 'numbers exist' or 'properties exist'. But the point is not that 'exists' is being used in a different sense by the nominalist and Platonist, but rather that the second accepts while the first rejects the linguistic framework that includes the relevant material concepts of property or number. Of course as a result of accepting the material terms of the new framework the Platonist will (having introduced variables for which number terms can be substituted) have a different domain of quantification than the nominalist, but this is not naturally thought of as a change in the meaning of the quantifier, and is a result of a more fundamental difference in whether the disputants accept the terms and concepts of the new framework. If the nominalist accepted those concepts (or the corresponding noun terms) with the same rules of use shared by the Platonist, she would also have to embrace truths like "there are numbers", as that would follow trivially from the rules that help constitute the framework. As a result, the nominalist cannot consistently assert that there are no numbers while using the linguistic framework that gives the term 'number' its sense.[29]

The dispute between Platonists and nominalists, on Carnap's view, is a pseudo-dispute if we take it as an ontological dispute about whether *numbers really exist,* since there is no way of making sense of the nominalist's position as both making use of the familiar concept of *number* and of denying that there are numbers. He suggests that the best way to understand the dispute is instead as a pragmatic dispute about whether to accept the number framework—one which differs from the thing framework not in using 'there is' with a different meaning, but rather in introducing new nouns, predicates of higher order to apply to them, and variables for which they can be substituted. Thus Carnap says:

29. What of other ontological disagreements that might result from this? Consider, for example, a disagreement between the eliminativist and realist that does not employ the term 'number'. Suppose instead we debate whether 'There is something non-physical', which the eliminativist (of a certain stripe, e.g. whose eliminativism arises from a thoroughgoing suspicion of abstracta) regards as false and the realist regards as true? (Thanks to Matti Eklund for raising this issue.) Figuring out how to understand this apparent conflict is trickier, given the variations (discussed in my 2009a and in chapter 2 below) about how to understand 'object', 'something' and other highly generic terms ('thing', 'entity'. . .). Various options are possible: if they are both using the term 'something' in the sortal sense (and assuming that it is tied to physicality), then the eliminativist speaks truly and the realist falsely—though it hardly seems plausible that the realist would use the term 'something' in the sortal sense while asserting this. If they use the term 'something' in different senses (e.g., if the realist uses it in a covering sense—with 'number' one of the sortals covered, while the eliminativist uses 'something' in a sortal sense, or in a covering sense that covers only sortals she accepts—not including sortals for abstracta) then they may indeed be talking past each other, and both speaking truly. But that is not due to a variation in the meaning each assigns the quantifier, but rather a variation in the meaning of 'something' each employs. If both are using 'something' in a covering sense that covers all possible well-formed sortals, then the realist is speaking truly and the eliminativist is speaking falsely. But in any case, we can analyze what is going on in their apparent disagreement without recourse to saying that they are using the quantifier or 'there is' with different meanings.

I agree, of course, with Quine that the problem of 'Nominalism' as he interprets it is a meaningful problem; it is the question of whether all natural science can be expressed in a 'nominalistic' language, that is, one containing only individual variables whose values are concrete objects, not classes, properties, and the like. However, I am doubtful whether it is advisable to transfer to this *new* problem in *logic or semantics* the label 'nominalism' which stems from an old metaphysical problem.

(1947/1956, 43)

Thus, however we slice it, there is no meaningful deep *metaphysical* debate to be had. If we make use of the relevant concept, the answer to the existence question is easy to come by; if we don't, the question is not an ontological existence question but the practical one of what conceptual or linguistic frameworks to accept.

The Carnapian way of deflating ontological debates, then, is not tied to the claim that the meaning of the quantifier varies, and the deflationist needn't deny that the quantifier and allied terms like 'exists' and 'there is' are formal notions that may be governed by the same rules of use in frameworks used by nomimalists, Platonists, and other disputants. Quite to the contrary, the idea that these are topic-neutral, *formal* notions, is one that can be traced back to the origins of metaontological deflationism itself. I shall have more to say in chapter 2 about how we may understand the rules of use for our English expression 'exists' in a formal, univocal way, and how this contributes to, rather than providing a barrier to, developing a Carnapian deflationary approach to ontology. In chapter 10 I shall show how a formal conception of the meaning of the quantifier can help defend easy ontology against Sider's accusation (2011, 83) that it cannot be metaontologically deflationary as it involves 'just more (hard) metaphysics'.

There is, however, one more sense in which one might think of Carnap as committed to quantifier variance. That is this: since, for Carnap, the meaning of a term is given by the meaning postulates that are analytic within the relevant framework, any change in the analytic claims that use a given term in a framework counts as a change of meaning for that term. When we introduce a term like 'number' with rules that make it analytic that, say, 'the number 5 exists', we thereby also change the analyticities for 'exist', and so, to that extent, effect a change of meaning for 'exists'. In that sense, one might think that the changes in material terms to which Carnap appeals in deflating ontological debates do lead to a form of quantifier variance.

Well, perhaps from the point of view of Carnap exposition we should accept this. But it does not affect the philosophical point at issue at all. For this sort of trivial change in the meaning of the quantifier is neither what Hirsch and Putnam were after in their forms of quantifier variance, nor what van Inwagen and other defenders of hard ontology deny in rejecting it. First, it clearly doesn't involve denying van Inwagen's view that 'affirmation of existence is denial of the number zero' (2009, 483); on the contrary, it is quite consistent with the view that 'exists' is a formal term governed by core rules of use (connecting it with rules for the quantifier, for number claims, and for disjunction) that *do not vary* even when we add new material terms to the language.[30] Indeed we need only propose a small shift—to count the meaning of a term as given by certain *core* rules of use (bringing us close to something like Horwich's [1999] view) rather than as tied to *all* analytic claims involving that

---

30. This of course is not to deny that there are differences between van Inwagen's and Carnap's views: Carnap treats existence claims as implicitly second order; van Inwagen rejects this (2009, 483–84). Van Inwagen also clearly would reject the Carnapian way of introducing new linguistic frameworks, holding instead that one must be justified in introducing new terms by thinking that there are things for them to refer to (2009, 491), a viewpoint Carnap clearly rejects (1950/1956, 214).

term—to license us to say that the meaning of the quantifier doesn't vary across those different frameworks that differ in adopting additional material terms.

Second, it is clear that this is not the sense of 'quantifier variance' that Hirsch uses as a way of trying to undermine hard metaphysics. For Hirsch is concerned not with the trivial changes in analyticities involving the quantifier that may be introduced when we introduce new terms to a linguistic framework, but rather with *changes in the truth-conditions* for (all) quantified statements (2002a, 54). He considers as an example two different uses of the quantifier: The A-use (antimereologist's use) and M-use (mereologist's use). While the A-language counts 'there exists something composed of the F-thing and the G-thing' as true only if those expressions refer to things that are united in some special ways, the M-language counts that sentence as true no matter how they are connected. As a result of these different standards, some existence statements that are true in the M-language, for example 'The mereological sum of my nose and the Eiffel Tower exists', are false in the A-language (2002a, 55–56). The two languages, as Hirsch presents them, do not differ in that one accepts and the other rejects the *terminology* of 'mereological sum'; both are apparently accepting (using) this terminology in making their declarations that there is or is not a mereological sum of nose and tower. Instead, they differ in the truth-conditions they require for statements that mereological sums exist, presumably in whether or not items must be "connected (united) in some special ways" in order for it to be true that there exists something composed of them (2002a, 54)

But this is not Carnap's diagnosis of the situation. First, he would be able to make no sense of the idea that those who employ the A-use would both *use* the term 'mereological sum' and yet deny that such a sum exists. So he wouldn't say that each of the competitors is saying something true given her own use of the quantifier.[31] Instead, he would deny that the A-speakers are making a coherent object-language (theoretical) claim at all (instead, they are at best implicitly rejecting the vocabulary). Second, he does not appeal to anything like changes in standards for existence to show that the debate here is faulty: the basic standards (rules of use) for 'exists' may (for anything Carnap says) remain the same across them. The disputants are not both speaking truths in their own idiolect—but with the debate being merely verbal owing to the different standards of existence each employs. Instead, the speaker of the A-language is not making any coherent theoretic statement at all; the speaker of the M-language may be seen either as stating a fairly trivial, obvious truth, or as implicitly making a different pragmatic suggestion that we adopt a framework including terms for mereological sums. Given that interpretation, we can also clearly see that the position of quantifier variance to which Sider thinks the deflationist must be committed (and against which he argues, in defense of hard metaphysics) is nothing Carnap himself is committed to. Sider initially describes deflationism as the view that

> [1] something is wrong with ontological questions themselves. Other than questions of conceptual analysis, there are no sensible questions of (philosophical) ontology. Certainly there are no questions that are fit to debate in the manner of the ontologists. To return to the case at hand: when some particles are arranged tablewise, there is no 'substantive' question of whether there also exists a table composed of those particles, they say. [2] They are simply different—and equally good— ways to talk.
>
> *(2009, 385–86; inserted numbers mine)*

---

31. To be precise, Hirsch holds that in fact, if both disputants in an ontological debate represent themselves as speaking English, one must be speaking a falsehood. It is just that

And he attributes this view to Carnap, Hirsch, Putnam, and me alike (2009, 386 n. 10). But one thing the above discussion should make clear is that there is a crucial difference between [1] and [2]. The Carnapian deflationist of course accepts [1] that something is wrong with ontological positions, and that there are no questions that are fit to debate in the manner of the ontologists. But she does not accept [2] that when one ontologist asserts that there are tables, and another denies this, they can each be charitably interpreted as speaking truths in their own language (with the variance amounting to a matter of how each chooses the meaning of the quantifier). Instead, the Carnapian deflationist does not interpret the table-denier as making any theoretic claim we can make sense of, since if she accepted the term 'table' with its customary rules of use, it would be an obvious truth that there are tables. And so there is no need for the Carnapian deflationist to accept that the disputants can be interpreted to "mean different things by the quantifiers" (Sider 2009, 391) to make sense of the idea that both speak truly (for the Carnapian denies that they do). There is a way of deflating ontological debates that does not rely on quantifier variance (in the robust, Hirschian sense). That way is Carnap's.

As a result, all of the recent discussion of quantifier variance turns out to be a complete sidetrack from the core issues between Carnapian deflationists and neo-Quinean ontologists. And the ambitious ontologist's defense of the idea that there is a single meaning for the quantifier, however successful it may be, does nothing to defeat Carnapian deflationism. Contrary to Sider's claim and the assumption of many contemporary metaphysicians, deflationism need not be tied to quantifier variance. Nor is

there is a possible language that disputant could speak in which her claims would be true (2002a, 69).

it the case, as Karen Bennett has suggested, that the only options for those who think that something is amiss with metaphysical debates are either (1) to deny that there is any fact of the matter about the disputed ontological issues, (2) to hold that the dispute is purely verbal, with each side talking past the other, or (3) to take the problem to be a merely epistemic one of a shortage of justification for believing that the ontological claim is true, or that it is false (2009).[32] The neo-Carnapian view is none of these—again, the true Carnapian option has been missed.

In what follows I will thus largely ignore questions about quantifier variance. This is not because I deny that the meaning of the quantifier does or could vary, or that some disputes might be understandable in this way—I will remain neutral on all of that. Instead it is because my interest here lies in developing an alternative sort of metaontological deflationism: one that does not rely on the idea of quantifier variance, and so sidesteps all of the recent criticisms of quantifier variance. It also has the potential for greater deflationary power than the quantifier variance view. For on the view developed here, to deflate an ontological debate does not require showing that "given the correct view of linguistic interpretation, each party will agree that the other party speaks the truth in its own language" (Hirsch 2009, 239). And so (as I will discuss in chapter 4 below) it may enable us to deflate, for example, disputes between Platonists and nominalists, whereas Hirsch doubts that his method can do so, as there seems to be no acceptable way of interpreting the Platonist's views so that the nominalist will accept that the Platonist speaks the truth in her own language (2009, 252–56).

32. Bennett (2009, 40–41) also mistakenly places me in the second category, classifying me with Hirsch as holding the view that at least some metaphysical disputes are purely verbal, on account of the disputants assigning different meanings to the quantifier, the relevant predicate, or negation. She does, however, acknowledge that I think that "some metaphysical disputes face different difficulties".

In all of the recent debates about quantifier variance, the true
Carnapian position has been missed. The truer legacy of Carnap's
metaontological approach is not carried by Putnam or Hirsch, but
rather by the neo-Fregeans in the philosophy of mathematics (who
of course were inspired by Carnap's teacher, Frege), as well as by
Stephen Schiffer's work on 'pleonastic' entities and my own defense
of ordinary and other objects. I will return to discuss this approach
and its generalization in chapter 3 below. Developing it and defending it will occupy the remainder of this book.

1.6. CONCLUSION

Above I have developed an interpretation of Carnap's deflationary
approach to existence questions, aiming to show that it does not rely
on verificationism, is not defeated by Quine's objections, and remains
tenable as long as we retain the distinctions between the analytic and
the synthetic and between use and mention. Moreover, I have tried
to show that (despite more recent developments of Putnam's) the
Carnapian deflationary approach to existence questions is not tied to
a general antirealism and does not rely on quantifier variance. These
results should make the approach immediately seem more promising,
and make evident that it has often been wrongly rejected by association with verificationism and antirealism. They also make it evident
that the vast majority of recent defenses of hard ontology, focused on
responding to threats of quantifier variance, are irrelevant to assessing
the original Carnapian deflationary position.[33]

33. Others also assume the main target is quantifier variance. For example, in her arguments for the epistemicist view that some metaphysical disputes just don't have sufficient justification for embracing either side, Bennett (2009) focuses on arguing
against the view that metaphysical disputes are purely verbal and never mentions the
neo-Carnapian line explicated above.

To really get at a neo-Carnapian deflationary ontological position we must leave behind the idea of quantifier variance, and see how a univocal view of the meaning of 'exists' and the quantifier may nonetheless form part of a position in which those disputes about existence that are meaningfully stated are easy to answer and not subjects for hard ontological debates. I begin that project in the next chapter, aiming to show a way to develop a neo-Carnapian deflationary approach in contemporary terms. I will argue that we may maintain that 'exists' is used as a *univocal*, formal term, while retaining an approach that makes existence questions easy to answer and not suitable subjects for deep and difficult ontological debates. I will also argue that, to the extent that it is a plausible view about the rules of use for 'exists', the deflationary proposal undermines a great many other approaches to existence questions—particularly those that take there to be across-the-board 'criteria of existence' such as causal efficacy, mind-independence, and so on, that may be used in resolving ontological disputes.

[2]

THE UNBEARABLE LIGHTNESS
OF EXISTENCE

In this chapter I aim to develop a contemporary version of a broadly neo-Carnapian approach to existence questions. In line with the conclusions of the prior chapter, it will be a view that does not rely on the idea that the meaning of the quantifier can be interpreted as varying in the mouths of disputants. Instead, it will treat 'exists' as having a fixed, formal rule of use. Yet it will also be a position on which most of those existence questions debated in metaphysics are answerable straightforwardly by conceptual and/or empirical means. This approach to existence questions also gives us reason to reject more substantive conceptions of existence of various sorts, and so to reject all ontological arguments based on whether or not putative entities satisfy some substantive 'criterion of existence' such as causal efficacy, mind-independence, and so on.

In chapter 3 I will go on to show how this general approach is related to contemporary approaches developed by neo-Fregeans for debates about the existence of numbers, and by Stephen Schiffer for debates about the existence of propositions, properties, fictional characters and other entities. I will also examine what follows from the approach for first-order ontological disputes and for metaontology. As we shall see, adopting this

THE UNBEARABLE LIGHTNESS OF EXISTENCE

approach to existence questions also deflates most ontological debates in the sense that existence questions (at least those that are well-formed factual questions: the equivalents of Carnap's internal questions) become too easy to answer to warrant serious metaphysical debate.

The goals here are relatively modest: I hope to motivate and develop an easy approach to existence questions in contemporary terms, showing that the view is tenable and attractive. If I can do that much then defenders of hard ontology may be forced at least to acknowledge a viable alternative and challenge to their view that does not rely on quantifier variance. Those who approach these issues from a more neutral standpoint may, by the end of the book, be brought to see the pragmatic appeal of the easy approach over the alternative. And finally, those in the silent majority of philosophers at large (though not of metaphysicians) who suspect that something has gone wrong somewhere in these metaphysical debates may be given some assistance in articulating where they have gone wrong, and what a plausible alternative might look like.

2.1. A CORE RULE OF USE FOR 'EXISTS'

As I have argued above, Carnap treats 'exists' as a formal term, and one may accept that 'exists' is a univocal formal term (governed by an invariant core formal rule of use) and yet still come to the conclusion that something is wrong with the vast majority of contemporary ontological debates. Most contemporary debates about existence in ontology concern whether entities of a certain *kind* exist: for example, are there numbers, propositions, tables, organisms, events, mental states, and so on? I will limit my focus to general existence questions (and claims) of this form, expressed in terms of affirming or denying 'Ks exist', where 'K' is a general noun.[1]

As we have seen briefly above in reviewing the history, there are good reasons to think that 'exists' is not a (normal, first-order) predicate, aiming to describe a feature of objects: to say that an object exists adds 'nothing to the idea' of the object, and cannot be used to distinguish objects that have and lack the feature. 'Exists' simply does not serve the same function as paradigmatic first-order predicates like 'red'. Denying that 'exists' is a first-order predicate also gives us hope of handling the ancient riddle of nonexistence: how a nonexistence claim such as 'Unicorns don't exist' could be both meaningful and true. For if we think of 'exist' (and 'don't exist') as a predicate describing objects, it is hard to see (barring Meinongianism) how this could be meaningful and true, since either 'unicorn' fails to refer (in which case we might treat the sentence as either lacking in truth-value or false, depending on how we treat cases of reference failure) or it does not fail to refer, in which case it is false.

But if we deny that 'exists' is a (first-order) predicate, how should we understand it? As we have seen above, Frege held that 'Ks exist' is equivalent to 'the concept K is instantiated', and assumed that Ks exist just in case $\exists x(Kx)$.[2] Carnap followed his teacher in treating the quantifier as a formal term, and treating the assertion that there is a human ($\exists x(Hx)$) as equivalent to the second-order assertion that the class of humans is nonempty or that the property or concept Human is instantiated.

---

1. Existence questions involving singular terms may, on my view, be handled similarly (see my forthcoming b). For further discussion of existence claims involving names, see my (2010).

2. This assumption is of course rejected by various philosophers including Meinongians and free logicians. It is, however, generally accepted by those who hold the approaches to ontology I will be criticizing below, viz., Quineans and most of those who propose substantive existence conditions (excepting Azzouni (2004)).

Whether this claim is tenable hangs to a considerable extent on how we understand concepts. If we thought of them as mental entities (as Frege evidently did not) we might reject the proposed equivalence on grounds that Ks might exist even in worlds in which the concept <K> did not exist. One could, of course, circumvent that sort of difficulty by being a Platonist about concepts—though one would still owe an account of what concepts are, why we should think there are such things, and why we should be Platonists about them. I suspect that all of these are debts that can be discharged successfully (particularly given the approach to existence questions given below), but nonetheless, to avoid long detours into a theory of concepts, I will take a different route to circumventing these difficulties below.

One might try to avoid entering into a theory of concepts by working instead with terms. Yet whether we deal in concepts or terms, we face a further difficulty. As we have seen, Frege held that the content of a statement of number or existence is "an assertion *about a* concept" (1884/1974, sec. 55, p. 67e), not about an object. But critics often reply that metalinguistic/conceptual views misrepresent existence claims as being *about* our terms or concepts, when they are really *about* the world and the things in it (see, e.g., Braun 1993, 455). For to the extent that we think of existence claims as being about the world and what's in it, it may seem misguided to think that they are tacitly *about* our concepts or terms.

Moreover, new difficulties arise by working with terms rather than concepts. For, critics allege, if we said simply that 'Ks exist' is equivalent to 'The term 'K' has a nonempty extension' we get in trouble, as Ks might exist in worlds in which the term 'K' does not.

Fortunately, all of these difficulties can be circumvented while retaining the spirit of the Humean/Kantian/Fregean idea. I prefer to avoid controversies about concepts, their existence, and nature, by speaking of terms and their application conditions. I have argued

elsewhere (2007a) that general nouns have certain kinds of constitutive rules, including application conditions and coapplication
conditions. (I will say more about what these are below.) With this
in place, one could say that (for a general noun 'K'): Ks exist iff the
application conditions for 'K' are fulfilled. But that would still leave
us with the problem that there may be worlds in which Ks exist, but
the term 'K' does not exist, or is associated with different application conditions. We can avoid this problem in turn by rigidifying
our reference to the application conditions for 'K': it is the application conditions *actually associated with 'K'*, here and now at our
world, that are relevant, regardless of the world at which the existence claim is evaluated. Thus we should suggest instead:

> E: Ks exist iff the application conditions actually associated
> with 'K' are fulfilled.

(Provided we retain the standard equivalence between quantificational claims and existence claims, we can also say: $\exists x(Kx)$ iff the
application conditions actually associated with 'K' are fulfilled.)
These application conditions may be fulfilled at other worlds,
regardless of whether or not the term (or concept) 'K' exists at those
worlds (or what application conditions it may have there). When
the view is expressed in this way, we need not worry about worlds in
which the term 'K' does not exist, or is used in a different way (with
different application conditions). For in evaluating the existence
claim, we must stick with the application conditions linked with 'K'
in the *actual* world, and evaluate whether these are fulfilled at some
other world. If those very application conditions are fulfilled at that
world, then Ks exist at that world.

But what about the objection that holds that our existence claims
are not *about* our terms or concepts but about the world? I think
there is something right about this. The right way to express the

view is not as a view about what the true content of existence claims is, but rather a view about a fundamental rule of use for 'exists'—just as the equivalence schema that (according to the deflationist about truth) connects "The proposition that snow is white is true" and "Snow is white" does not entail that 'Snow is white' is *about* a proposition rather than being about snow. An equivalence schema involving 'exists' need not be taken as reporting a synonymy. Instead, schema (E) demonstrates a connection between the rules of use that enables us to move up and down the semantic slide, from *mentioning* terms and evaluating whether their application conditions are fulfilled, to *using* those terms in talking about whether or not entities of the sort exist. As long as the terms are *used*, the statements made using them are indeed, as the critic would have it, about the world, not about language.

Indeed I think a helpful way of looking at this proposal is as offering a deflationary view of 'exists', analogous to deflationary treatments of 'truth' and 'reference'. While the term 'deflationism' is used in many ways, here I will use it to describe theories that deny that the relevant concept (of truth, reference, or existence) is even attempting to refer to a substantive property the nature of which we can investigate and hope to discover. On deflationary views of truth, reference, or existence, the term in question has a very different function than to attempt to refer to a property we can track and investigate—so we do well to be functional pluralists, acknowledging the different functions of different predicates. Instead, the function of the truth predicate, on Horwich's deflationary view, is to serve as a device of generalization (1998). What might the function of 'exists' be? It may be better to begin by examining the function of claims that things of some kind do *not* exist. For positive existence claims are seldom used in ordinary English conversation, except to rebut claims of nonexistence, and so the latter seem to play a more basic role. What then might the function of nonexistence claims be? Typically, they are used to disabuse listeners of mistakes we think they are making, in expecting people to have been talking about (or drawing or . . .) something, when in fact they are making a mistake, telling a story, engaging in a pretense, or something along those lines. So, for example, we might comfort a child by telling her that monsters don't exist—they are just talked about in stories and movies. Where existence claims are used, they are typically used with a 'doch' function, of rebutting a nonexistence claim or insinuation; in that case they may (as Hume had it) function to (re-)join 'belief to the conception'. A term governed by the rule of use articulated above (that Ks exist iff the application conditions actually associated with 'K' are fulfilled) may ably perform the function of correcting mistaken assumptions about when terms (or other referential devices) do and do not really refer.

Since they deny that the target terms even attempt to describe a property we can hope to investigate the nature of, deflationary theories renounce the search for reductive generalizations of the following form: x is true iff . . . (x corresponds to the facts, is made true by truthmakers, is verifiable, is ideally warranted . . .); 'n' refers to x iff 'n' bears . . . to x (is causally linked to x, evolved with the function of indicating the presence of xs . . .); Ks exist iff . . . (Ks are causally potent, mind-independent, posited by our best scientific theory . . .). Instead, each holds that the relevant concept may be grasped by grasping certain trivial platitudes governing the concept. Each thus gives a sort of no-theory attitude towards the concept in question, holding that we were wrong to think that we need a theory to uncover what truth, reference, or existence consists in. As a result, adopting the relevant form of deflationism leads one to reject any number of different philosophical proposals to identify the deeper or more substantive nature of truth, reference, or existence.[3]

3. At the end of the day, however, the deflationist need not deny that there is a relevant property or relation (of truth, reference, or existence). For we may trivially acquire reference to the relevant properties or relations—though these cannot serve an

In section 2.5 below, I shall say more precisely why the above proposal of a core rule of use governing 'exists' should lead us to reject all substantive theories of existence (captured in various proposed 'criteria of existence'). For now this much may be said. The application conditions for nouns of different kinds may vary widely, again at least in part owing to the different functions our terms serve. As a result, we should expect no uniform, across-the-board answer to the question of what it takes for entities to exist. Thus, again we have a purely formal answer, not one with across-the-board material content. The examples discussed below will help make clear some of the ways in which the application conditions for terms of different sorts may vary. As a result, while we can say in general that a term refers if its application conditions are fulfilled, the conditions under which things of different kinds exist will be as various as those application conditions are. This leads us to deny that there are any across-the-board, shared criteria of existence.

2.2. WHAT ARE APPLICATION CONDITIONS?

To make this proposal plausible requires that more be said about what application conditions (in the present sense) are, why we should think that our terms have application conditions, and why we should think that they vary for terms of different sorts. Application conditions, as I understand them, are certain basic rules of use that are among those that are meaning-constituting for the term.[4] In the

---

explanatory function and we would be misguided to think of ourselves as discovering the true natures of these properties (in the way that we might discover the nature of water). See below.

4. I do not mean, however, to say or imply that these are the only meaning-constitutive rules for a term. In (2007a) I also discuss other rules in the form of coapplication conditions

case of sortal terms, these establish certain basic conditions under which the term will succeed or fail in referring: both in its initial grounding, and in subsequent attempts at using it referentially. As I conceive of them, application conditions are among the semantic rules of use for the terms we master as we acquire language. Infants may learn which rules govern which terms as they observe the use of various terms, attempt to use the terms themselves, have their uses approved or corrected or misunderstood by others, and so on (and of course this is a process that, for more recondite terms, by no means ends in infancy). I can remain neutral on whether the rules for the corresponding concepts are all learned, or if some are innate.[5] The association with the particular phonemes of a word must be learned even if the corresponding concept is innate, and a great many concepts are clearly acquired, culturally local, and conventional, including those for many specific sortals such as 'bottle' and 'car'.

Mastery of these rules of use enables competent speakers to evaluate actual and hypothetical situations as ones in which their term (given the rules that govern its use in the actual world) would or would not refer; if the (actual) application conditions are fulfilled (in a particular circumstance), a speaker is entitled to say 'there is a K' (in that circumstance). Given the conceptual links elucidated

(conditions for when one may refer again to the same K); other meaning-constituting rules may also be involved, including not only application conditions (which serve as something like introduction or entry rules for a term) but also exit-rules, which tell us what we are committed and entitled to on the basis of applying a term. I come back to this idea in chapter 6.

5. Susan Carey argues that certain basic concepts (including 'object' in a sortal sense, 'agent', etc.) are innate concepts that humans and many other higher mammals have evolved to have. Possession of these concepts, on her view, is a matter of having evolved certain innate 'input analyzers' that license the application of these concepts on the basis of certain spatiotemporal information. So, for example (she argues), the spatio-temporal information that yields representations of objects includes being bounded in three-dimensional space and spatiotemporal continuity (2009, 451). This interpretation of the data is contested, however. See Hirsch (2011).

above, a speaker who is entitled to say 'there is a K' (in a given situation) is also licensed to infer that Ks exist.

While I have discussed application conditions extensively elsewhere (2007a, 2008), I nonetheless should summarize some important features of the idea here, to avoid misunderstanding:

1. They are semantic rules of use which speakers *master*, but these rules needn't take the form of necessary and sufficient conditions, and needn't be statable.
2. They are not merely conditions under which we would have *evidence* that the term applies, but rather conditions under which the term *would be correctly applied* (entitling us to truly say 'there is a K').
3. They need not be descriptive, and may involve deference to experts and to the world.

Each of these points deserves commentary.

1. Application conditions are semantic rules of use which speakers *master*, but these rules needn't take the form of necessary and sufficient conditions, and needn't be statable.

Many are skeptical that our terms have *informative* application conditions. The history of philosophical attempts to discover necessary and sufficient conditions for the application of various central terms (it is often thought) is a history of failures, and competent speakers typically can state application conditions for hardly any of the terms they use.[6] Often the most that can be agreed on is the

---

6. But see McGinn (2011) for a counter to this scepticism, including an argument that even an apparently insuperably difficult term like 'game' may be given a conceptual analysis.

uninformative disquotational claim, for example, that 'dog' applies if and only if there's a dog.

But for a term to *have* application conditions is not the same as for those application conditions to be (informatively) *statable* by competent speakers. The fact that competent speakers typically cannot *state* application conditions for most of the terms they use is no evidence at all against the idea that our terms *have* application conditions.[7] Application conditions should be thought of as semantic rules analogous to grammatical rules; just as competent speakers must be masters of following grammatical rules, but need not be capable of stating them (although it is plausibly those speakers' normative practices in speaking, correcting the speech of others, etc., that fixes the grammatical rules for a particular language), so must competent speakers be masters at following the semantic rules—but need not be capable of stating them.

Most importantly, however, for a term to have application conditions does not require that those conditions be statable at all. For it is plausible that any language must include some 'semantically basic terms',[8] that is, terms that cannot be learned just by way of learning definitions stated in other terms.[9] And if that is so, we must allow that for at least some terms, the application conditions (considered as semantic rules of use) needn't be capable of being (informatively) stated to be learned and to be in force. Instead, speakers may learn to master the rules of use for those terms by other means, for example, ostensively as we learn that a term is to be applied in situations like *this* (and not in situations like *that*), or via judgments of similarity to ostended paradigms; in some basic cases

---

7. So *pace* Kaplan (1989b, 577–78), the inability of most competent speakers to state the relevant rules is no evidence against these rules forming part of the semantic content of the name—on a conception of semantic content that ties it to rules of use.
8. To use a term of Philip Pettit's (2002, 128).
9. Michael Dummett (1976, 80) makes a similar point.

(as mentioned above) it may even be that what Carey (2009) calls our innate 'input analysers' give us the conceptual rules which we need only link with the relevant term of our language. And in fact, we teach our children words not by telling them (unhelpfully) that they should apply 'dog' wherever a dog exists, but rather by simply demonstratively applying 'dog' in some situations and refusing it in others, and applauding or correcting their attempted uses of phrases like '[there is a] dog' in various situations.

In short, rather than thinking of application conditions as definitions competent speakers (or anyone else) could recite, we should instead think of them as rules for when it is and is not proper to use a term, which speakers master in acquiring competence with applying and refusing a new term in various situations, and that (once mastered) enable competent speakers to evaluate whether or not the term would properly be applied in a range of actual and hypothetical situations. Although the application conditions for many basic nouns might not be statable at all, they will be learnable, as infants learn (through the approval and disapproval, the comprehension or bewilderment of their caregivers and eventually peers) that in circumstances *like these* it is appropriate to say 'this is a K' or 'there is a K', while in circumstances *like these* it is not. They thereby learn when the term is to be applied and when refused, and so master the application conditions for these semantically basic terms.

> 2. They are not merely conditions under which we would have *evidence* that the term applies, but rather conditions under which the term *would be correctly applied*.

Not much more needs to be said here. This point is only to make clear that 'application conditions' should not be understood as conditions under which it would be warranted or generally accepted to apply the relevant term, or in which we would have some evidence that it applies. Instead they are conditions under which it (really) would be proper to apply the term. Notice that this distinction applies wherever we have a rule: when we have *evidence that* someone has scored a touchdown, or committed a crime, is not the same as when it would be *correct to say* that someone scored a touchdown or committed a crime.

> 3. They need not be descriptive, and may involve deference to experts and to the world.

This thesis is intended to make it clear that one can accept application conditions while also accepting the validity of the main arguments that have led to the popularity of externalist and causal theories of reference for natural kind terms. The relevant application conditions for 'platypus', for example, do not state superficial observable characteristics (like being brown and furry), and we may decide to precisify or revise the application conditions for our terms in response to empirical discoveries. Nonetheless some application conditions *are* associated with the term, which distinguish it as a biological-kind term and make clear under what conditions the reference chain would have ended in a block, and nonexistence claims made involving the term would have been true. Where terms have world-deferential rules like these, one may then defer to the world (or to experts who have specialized knowledge of the world) to discover exactly what it is that distinguishes the kind *platypus* from other biological kinds, what its essential features are, and so on. And if one ultimately discovers that there are two species of furry monotremes with duck-like bills swimming in the rivers of Australia, one may have to make a decision about whether to apply the term 'platypus' to both species or to introduce a new term or terms for one or both.[10]

---

10. This parallels some important observations of Tim Button's (2013, 184–90) about the difficulties of determining the reference of the term 'zebra'.

Why think that our terms have application conditions, so conceived? The usual grounds given for thinking that our terms have no application conditions—conceived of as above—come from those who are inclined to purely causal theories of reference, which would hold that our terms and concepts derive their entire content from the things and kinds they pick out. I have argued extensively elsewhere (2007a, chapter 2; 2010),[11] however, that causal factors alone cannot sufficiently disambiguate whether a term refers and if so to what. For purely causal theories of reference notoriously face the so-called '*qua* problem'. In any situation, a speaker who would ground the reference of a term is apparently related to a great many things: a person, her clothes, the color of her hair, her current temporal part, the air between them, and so forth. Something more is needed to help disambiguate what is referred to (e.g., that the name is introduced as a person-term).[12] Moreover, a similar problem arises in determining whether our terms refer at all. For speakers are always in causal contact with a great many things, so how could attempts to ground reference ever fail, and a term fail to refer? As I have argued elsewhere (2010, 115–25), in order to allow that terms may sometimes fail to refer, we need to allow that our terms also come with rules in the form of something like application conditions, which play the needed role in determining whether or not a term succeeds in referring at all (or if its uses end in a block).[13]

11. In part following Devitt and Sterelny (1987/1999).
12. That is not to say that the reference of our terms always is or must be fully determinate, but the reference of our common terms certainly does not seem to be *that radically* indeterminate.
13. That earlier argument targeted those sympathetic to causal theories of reference, giving them reason to take the idea of application conditions on board (and to at least shift to a hybrid theory). I am now, however, more inclined to an inferentialist or use theory of meaning (see Brandom 1994; Horwich 1999), which enables us to preserve a pluralism about how terms of different types work (as the forms of the rules may vary) (Horwich 1999, 52). If one takes this general approach, application conditions for general nouns can be treated as among the introduction rules licensing us to apply a certain term or concept (and partially constitutive of its meaning). But application conditions for

2.3. DO APPLICATION CONDITIONS FOR 'K' INCLUDE THAT KS EXIST?

I have argued that Ks exist iff the application conditions actually associated with 'K' are fulfilled. But at this stage a crucial objection may arise. Some might argue that the application conditions for a term 'K' must include that Ks exist. If we must understand application conditions in terms of existence, however, we will need a prior and more substantive understanding of existence to determine whether application conditions are fulfilled.

To show that we can use E to gain an easy approach to existence questions, I must show how we can hope to understand application conditions for a term 'K' without their including the requirement that Ks exist (though their fulfilment of course *entails* that Ks exist—given the relevant conceptual links). That is the first challenge I will aim to meet below. To make this requirement explicit, in addition to the three features discussed above we can add a fourth:

4. Application conditions must not take the following form: 'K' applies iff Ks exist. (While this will always be true, it will not count as an application condition, in our terms.)

different sortal terms may take many different forms. For certain observational terms (e.g., 'red patch'), application of the term may be justified by the presence of certain visible conditions; for natural kind terms it may require the presence of entities of the same natural-scientific kind as those present in an original sample; for others (including many terms for institutional and abstract entities), we may be licensed to introduce a term by the truth of another proposition or application of another term, and so on. Such general issues in the theory of meaning are, however, beyond the scope of the present book. All that is required here is that we accept that our general noun terms have application conditions in something like the sense above, and that in certain cases the truth of a given sentence (not using that term or any supposed to be coreferential with it) may guarantee that those application conditions are met.

In short, we need to show that we needn't first settle existence questions of the form "Do Ks exist?" in order to settle questions about whether the application conditions for 'K' are fulfilled. This is cohesive with Carnap's approach, as he explicitly denied that we must raise and answer an ontological question regarding the existence or reality of a system of entities to legitimate introducing a new language form (1950/1956, 214). Yet (he holds) once we have introduced a new language form, we may be licensed—just given the rules of the framework—to introduce terms that are guaranteed to refer (e.g., 'five') and to make quantificational claims regarding entities of that type (to quantify over numbers). Thus, clearly on his view, as on that developed here, we need not settle existence questions before we can settle questions about whether we may introduce new concepts or terms and indeed about whether those concepts or terms refer.[14]

Although, as discussed above, there is no need for application conditions to be statable at all, the clearest way to make it evident that application conditions for 'K' need not appeal to the existence of Ks is to show a way in which they may be stated without appealing to the existence of Ks—or of some *thing* that meets the application conditions for 'K'. So, to respond to the objection more fully, it will help to give a way to understand application conditions for various sorts of terms 'K' in terms that do not appeal to the existence of Ks. I do not claim that the response given below is *completely* general; there may be more kinds of term than are mentioned here. But it is designed to show how we can address the question of whether

14. A similar line is taken by neo-Fregeans, who argue that it is out of place to demand a metaphysical justification for thinking that numbers, say, exist, before introducing the abstraction principle that enables us to make true identity claims about numbers and concluding that our number terms refer. (See, e.g., Hale and Wright 2009.) I will say more about the relation between the present position and the neo-Fregean one in chapter 3 below.

application conditions are fulfilled in ways that do not appeal to the existence of Ks, to make it clear that the project is not hopeless.

A distinction is commonly raised between substance sortals ('person', 'artifact' . . .)—sortal terms that must apply to that very entity as long as it exists at all—and phase sortals or other accidental sortals ('child', 'teacher', 'redhead'), which may apply to an object for a particular phase or in a particular role, but may cease to apply without that individual ceasing to exist.[15] One fairly uncontroversial way in which application conditions for a general nominative term 'K' may be stated without appealing to the existence of Ks is when the term is an accident sortal. So, for example, we may say that 'teacher' applies if there is a *person* who is employed to instruct—and thereby infer the existence of teachers from claims that made no use of the term or concept 'teacher'. Such inferences are relatively uncontroversial, for they are not, as it is sometimes put (Chalmers 2009), 'ontologically ampliative': the person *just is* the teacher—we are not inferring the existence of anything new. In this case, we do seem to answer the existence question simply by determining whether there is something that meets the additional criteria for the accidental sortal to apply.

What is far more controversial—and distinctive of the easy approach to existence questions—is the idea that even substance sortals (such as 'person') may have application conditions that do not appeal to the existence of things of that sort, so that we are not merely making the inference to existence from determining that there is some thing, and that it meets the relevant criteria. It is in these cases that we are truly inferring the existence of a new entity (not an old one under a new label), the existence of which is not adverted to in the application conditions, and from a sentence that referred to nothing of the sort.

15. Thanks to Simon Evnine for suggesting that I include this discussion here.

If we accept the view that even substance sortals have application conditions, and can show how to understand these conditions
in ways that don't involve saying that 'K' applies when Ks exist
(or when something exists that meets the criteria for being a 'K'),
then we can make plausible the idea that the above view about the
basic rule of use for 'exists' can form part of a deflationary approach
to existence questions. I will divide nominative terms into two
cases: concrete nouns of what Carnap called the 'thing' language
(1947/1956, 206–8), and derivative nouns (those that would have,
in Carnap's terms, been introduced as part of a new framework)
that may be introduced on the basis of these. I will take them in
reverse order, as the latter case is easier. In each case, I will suggest
a way of understanding the application conditions for 'K' without
appealing to the existence of Ks. This is not to say that the way suggested is the only way to state the application conditions (there need
not be a single or most privileged way), nor to provide a history of
how the terms were or are actually introduced. Instead, the idea is
that by stating some sufficient conditions for application of 'K' that
don't appeal to the existence of Ks we can make it clear that one
may grasp the application conditions and make correct judgments
about whether they are fulfilled without *relying* on prior judgments
about whether Ks exist. For this is crucial to the idea that existence
questions may be answered easily by making use of application conditions, without this turning out to be circular.[16]

2.3.1. Case 1: DERIVATIVE NOUNS

Rules of use for our noun terms may take different forms. Once
basic nouns are in place (more on these below) we can introduce new nouns on the basis of others. Call these 'derivative

---

16. Thanks to Huw Price for raising the circularity worry.

nouns'. Put in linguistic terms, this procedure is roughly what Carnap speaks of as introducing a new framework by "introducing into the language new expressions with suitable rules" (1950/1956, 208).

Some may balk at the idea that we could ever understand application conditions for 'K' in terms that do not appeal to the existence of Ks. Yet it is not hard to find everyday cases in which we can introduce a new substance sortal term 'K' and make clear under what conditions it refers without making any appeal to the existence of Ks (or of some thing that meets the new criteria and so may be identified with a K, as the person meets the criteria for being a teacher). In the case of many social and institutional terms, it is clear that this may happen. For example, institutional terms typically come with application conditions enabling us to say, for example, that if such and such paperwork is filed and the relevant fees paid, a corporation comes to exist (and 'corporation' comes to refer), without saying (trivially) that if a corporation exists, then 'corporation' may be applied. In such cases, we may determine whether the application conditions for 'K' are fulfilled without having to first answer the question "Do Ks exist?". Nor do we answer it by finding that any of the entities we begin by referring to (paperwork, fees) meet the relevant criteria and so *are* a corporation. Instead, we are genuinely introducing reference to a new entity, not just relabeling an old entity with a new accidental sortal. Terms for laws, marriages, debts, touchdowns, and so on similarly are explicitly introduced by way of specifying (in other terms) conditions under which a law is created, a marriage is entered into, a debt incurred, a touchdown scored. These conditions may be stated in the form of rules that enable us to move from talk that did not make use of the *relevant* noun term (or any synonymous or co-referring term—though it may make use of other noun terms) to talk that does—introducing use of the new noun.

Although rules may only give us (e.g.) an open list of suf-ficient conditions for application of the term, rather than a set of necessary and sufficient conditions, they may still be useful in evaluating existence claims. So, for example, there may be the rule: if the members of the legislature vote for a bill that the president signs, then a law comes into existence. Combined with more basic facts such as 'The members of the legislature voted for bill #362, and the president signed it', we can infer 'A new law came into effect', introducing the term 'law'. The rule that helps introduce the new noun term guar-antees that the term may be applied and so that there is a law if those conditions are fulfilled, thereby settling the question of whether laws exist. Notice that in these cases it is clear that we can evaluate whether the term 'law' applies without previously evaluating whether the law exists, as the condi-tions (that there be members of a legislature who vote for a bill signed by the president) don't appeal to the existence of a law—though (given the rules of use introduced for 'law') their fulfilment *guarantees* that there is a new law. So simi-larly, a term like 'marriage' may be introduced and partially governed by the rule 'If two suitable people A and B visit the justice of the peace and fill in the relevant paperwork and say the relevant vows, then A and B got married'. Combined again with more basic facts—say, that Jack and Jill visited the justice of the peace, filled in the paperwork and said the vows—we are entitled to infer that Jack and Jill got married, and so that there is a marriage (of Jack and Jill), thus easily resolving the question of whether marriages exist.[17]

---

17. For more discussion of the various rules that introduce terms for social entities, see my (2003a).

In each of these cases, existence questions posed *using* the relevant terms ('marriage', 'law') may easily be resolved by competent speakers, provided only that they know the truth of the more basic claims that can be fed into the rules. For if the basic claim is true, the application conditions for the new term are guaranteed to be fulfilled. So if we know that the legislature has ever voted to approve a bill, we know there is a law; if we know that individuals have ever fulfilled the relevant requirements, we know that there is a marriage; if we know that someone has ever filed the relevant paperwork, we know that there is a corporation. Provided we are using the terms with their customary rules of use, the existence questions posed may be straightforwardly answered. In each case the truth of the basic claim ensures that the application conditions for the term are fulfilled, so that we may conclude that the entity exists and the term refers without relying on a prior judgment that an entity identical with the one in question exists.

It is useful to consider social and institutional terms since these are typically terms that are explicitly defined, enabling us more easily to state at least some rules introducing the term, and some conditions the satisfaction of which guarantees that the new noun term applies. But other nominative concepts that don't aim to refer to institutional entities may follow similar rules. They may be introducible by way of rules that license us, from a true basic sentence involving no nominative term for anything of that type, to apply the new term 'K', and thus to infer that there is a K. So, for example, we can move from "Katie was born on a Tuesday" to "Katie's birth occurred on a Tuesday", and thus infer that there is a birth, and so that there is an event. We can similarly move from 'the crowd panicked' to 'the crowd was in a state of panic', inferring the existence of a state. From a sentence like 'the table is brown' we may also infer 'the table has the property of brownness', and thus that there is a property, and so on.[18] I shall have more to say in chapter 3 below about inferences like these, which have played a core role in prior 'easy' ontological arguments. In each of these cases we can thus give a straightforward answer to the challenge of saying how particular application conditions for 'K' might be articulated in ways that don't require a prior answer to "Do Ks exist?", or to "Is there some object that meets the criteria associated with the new sortal 'K'?".

2.3.2. Case 2: BASIC NOMINATIVE TERMS AND CONCEPTS

I have argued that application conditions for institutional terms such as 'corporation', as well as for noninstitutional terms such as 'property' and 'event', can clearly be introduced on the basis of application conditions that don't require any appeal to the existence of things of the disputed sort. In each case considered so far, however, in showing that the application conditions considered for the introduced term are fulfilled, we have begun from more basic truths that claim that there are things of *some* kind or other: for example, some papers that were filed, something that was red, or someone who was born. Thus, one might worry that this approach won't work for more basic sortal terms.

Indeed, one might worry that the application conditions for basic sortal terms 'K' *must* appeal to the existence of Ks (rather

---

18. But suppose the sentence "the table is brown" was false. Could we still infer "the table does not have the property of brownness" and so infer that there is some property *not* possessed by the table? It may not be clear how the standard rules of use for our English property terms go in such cases. Platonists about properties of course would allow such inferences, while Aristotelian or *in rebus* realists about properties would not. Indeed from the present point of view we may see the debate between Platonists and Aristotelians about properties as arising from that difference of interpretation of the

than their being fulfilled by the existence of entities of other sorts)—making it impossible to appeal to whether or not application conditions are fulfilled to determine whether things of the relevant sort exist, and so rendering the easy approach to existence questions unworkable for this range of terms. Of course it might still provide an easy way of resolving existence debates for many disputed entities, including numbers, properties, propositions, events, states, nations, and so on, and so still might be quite a significant contribution to metaontology. But, the objection goes, hard ontology on this view still has a place: existence questions posed using basic sortals must be addressed using hard ontological methods, and the rest may be answered easily.[19]

There are (at least) two things one might mean by 'basic sortal terms': (1) those that are basic in the sense that they are expressed by those basic terms we tend to learn early in our cognitive or linguistic development, and that we make use of in acquiring other concepts and learning to use other terms and (2) those that purport to refer to basic or fundamental entities. These two senses come apart. Of course there are many questions about which entities are fundamental. If by 'fundamental' we mean independent of other entities, then it seems that numbers and propositions might be candidates for being fundamental in that sense, though (as defenders of the easy approach have shown) the relevant concepts may be derived and we can make easy inferences to conclusions about their existence. If, on the other hand, one thinks of the fundamental as involving the basic posits of physics, for example, then (putting aside the concern

---

rules of use for our property talk (though obviously many of those disputants would not find this a friendly interpretation). I will return in chapter 3 to discuss cases in which the rules apparently license us to introduce the new term regardless of whether the initial sentence is true or false.

19. Thanks to Uriah Kriegel for pressing an objection along these lines.

that it is by no means clear what those are) it is clear that the concepts of even relatively basic physical entities are not at all basic to our conceptual scheme. Instead, acquiring mastery of them requires many years of education and mastery of many other concepts.

It seems to be sense (1) that is relevant here.[20] For the concern is that, while we may be able to introduce derivative nouns in ways that enable us to address existence questions using those nouns without appealing to the existence of that very kind of thing, we cannot do the same for our conceptually basic nouns (since we can't acquire them by rules that take us from the application of other terms to conclude that our new term applies).

So, focusing for now on basic sortal terms in sense (1), is it true that one cannot hope to get easy answers to existence questions expressed using these terms, but rather must answer first

---

20. But suppose one thinks it is (2) that is relevant. Must we accept that the sortal terms (if any) used to refer to the basic entities posited by physics have application conditions that can only take the form: 'K' applies if Ks exist? It seems not. Consider the term 'particle', which is introduced as part of a total theory, evaluated largely on the basis of its empirical adequacy, and applied in situations on the basis of certain empirical conditions. The term 'particle' is used in many different scientific theories, varying in terms of what fundamental ontological descriptions they use. J. S. Bell (1986) in fact lays out six ways the world could be, each consistent with the phenomena of quantum mechanics. So, for example, in quantum mechanics those who espouse hidden variables theories, many-worlds theories, and spontaneous collapse theories each accept the existence of particles. But even if 'particle' turns out to be a term for the most fundamental sort of *object*, one need not take particles to be what is most fundamental, or take application conditions for 'particle' to only be statable as 'particle' applies if particles exist. For defenders of many-worlds and spontaneous collapse theories will license us to infer the existence of particles from the behaviour of the wave-function, taking descriptions in the latter terms to be more ontologically basic (and not themselves to appeal to any particle-like entities, or indeed to any objects, sortally construed, at all). Once again, as in the case of ordinary terms like 'table', the application conditions may be ontologically neutral in the sense that one may be licensed to infer that they are fulfilled from a variety of different ontological descriptions, and so to infer the existence of particles from the fulfilment of application conditions that need not simply take the form of saying 'particle' refers just in case particles exist. Thanks to Peter Lewis for helpful discussion of this point. For further discussion of these issues see his (2006).

whether a K exists in order to say whether the application conditions for 'K' are fulfilled? If so, perhaps we must do hard ontology at least for those existence questions expressed using our basic sortals.

What might the basic sortals be? We could start by considering basic sortals of what Carnap called 'the thing language' (a language for 'the spatio-temporally ordered system of observable things and events') (1947/1956, 206–7)—such as 'piece of paper', 'desk', and the like. Terms of this category, such as 'dog', 'cup', or 'teddy', tend to figure prominently in early language acquisition, giving us additional reason to think (some of) these sortals are at least relatively fundamental.[21]

As mentioned above, we can show that one may answer an existence question 'Do Ks exist?' easily, by appeal to whether the application conditions for 'K' are fulfilled, if we can show a way to state and understand the application conditions for 'K' that does not appeal to Ks. A little ingenuity enables us to see how application conditions even for these (relatively) basic nouns of the thing language *could be* stated in terms that don't appeal to the existence of those very things. (Though again, it's worth emphasizing that there is no requirement that these application conditions be statable at all. Showing that the application conditions for 'K' may be stated without appealing to the existence of Ks *demonstrates* that the easy approach is workable for questions about the existence of Ks, but it is not *required* for the easy approach to be workable.)

I have argued elsewhere (2007a) that even if one lacked a term like 'cup', but instead (with the eliminativist) merely used such phrases as 'there are particles arranged cupwise', one could perfectly well introduce a term 'cup' as follows: if there are particles

---

21. Though this is not the only category of term represented in early language acquisition. Names, action words and social words, for example, also figure prominently. See Benedict (1977).

arranged cupwise, we are entitled to infer 'there is a cupwise arrangement of particles', and so to infer: 'there is a cup'. This enables us to state a sufficient condition for the application of a new noun (indeed one for a common-sense concrete object) without that statement making any appeal to the existence of the disputed object (the cup). Of course this is not to say that there *must be* particles (arranged cupwise) for the application conditions for 'cup' to be fulfilled; plenum stuff arranged cupwise would equally well ensure the application of the everyday term. So these are sufficient (not necessary) conditions for the application of the term.

Though we do not *actually* start from such terms as 'particles' (or 'plenum stuff') in English, this suggests that there are ways in which application conditions for common-sense terms might be statable without appealing to the existence of that very kind of thing. Indeed it seems that there are various different ontological descriptions we could use to express sufficient conditions for the application of the ordinary sortal 'cup': if particles are arranged cupwise, there is a cup; if there is plenum stuff arranged cupwise, there is a cup; if there is a state of affairs of an object instantiating cuphood, there is a cup; if there is a bundle of tropes including cupness, etc., there is a cup, or if there is a certain kind of mode or disturbance in a region of space-time there is a cup, and so on.[22] Or one could perhaps instead express the application conditions in what Hawthorne and Cortens (1995) call a 'feature-placing language', and hold that if it is cupping around here, then there is a cup. If so, we could state the application conditions for 'cup' without appealing the existence of a cup *or indeed of any object at all*.[23]

22. John Heil (2003, 177) makes a similar point.
23. This point is along the same lines as and inspired by Heather Dyke's (2008, 88–90) arguments that many nonsynonymous truths may have the same truthmaker, and that there is no unique and privileged way of describing the truthmakers (or here: of stating the application conditions). As she puts it: "the words we use to describe... truthmakers need not commit us to any particular ontology" (2008, 83).

Yet some might suspect that there is an underlying problem here. Talk about particles (or stuff) being 'arranged cupwise' (or similarly about bundles of tropes, states of affairs, placements of features, etc.) is a relatively recent introduction, and (the objector might hold) introducing such ways of speaking requires relying on the conceptual resources of those who already competently wield terms like 'cup' and other distinctively *objectual* terms.[24] Indeed, the objector might suggest, if we try to answer a question such as 'are the application conditions for 'cup' fulfilled?' by saying 'yes, because there are particles arranged cup-wise', we are still relying tacitly on a prior judgment that *there are cups*, in order to affirm the claim that there are particles arranged cup-wise.[25] If that objection is on the right track (a point I do not wish to commit myself to here) then we still have worries about whether one may answer existence questions about cups, tables, and the like by assessing whether the application conditions for these terms are fulfilled without those application conditions (at least tacitly, at some level) appealing to the existence of a cup, table, and so on.

Indeed the objector might (with some justice) suggest that what is conceptually basic to us is an *object* concept, and that the application conditions for an ordinary term like 'cup' are really *best* understood as requiring that there is an *object* (of a certain kind) there. For 'object' is plausibly the most basic sortal concept, possessed prior to specific sortals such as 'cup' or 'ball' (Carey 2009). But then (the objector might suggest) for this very basic concept 'object', the application conditions must appeal to *there*

---

24. Sometimes the 'arranged-F-wise' language is even introduced in a way that appeals to prior possession of the relevant F concept. Trenton Merricks, for example, writes, "Atoms are *arranged statuewise* if and only if they both have the properties and also stand in the relations to microscopica upon which, if statues existed, those atoms' *composing a statue* would non-trivially supervene" (2001, 4).
25. Thanks to Amanda McMullen for clearly articulating this concern.

being an object; here we can only say 'object' applies if an object exists, and so we cannot make use of the easy approach to address the most basic existence questions about what *objects* exist: here, they might suggest, is where room for hard ontology enters in.

I have argued elsewhere (2009a; 2007a, 157–58) that we must distinguish different uses of 'object' (or 'thing' or similar terms). On one of them (which I have called the 'covering' use) 'object' or 'thing' serves as a dummy sortal that may be replaced with any normal first-order sortal, and the rules of use for which entitle us to infer 'there is some thing' ('thing' seems to be used more commonly than 'object' in this totally generic role) from 'there is some S', where 'S' is any first-order sortal. So from 'there's an eyelash in my eye' we may infer 'there is something in my eye', and from '*The Rocky Horror Picture Show* is showing at the cinema' we may infer 'there is something showing at the cinema'. But 'thing' or 'object' in this sense clearly is not conceptually basic; instead we may acquire easy inferences to the existence of an object from more basic truths about the existence of an S. If 'object' is being used in this sense, as a covering term guaranteed to apply if some first-order sortal does, then we cannot try to answer the question of whether there is, for example, a table, symphony, or proposition in a given situation by asking whether there is an object. Instead we can only answer the question 'is there some object?' by way of answering the various sortal-specific existence questions.

The sense of 'thing' or 'object' that plausibly *is* conceptually basic is the sortal sense of 'object' studied by cognitive psychologists (e.g., Spelke 1990; Carey 2009; Xu 1999). Carey (2009) argues that this sortal concept of 'object' (along with 'number', 'agent', and 'cause') is part of 'core cognition': those basic concepts possessed by prelinguistic infants, shared with other animals (who share our evolutionary ancestry) such as cottontop tamarins and rhesus macaques, and remaining intact in adult cognition. This basic object concept apparently comes with individuative principles that enable infants to create 'object files', to individuate and track different things in the world through changes in location, properties, occlusion, and so on—treating them as the same individual across these changes, and judging when they persist or cease to exist.

But the application conditions governing this sortal concept of 'object' needn't be understood as simply appealing to the existence of an object. On the contrary, as Carey makes clear, infants make judgments about whether an object is present or persists based on the cohesiveness, well-boundedness, and rigidity of what they observe. In this sense, the basic sortal use of 'object', Carey argues, is applied based on observed criteria such as spatiotemporal continuity, boundedness, and cohesiveness (2009, chapter 3). We needn't enter into debates here about whether such an object concept is innate (given a process of evolution) or acquired. The point is that it provides at least a good candidate for a conceptually basic sortal.

Is it true, then, as the objector alleges, that existence questions asked using that basic object sortal (term or concept) cannot be answered 'easily' and so require hard ontology? That hardly seems the right conclusion to draw. Infants individuate these objects, track these objects, keeping track of how many there are (at least for very small numbers) and note when an object ceases to exist. In determining whether the object concept applies (or continues to apply, or how many objects there are) they make use of perceptual information, using what Carey calls 'perceptual input analyzers' that track such input as spatiotemporal continuity, boundedness, and cohesiveness (2009, 115). In short, infants apply the basic object concept empirically on the basis of observable conditions. Those who become more linguistically sophisticated and use this conceptually basic object concept are entitled to conclude that there is an object in a given situation by tracking the relevant features, without needing to first determine whether an object exists in order to determine whether the application conditions for this basic concept are met.

Some might be tempted to object that infants apply the object concept by *seeing that there is an object there*, and that the application conditions for their concept require *that there be an object there*, so that again in this case the application conditions for 'object' require saying that 'object' applies just in case there is an object there.

But I think this is a misunderstanding. Infants apply the basic object concept based on perceptual input, observable features. The object concept they possess includes criteria of individuation and identity for objects (Carey 2009, 117): modal features. But as is notorious since Hume, such modal features cannot be simply observed. The more proper way to understand the application conditions for this basic object concept (applied using their perceptual input analyzers) is in terms of the perceptual input that leads them to apply the concept. That does not appeal to prior criteria about whether an *object* exists (taking this to be a concept with criteria of individuation and identity). Instead the fulfilment of the application conditions is what leads to conclusions about whether there is an object in a given situation.

We need not be wedded to any particular psychological empirical theory to get to the conclusion that there is a plausible way to see how even existence questions asked using the (plausibly) conceptually basic 'object' sortal may be answered easily—not by making trivial inferences from other claims that did not involve that sortal, but rather by answering them empirically. So, we may reject the claim that one must do hard ontology to answer existence questions that are expressed using conceptually basic sortals. Instead, it is perfectly coherent with (indeed suggested by) the best empirical evidence that existence questions expressed using our most conceptually basic object concept are instead answerable by straightforward empirical means.

At this stage a fan of hard ontology might respond that that may be how, in fact, infants make judgments about whether an object exists or persists, or how many objects are in a given situation—but the question is *should they? Are they right to do so?* But if we understand their object concept to be governed by the rules elucidated by cognitive psychology, they *are* right to conclude that there is an object in a given situation, that an object has ceased to exist (when it is dispersed into parts), and so on. The objector cannot be coherently suggesting that, given the rules for identifying and individuating objects (that delineate our basic object concept), the infant gets it wrong. At best, the objector can be suggesting that we should replace this basic object concept of core cognition with some other concept suitable for doing grown-up ontology. I will consider below some prominent suggestions for replacing our conceptual scheme (e.g., by shifting to use a 'joint-carving' quantifier).

2.4. ANSWERING EXISTENCE QUESTIONS EASILY

All of this, of course, has merely been in defense of the idea that existence questions may be answered by (noncircular) appeal to whether the application conditions for the relevant term are fulfilled. Application conditions are conditions mastered by competent speakers (we may think of competent users of a term as those who do not use it merely parasitically on other speakers). So competent speakers are in a position to make use of their linguistic mastery and empirical or conceptual work to answer existence questions straightforwardly.

For a competent speaker has only to make use of her mastery of the rules of use of the term—combined with her access to any relevant empirical information—to determine whether the application conditions are met, and thus to evaluate whether the corresponding entities exist. A competent speaker, for example, who has mastered the use of the noun 'table', is in a position to know that the term may be successfully applied in restaurants all over the country, and so to conclude that there are tables without the need to read the copious metaphysics literature on composite objects. (Though she may need to read it to answer one or more challenges against the view that there are tables, such as arguments that the concept is incoherent.) Indeed for most common terms of our language, competent speakers are in a position to answer existence questions easily by making use of their mastery of the rules of use for the terms employed in asking those questions.

Thus, on this view a first sense in which existence questions are easy to answer is that a great many may be answered simply by making use of our conceptual competence, often combined with simple, straightforward empirical work. (I will discuss another sense in which they become easy in chapter 3 below). There is nothing 'epistemically metaphysical' in Sider's sense required for answering existence questions; we need only make use of our conceptual competence, reasoning skills, and empirical information—typically of a fairly uncontroversial sort. Of course, the relevant empirical work may in certain cases be tricky—in that sense it might not be entirely 'easy'. Nor is this to deny that there may be cases in which it is unclear whether the application conditions are fulfilled, such as if we ask, 'Do ivory-billed woodpeckers [still] exist?' But even where the empirical work is difficult, it is work for scientists or investigative journalists, not for a distinctively philosophical discipline of ontology.

Some questions (e.g., 'Is there a heap on my patio?') may be difficult to answer, even for those who have mastered the rules of use for the terms, due to vagueness or open-endedness in the rules of use for the term 'heap'. In such cases distinctively philosophical work may help in attempting to figure out and make explicit what the rules of use for our terms and concepts are, and also in determining which questions may simply be unanswerable owing to the vagueness or indeterminacy in the corresponding concept. But this is conceptual philosophical work. Many ontological disputes might be understood as implicitly disputes about what it takes for there to be, for example, fictional characters, numbers, properties, propositions, and so on, and the work may be difficult and contentious—especially where the terms used are distinctively philosophical terms that lack rules of use established by ordinary English speakers. But it is not a matter of figuring out what 'really exists' by distinctively philosophical means. Indeed, as Carnap himself would have allowed, conceptual work may be required at several levels: in working out the rules of use for our terms (where this is obscure), in determining which linguistic framework—or which sorts of terms, with which rules—to adopt (for which purpose), and even in determining the relations among our concepts and determining whether or not the rules governing various terms are (individually or mutually) consistent. But while serious conceptual work may be required, there are no deep metaphysical mysteries to be solved here, nor is there any need to appeal to the best 'total theory' or undertake any epistemically metaphysical investigations to resolve existence questions.

2.5. AGAINST SUBSTANTIVE CRITERIA OF EXISTENCE

It is safe to say that the deflationary approach to existence questions has not been dominant—or even widely recognized—over the past sixty years or so. Many philosophers approach existence questions in a neo-Quinean way, attempting to determine whether our 'best theories' unavoidably involve us in quantifying over the disputed entities. But often negative answers are arrived at in a different way: they are justified by the failure of the alleged entities to meet some substantive 'criterion of existence', such as mind-independence, contribution of (distinctive) causal powers, and so on.

Many different substantive criteria have been proposed and utilized as conditions for what it takes for entities to exist. So, for example, it is often supposed that one may answer questions about whether mental states, propositions, or properties exist by considering whether or not the purported entities meet the 'Eleatic' criterion, promoted by David Armstrong: "Everything that exists makes a difference to the causal powers of something" (1997, 41; see also his 1978, vol. 2, p. 5).[26] On this view, as it is usually interpreted, we should accept into our ontology all and only those entities that *make a causal difference*, or that have 'distinct causal powers' 'over and above' those of other entities we accept.[27] Another common

---

26. For discussion of difficulties with interpreting Armstrong's criterion, see Oddie (1982).

27. E.g., Trenton Merricks (2001, chapter 3) uses a version of this principle restricted to macrophysical objects to argue against the existence of ordinary objects such as tables and chairs, by arguing that they lack distinctive causal powers 'over and above' those of the atoms that make them up. The principle has also (sometimes under the name "Alexander's Dictum": to be real is to have causal powers) played a prominent role in discussions about whether we should grant real existence to phenomenal consciousness (Kim 1993, 348–49).

proposal is that for things to exist they must be (in some sense) mind-independent—as George Lakoff puts it, "Existence cannot depend in any way on human cognition" (1987, 164). Jody Azzouni, while denying that there are philosophically conclusive arguments for any criterion of existence, nonetheless holds that the criterion at work in *our* society is ontological independence from "any psychological or linguistic process *whatever*" (2004, 113). Crawford Elder (2004) proposes the distinct but related criterion that objects are real only if they have "real natures", where this is a matter of having essential properties whose status as essential is mind-independent. Still other criteria for existence are sometimes considered, for example, trackability, observability,[28] or other forms of epistemic robustness (Elder 1989, 440).[29]

A deflationary treatment of existence, however, involves the idea that there is no call for a theory aiming to uncover a deep and substantial nature of existence, for there is nothing more to the notion than is captured in the rules of use that enable it to fulfill its function. If the deflationary approach to existence is right, we may reject all attempts to find an acceptable principle telling us what it is to exist, or what features are definitive of existence. So we deny that we should even be looking for any principle of the following form: for every x, x exists iff x is such and such (causally relevant, mind-independent, in possession of a real nature . . .). The deflationary approach thus involves rejecting the idea that there is a shared *substantive* criterion for existence.

We do, however, have a purely *formal* criterion for existence, namely that given by schema (E): entities of kind K exist iff the

---

28. Bueno (2005, 477) proposes that it is a *sufficient* criterion for existence that we have observed an entity, tracked it, interacted with it, or developed methods of instrumental access to it. But he takes these only as sufficient, not as *necessary* criteria for existence, and so is not subject to the objections below.

29. Azzouni (2004, 129ff.) lays out four conditions on thick epistemic access as criteria for entities being 'thick posits', but also allows that we should accept the existence of 'thin' (but not 'ultrathin') posits.

application conditions actually associated with 'K' are fulfilled. Given the variety of different application conditions associated with different terms, the *substantive* conditions on the world that are relevant to whether terms of different kinds refer will vary considerably—and so (via semantic descent) we can also say that the conditions of existence for things of different kinds will vary considerably. Given that variability, the search for a single across-the-board material criterion of existence is misguided. Thus the deflationary approach to existence may be used to undermine any such substantive or material criteria of existence and their use in ontological debates.

I will not discuss the different proposals for substantive 'criteria of existence' separately and in detail. Instead, I will aim to show how the deflationary approach to existence leads us to reject all of these proposals. For on the above view, if the application conditions are fulfilled, entities of the corresponding type exist.

This gives those who accept the deflationary approach to existence questions a blueprint for generating counterexamples to any proposed across-the-board criterion of existence: we can show that any proposed criterion is mistaken if we can show that there is some term whose application conditions (established by speakers) are fulfilled, although the proposed existence criterion is not met. For if the application conditions are met, then we can infer that the entities in question exist despite failing to meet the proposed existence criterion—showing that meeting the proposed existence criterion cannot be necessary for existence.

Consider, for example, terms for everyday social and cultural entities, including artifactual kinds like tables and chairs, for works of art like paintings and sculptures, and for social and institutional entities such as baseballs and money. Even if we can't properly *state* the application conditions for terms like 'table' and 'chair', it's clear that most dining rooms provide sufficient conditions for these terms to apply according to the speakers' ordinary standards, most art galleries meet conditions that ensure 'painting' and 'sculpture' apply, and so on. And so it seems that (barring radical skeptical hypotheses that would take speakers to be badly deceived in thinking that the relevant conditions are fulfilled in dining rooms and art galleries when they are not) the conditions ordinarily required for these terms to apply are fulfilled.[30] As a result, we can conclude that tables, chairs, paintings, and sculptures exist. But the corresponding terms *require* for their application that there be intentional actions or practices of various sorts, and so if there are the corresponding entities, these entities must fail the mind-independence condition—at least on the usual construals that take mind-independence to mean that they could exist even if no minds, or psychological events or processes, existed.

Of course it is open to the defender of the mind-independence criterion to define 'mind-independent' in some other way, such that these purported entities would not violate it. We could, for example (with Elder 2004) take it to require possessing a *nature* independently of minds (not to require *existing* independently of minds) or (with Elder 1989) take it to require certain kinds of *epistemic* independence. I won't discuss these options in detail here, though I have argued at length elsewhere (2003c, 2007d) that artifacts (to name but one case) violate these criteria, although the application conditions actually associated with the term 'artifact' are nonetheless met in spades.

What about the Eleatic criterion? This is interpreted in a number of ways—some take it as the requirement that any entity that exist contribute *novel* causal powers—that is, powers 'over and above' those already contributed by any other entity (or entities) posited.

30. Some defenders of hard ontology suggest that speakers are deceived in thinking that there is some 'thing', 'object', or 'individual' in the relevant situations (where the presence of such a 'thing' is supposed to be an application condition for the term), when there is none. I address this line of thought briefly above, and more thoroughly in my (2007a, 157–58) and (2005).

It is often argued (Merricks 2001, 81; van Inwagen 1990, 122), however, that all purported inanimate composite objects (including not just artifacts but also natural objects like sticks and stones) violate this criterion, since all of their alleged work may be better accounted for by the work of the microscopic entities that (allegedly) compose them.[31] But (as I have argued elsewhere [2007a, 155–59]), the ordinary term 'table', for example, is guaranteed to apply given merely what the eliminativist calls 'particles arranged tablewise', that is, intentionally arranged in a characteristic shape and so that they may (collectively) perform certain characteristic functions—without any requirement that a table contribute causal powers 'over and above' those of its parts working together. But if the application conditions actually associated with 'table' are met, then tables exist even if they do not contribute 'novel' causal powers, and so we should abandon this version of the Eleatic criterion as an across-the-board criterion for existence.

On other formulations, the Eleatic criterion is taken to require not that a purported entity contribute *novel* causal powers, but only that it contribute *some* causal powers. This is more plausibly thought to be a requirement for terms like 'table' and 'stone' to apply; it seems that on this formulation, macroscopic inanimate physical objects would pass the Eleatic criterion. But there are nonetheless a great many common-sense terms that have actual application conditions that may be fulfilled without that criterion being met. Consider, for example, terms such as 'story' and 'symphony'.[32] Barring radical skeptical hypotheses, it seems that

31. Though it should be noted that van Inwagen and Merricks only accept the Eleatic principle as a criterion for the existence of macroscopic *physical* objects, not as a general criterion of existence.

32. Of course much the same could be said of other abstracta, including propositions, universals, numbers, etc. But since it is a contentious matter what exactly the application conditions for these terms are, I have stuck with more common-sense terms of ordinary language above.

the standard application conditions associated with these terms are regularly fulfilled (given the relevant creative acts, performances, etc.), and so that such things exist. But if such things do exist, as normally understood they cannot be identified with any spatiotemporally located entities such as copies of texts or performances. And so (if we assume that causation requires spatiotemporal location), they cannot be thought to directly have any causal impact on the world at all, although their copies and performances, and our thoughts and beliefs about them obviously may have a great deal of impact. So again, if we attend to the established application conditions for common-sense terms like 'story' or 'symphony', it follows that stories, symphonies, and the like exist, despite their apparent violation of the Eleatic criterion (as well as the mind-independence criterion, and presumably the trackability criterion as well).

On the deflationist's view, the mistake that lies behind proposing the various uniform criteria for existence seems to come, in each case, from finding an application condition that holds for *terms of a certain kind*, and a corresponding condition for the existence *of things of a certain kind*, and illegitimately generalizing it as an across-the-board criterion for the existence of 'anything whatsoever'. But even if, for example, mind-independence or contribution of causal powers are genuine criteria for the existence of basic physical entities, it does not follow that these are criteria for the existence of anything whatsoever. Careful consideration of a broader range of examples suggests that there are different application conditions for terms of different kinds. Given the connections between application conditions and existence, the application conditions for our terms may (by semantic descent) be expressed in the object-language as existence conditions for the objects (if any) referred to by those terms, and the conditions for the existence of objects of different kinds may be as various as the application conditions for our terms. So while each of these proposed criteria might be relevant as conditions for the existence of *some* sorts of things (e.g., mind-independence might be a relevant criterion for fundamental particles or mountains), they are not legitimately used as criteria for the existence of *anything whatsoever* (e.g., mind-independence may not be legitimately used as a criterion for the existence of money or works of art).

In fact, the application conditions for our terms seem to be so various (consider the differences in conditions under which terms like 'electron', 'mountain', 'debt', 'Thursday', 'public holiday', 'jury', 'fictional character', and 'symphony' would properly apply, given the actual application conditions associated with each) that the prospects seem very dim indeed for finding a single feature required for the application of *each* of these terms, and thus required for things of *any* sort to exist (*pace* Azzouni 2004, 112–13). So if we accept E and the link between the concepts of existence and application conditions proposed above, we have reason to doubt that there is any single criterion of existence that is shared across the board for (putative) objects of *any* kind. We also have reason to call into question many arguments for eliminating entities of various sorts (including mathematical entities, propositions, fictional characters, artefacts, composite macroscopic objects, etc.) on grounds of their failure to meet some across-the-board criterion of existence.[33] We thus also get a first sense in which the resulting view is metaontologically deflationary: it suggests that something is wrong with certain debates in ontology, namely, with all of those based in arguing that disputed entities do or do not meet some proposed substantive criterion of existence.

33. Some eliminativist strategies, however, remain untouched by this argument, including arguments based on alleged contradictions in the very idea of the sort of thing in question. I deal with these arguments elsewhere (2007a).

2.6. LINES OF REPLY

In this chapter I have tried to make clear how we may develop an easy approach to answering existence questions that does not rely on quantifier variance. Moreover, if the analyses I have proposed for the rules of use for 'exists' and for general nouns are correct, I have argued, it follows that common proposals for substantive across-the-board criteria of existence are wrong and a great many arguments for eliminating various sorts of entity should be rejected. It may be useful, however, to close by mentioning some lines of reply that remain open to those metaphysicians who find the lightness of this approach to existence questions unbearable.

One option is to accept that schema (E) expresses a rule of use for an everyday, 'thin' sense of existence, but to hold that there remains a deeper, more robust, or serious sense of what 'exists' or 'really exists' in which we can frame a distinctively ontological question. Ross Cameron, for example, suggests that we accept the easy ontological approach to (ordinary) existence questions. Nonetheless, he suggests, ontologists can and should pursue instead the question of what there *really* is, where that is to be determined by asking what we need as truthmakers for our sentences. Following John Heil (2003), Cameron accepts that in many cases <x exists> may be made true by something other than x (Cameron 2008, 4)—for example 'there is a sum of a, b, and c' may be made true by a, b, and c without any need to appeal to the sum as a truthmaker.[34] In such cases, Cameron argues, we are only ontologically committed to the truthmakers (a, b, and c)—not the sum; the truthmakers are all that 'really exist' as 'parts of fundamental reality' (2008, 17). In general, Cameron argues, if we must appeal to x as the truthmaker for the claim 'x exists', then we

---

34. In this Cameron is going against David Armstrong (2004), who holds that x is always a truthmaker for <x exists>.

should accept that x really exists. But if we can account for the truth of 'x exists' by only appealing to y, z . . ., then we aren't ontologically committed to x; x doesn't *really* exist (although the application conditions for 'x' are fulfilled and we should accept that x exists).

This way of locating a project for hard ontology thus relies on the idea that there is a distinction between sentences of the form 'x exists' for which we must appeal to x as a truthmaker, and those for which we do not (where the truthmaker may be y, z . . .) (2008, 17). But I have argued that we never need to evaluate the truth of 'x exists' by determining whether an x exists to make it true. (Moreover, as I will make clear in chapter 3 below, when the easy ontologist claims that certain entities exist she does not *posit* them as explanatory truthmakers). Instead, 'x exists' is true just in case the application conditions for 'x' are fulfilled, but (I have argued) these application conditions need not appeal to *there being an x*—we do not need to begin with hard ontology by asking if there is an x to serve as truthmaker for 'x exists' or to fulfill the application conditions for 'x'. The easy ontologist works in the other direction: given that 'x' applies, we infer that x exists (we don't presuppose it in determining whether the application conditions for 'x' are fulfilled).[35]

Others have taken different routes to articulating a deeper sense of 'exist' that remains for ontologists to investigate, even if one accepts the above approach to everyday existence claims. In fact, it has become commonplace for those defending hard ontology to

---

35. In fact, Cameron's project for ontology seems to rely on the idea that there is a uniquely, ontologically, best description of what the truthmakers for our sentences are—or else we could not determine our ontology by determining what the ultimate truthmakers for our sentences are. But even prominent truthmaker theorists such as John Heil (2003) and Heather Dyke (2008) reject that assumption. Dyke argues that there is "a variety of ontologies that are, arguably, able to supply truthmakers for truths" (2008, 82). As Dyke points out, even a claim of such a simple form as 'Fido exists' one might describe as made true by Fido, or by the fact of Fido existing, or by a state of affairs, or by tropes bundled, etc. (Dyke 2008, 83).

argue that they are using 'existence' or the quantifier in a 'thick' or 'strict' sense (Dorr 2005; Sider 2009), distinct from the ordinary use that might be captured by schema (E).[36] Indeed it has become increasingly popular among those who hope to preserve the seriousness of metaphysical debates to endorse a special technical language 'Ontologese'. This approach warrants and will be given fuller discussion. I will discuss Hofweber's arguments that there are two senses of 'existence', or two uses of the quantifier in chapter 9 below. In chapter 10 I will examine Sider's attempt to articulate an 'Ontologese' sense of the quantifier distinct from this thin everyday sense, and suitable to ground hard ontological debates.

In any case, if schema (E) really does lay out a core rule of use for the English term 'exists', then as long as we think of meaning as fixed by core rules of use, those engaged in hard ontology cannot be properly using the standard English term 'exists' (with its actual meaning) in their ontological work. Where they employ the same typography or sounds, they must (if they are not to be thought of as *misusing* the familiar English term by intending to use the familiar term and thus subjecting themselves to its standards of use, yet violating a core rule of use) be explicitly or implicitly introducing a new homophonic term 'EXISTS' governed by different (though perhaps related) rules.[37] In the latter case, the claims seem best understood as (explicit or implicit) proposals that we adopt a new language, not as claims that might surprise or enlighten speakers of English who consider existence questions using that language.

36. Hofweber (2005a), though no defender of hard ontology, also thinks that there is a distinct sense of the quantifier at use in ontological claims as compared with in the inferences that give us easy arguments for objects of various kinds. See chapter 9 below.

37. Thus in this sense I of course allow (as anyone should) that one can attempt to introduce new meanings for the existential quantifier or 'exists'. Nonetheless, this is not to endorse the idea that typical ontological debates are to be deflated by showing that each disputant uses the term 'exists' or the quantifier with a different meaning.

An additional worry arises, too: if those engaging in hard ontology are not using our familiar English term 'exists', is it clear that they have successfully introduced a new meaningful term at all? David Chalmers suggests that once we recognize the difference between ontological and ordinary existence assertions, that

> should make us suspicious about whether we really have a nondefective grasp of the notion of absolute quantification [or 'EXISTENCE']. If ordinary practice involving 'exists' always involves lightweight quantification [the sense of 'exists' that I have discussed above], then the coherence and nondefectiveness of this practice gives little support to the coherence and nondefectiveness of [the] practice involving the absolute quantifier. It is tempting to hold that the absolute quantifier is something of a philosopher's invention, one that otherwise plays very little role in our thought and talk. If so, then one may reasonably have doubts about whether it has a determinate content.
>
> (2009, 102–3)

Finally, even if the defender of hard ontology does successfully introduce a new term, with new rules of use, we might ask why those who look to ontology to find out what exists (using the standard English term) should care about the claims of hard ontology, or why the hard ontologist should not describe what she is doing in less misleading terms. In any case, if those who do hard ontology are (implicitly or explicitly) changing languages, then their work gives no reason for doubting that the above account gives an appropriate and easy method of answering existence questions, whenever these are asked using our familiar *English* language.

What I hope to have done in this chapter is to have made it plausible that existence questions (asked in ordinary English) can be answered easily, by motivating and developing a deflationary understanding of existence consistent with the idea that 'exists' and the quantifier are univocal formal terms. This leaves us with a view that makes existence questions 'easy' to answer in the sense that it enables those existence questions that are well formed to be answered straightforwardly by conceptual and/or empirical work—leaving no need for distinctively philosophical inquiries into existence. It also gives us a contemporary understanding of something along the lines of Carnap's approach to internal existence questions, showing how they may be answerable by 'logical or empirical means' in a way that doesn't leave room for any special 'hard' discipline of ontology.

[3]

EASY ONTOLOGY AND ITS CONSEQUENCES

Having now laid out a view on which existence questions may be answered easily, in this chapter I aim to make clear the relation between that view and recent easy ontological approaches used by neo-Fregeans in the philosophy of mathematics and by Stephen Schiffer in his defense of 'pleonastic' entities.[1] These other easy approaches to ontology do not rely on the same theses about application conditions and the rules of use for 'exist' that I have defended above. They do, however, share the feature of my view that they make existence questions easy to answer in the sense that answering them requires nothing more than conceptual and/or empirical work.

But there also is a more well-known sense in which recent easy approaches make ontological questions manifestly easy to answer: according to easy ontological views, in many cases ontological debates may be resolved by engaging in trivial inferences from uncontroversial premises. I will call an approach to answering

1. A still more recent defense of an easy approach to ontology is in Rayo (2013), who defends what he calls 'trivialist Platonism' in philosophy of mathematics, along with defending trivial inferences to the existence of events, properties, and ordinary objects. (Rayo explicitly develops this in the neo-Fregean tradition, but apparently independently of and without apparent awareness of the prior work of Schiffer or myself.) Since it has appeared so close to the time for this volume to go to press, I am unable to engage in extended discussion of Rayo here, but refer interested readers there.

(a particular range of) existence questions an 'easy' approach provided it shares the following two features: holding that all well-formed existence questions may be answered by conceptual and/or empirical work (requiring nothing 'epistemically metaphysical'), and that at least some disputed existence questions may be answered by means of trivial inferences from uncontroversial premises. In this chapter I will begin by discussing the relation between other easy approaches and the particular form of the easy approach to existence questions defended here. I will also try to make clear what advantages there are to developing the view in my way. Much of what I will say in the remainder of the book applies equally well to defending easy approaches of all forms against common objections, regardless of the form defended, since most criticisms have focused on the idea that some ontological debates can be resolved by way of trivial inferences from uncontroversial premises, a point all versions of the easy approach share.

In this chapter I also aim to make clear what follows from this easy approach to existence questions: a first-order simple realism about most disputed entities, and a deflationary metaontological approach that treats something as being amiss in standard ontological debates. Adopting an easy approach to existence questions leads to a deflationary attitude towards ontological debates: seeing prolonged philosophical debates about what *really* exists as pointless, since the questions may be resolved so straightforwardly.[2] Thus on the view developed here, we deflate not only the notion of existence, but also debates about existence questions. Since my particular version of the approach begins with deflating existence, and ends with deflating ontological debates, I will (for brevity) sometimes refer

---

2. Of course this is not to suggest that explicitly or tacitly conceptual debates about how the relevant terms and concepts work, what application conditions they have or what rules they are governed by are pointless. These may sometimes present quite difficult work.

to my view simply as the 'deflationary' position. But of course this term can be and has been used in a variety of ways, and on my view we should *not* say that the *entities* in question are 'deflated'—that is part of the point of the first-order 'simple realism'.

3.1. USING TRIVIAL INFERENCES TO ANSWER EXISTENCE QUESTIONS

I have argued that the view defended in chapter 2 about the fundamental rule of use for 'exist'—combined with the above understanding of application conditions—enables us to develop an easy approach to existence questions that enables those existence questions that are well formed and answerable to be answered straightforwardly by conceptual and/or empirical means, without the need for distinctively philosophical inquiries into existence, or for any 'epistemically metaphysical' knowledge.

But there also is another, more familiar, sense in which this approach enables existence questions to be answered easily: it enables a great many ontological debates to be resolved by trivial inferences that start from uncontroversial premises. For start from the truth that there are particles arranged tablewise in the restaurant, a truth that (if they check out the restaurant) eliminativists and realists about tables will both accept. But from 'there are particles arranged tablewise', competent speakers who have mastered the application conditions for 'table' can see that they are licensed to infer 'there is a table', thus settling the debate about the existence of tables. (Those who don't *feel* it is settled because they think some other condition must be met, for example, that there must be some *object* there, are referred to my 2007a, chapters 6 and 9, and chapter 2, section 2.3 above). Similarly, debates about whether there are events or properties may be resolved by trivial inferences from undisputed truths. For we may start from the undisputed truth that May was born on a Monday, and conclude that a birth (an event) occurred on a Monday, and thus that there are events. Similarly, a competent speaker who has mastered the use of property language is in a position to start from the undisputed observation that Beyoncé's dress is red and move to the conclusion that the dress has the property of redness, and so that there are properties, without reviewing metaphysical debates about properties.

Given the approach to existence questions I have defended above, such moves are legitimate, in each case, provided that the truth of the undisputed claim guarantees that the relevant application conditions for the new noun term are fulfilled. Since the very rules of use for the noun terms being introduced guarantee that that is the case, we can readily arrive at positive answers to many disputed existence questions.

This also makes evident two clear points of contrast between this easy approach and the neo-Quinean mainstream approach to existence questions, which holds that we should accept the existence of all *and only* those things over which we *must quantify* to make our *best scientific theories true*. The first is the idea that we should only accept those entities over which we *must* quantify to make statements we accept true. The trivial inferences allowed by the ordinary rules of English, however, suggest that whether a term is introduced as a noun (replaceable by a variable in a sentence of quantified form) or in some other grammatical role is often irrelevant. For we may have, or introduce, rules permitting us to make inferences from a sentence without a noun term into a sentence with a corresponding noun—one guaranteed to apply if the prior sentence was true. This gives us a way of introducing the noun into our language as a referring term (provided the prior sentence was true), which in turn licenses us to introduce variables ranging over the entities referred to. So, for example, the Quinean will say that we needn't accept the existence of properties, since we may avoid property talk in our best theories by saying, for example, 'There are red houses', which only quantifies over houses (not properties) when properly rendered in standard quantificational form. But from this statement we may trivially infer 'There are houses which have the property of being red', and from there infer 'there is a property (of being red which some houses have)'—leading us to quantify over properties. On my view, whether we *must quantify* over numbers, tables, propositions, properties, or whatever is largely irrelevant, if any statement we'd use to replace the quantificational statement leads us by trivial inferences to one in which we *do* use the relevant noun terms in a referring way or quantify over entities of that sort.[3] The placement in a part of speech is (to alter Quine's phrase [1966/1976, 210]) 'of little concern', as it varies according to *ontologically* irrelevant changes of *grammar*.[4] So we may accept one direction of Quine's dictum: that we should accept the existence of entities if we must quantify over them in our best scientific theories, but reject the *only if* direction. This is a critical difference since it means rejecting all ontological arguments that work by showing how we may (through paraphrase) avoid quantifying over entities of a disputed sort and concluding that we may deny the existence of those entities.

The second crucial difference is in Quine's constraint to accept only those entities over which we must quantify to make our *best scientific theories true.* The language used in scientific theories is only one small part of our language, and the use of language in formulating scientific theories covers only a small range of all the uses of language.[5] The deflationary approach defended above instead leads

---

3. For further discussion of this point, see my (2007a, chapter 9). To my knowledge, the first time a point along these lines was made was by Searle (1969, 107).

4. Cf. the arguments in Rayo (2013, chapter 1) that one should not reject easy arguments (or rather the 'just is' statements he considers) on purely syntactic grounds.

5. See also Price (2009), who argues that Quine's very naturalism should have led him to accept a pluralism about linguistic functions.

us to accept the existence of entities of any kind K, provided that the application conditions for 'K' are met—regardless of whether 'K' is a term used in our scientific theories, in our graduate admissions meetings, in our political discourse, in our department stores, in our art criticism, or whatever. So while the neo-Quinean holds that we should accept the existence of all and only things over which we must quantify to make the statements of our best *scientific* theories true, even if some term, say, 'hat', doesn't appear at all in our best scientific theories, if we accept schema (E) we should conclude nonetheless that hats exist, provided the standardly accepted application conditions for 'hat' are met. Barring radical skeptical hypotheses or conspiracy theories, it is clear that they are.[6] We might hope that the Quinean approach will help us to sort out those entities that are scientifically basic from those that are not, but if we accept the above understanding of the rules of use for 'exist' and the standard application conditions for our terms, we can't use it to tell us what does (and does not) exist. To say that something exists is not the same as to say it is basic or a scientific posit.

3.2. THREE FORMS OF EASY ONTOLOGY

The idea that certain ontological debates may be easily resolved by way of trivial inferences from uncontroversial truths is familiar from certain debates in recent metaphysics. Until recently, the idea was developed mainly in isolated pockets, for example, by neo-Fregeans in philosophy of mathematics and by Stephen Schiffer in his discussions of various pleonastic entities, and by myself in defense of ordinary objects. It is only relatively recently that the view is

---

6. I provide a more thorough criticism of the Quinean approach to existence questions and to ontological commitment in my (2007a, 159–68).

starting to become recognized as a unified approach—and it is also attracting increased sympathies.[7] While I have developed my own way of getting an easy approach to ontology above, it is both useful and important to see how these three views are related, all of which yield easy routes to answering at least some existence questions.

Bob Hale and Crispin Wright (2001, 2009) have developed an approach to the philosophy of mathematics that is commonly called 'neo-Fregean', since it takes off from Frege's view that objects are simply the correlates of singular terms, and that in general ontological categories are to be identified by way of the logical categories of our expressions (e.g., as singular terms, predicates, etc.). As Hale puts it, this view about the relationship between logical categories of expressions and ontological categories 'encourages' a certain approach to determining what kinds of things there are:

> If entities belonging to a certain ontological category just are
> what expressions of a certain logical category stand for, then
> we can argue for the existence of entities of that kind by argu-
> ing that there are true statements involving expressions of the
> relevant kind. If, for example, there are true statements incor-
> porating expressions functioning as singular terms, then there
> are objects of some corresponding kind. If the singular terms
> are such that, if they have reference at all, they refer to num-
> bers, there are numbers.
>
> *(2010, 406)*

This enables neo-Fregeans to offer 'easy' arguments for the exis-tence of numbers. For we can begin from an uncontroversial truth

---

7. In addition to those who have directly defended easy arguments for various entities, several prominent metaphysicians accept that easy arguments like these answer stan-dard existence questions asked in English, and suggest that as a result the real work of ontology must move on to other territory (Schaffer 2009a; Cameron 2010; Fine 2009).

that makes no use of the number concept, and then use a conceptual truth to derive a true statement using singular terms for numbers. So, for example, we may argue as follows:

Uncontroversial truth: The cups and the saucers are equinumerous.

Conceptual truth (Hume's principle): The number of ns = the number of ms iff the ns and the ms are equinumerous.

Derived claim:[8] The number of cups = the number of saucers.

But since the derived claim is a true identity claim, they hold, we are entitled to conclude that the singular terms in it ('the number of cups' and 'the number of saucers') refer, and so that there are numbers. This approach to getting an ontology of numbers apparently resolves an ancient ontological problem by starting from an uncontroversial truth that does not make use of the disputed concept (*number*) or make reference to the disputed entities (numbers) at all, and making use of trivial inferences.

A second version of an easy route to answering certain existence questions has been developed by Stephen Schiffer (1994, 1996, 2003) for such entities as propositions, properties, events, states, and fictional characters. In Schiffer's terms, we can begin with undisputed truths, and then engage in pleonastic 'something from nothing' inferences, to reach a truth that is intuitively redundant with respect to the first, yet leaves us with (apparently new) ontological commitments to the disputed entities—again apparently

8. By calling this a 'derived claim' I do not mean to suggest that such claims could not be arrived at directly, without inference, by competent speakers. I only mean to point to the fact that they may be derived from the uncontroversial claim combined with the conceptual truth.

resolving ontological questions by way of trivial inferences from undisputed truths.

In each case, an undisputed claim in which there is no mention of an entity of type J (and no use of the concept J or any supposed to be coreferential with it) may be combined with an analytic or conceptual truth that functions as what Schiffer calls a 'transformation rule', to give us a derived claim that is, intuitively, redundant with respect to the undisputed claim. Yet the derived claim apparently entails the existence of Js (numbers, propositions, events, possible worlds . . .)—thus settling what seemed like hard disputed ontological questions easily, by way of undisputed basic claims and their analytic entailments.

So, for example (making the intervening steps somewhat more explicit than Schiffer [2003] does), we can move from

- Undisputed claim: Snow is white.
- Conceptual truth: If P then *that P* is true.
- Derived claim: *That snow is white* is true.
- Ontological claim: There is a proposition (namely that snow is white).

Or from:

- Undisputed claim: May was born on a Monday.
- Conceptual truth: If P was born on D, then P's birth occurred on D.
- Derived claim: May's birth occurred on a Monday.
- Ontological claim: There is an event (namely of May's birth).

This seems to correspond to Carnap's talk of introducing new noun terms with new rules of use, as parts of new (or expanded) linguistic frameworks. So, on Carnap's view, numerals like 'five' may initially be used in the determiner position, as in "there are five books on the table". But we can go from there to introduce a general noun term "number" and sentences in which it appears, as in 'Five is a number', and then introduce variables to range over the numbers in quantified sentences (1947/1956, 208). Similarly, adjectival words like 'red', 'hard', and the like may be used in describing concrete objects. But we can go on to introduce a general term 'property', variables ranging over properties, and new rules for forming sentences with these terms in the nominative position, for example, 'Red is a color' and quantified sentences like 'These two pieces of paper have at least one color in common', from which we may infer that there is a color—and thus that there is a property (1947/1956, 211–12). The conceptual truths cited above in easy arguments may be seen as object-language articulations of the rules that may be used in introducing terms for propositions or events to our language. Given the introduction rules for the new terms, existence questions formulated *using* those terms are easy to answer, for the rules of use for the terms license us to make easy inferences from basic, uncontroversial truths to the existence of the entities in question.

Similar easy inferences also play a role in sophisticated versions of positions often labeled as 'expressivist', 'pragmatist', or 'quasi-realist' about an area of discourse.[9] Traditional expressivism starts by suggesting that a given range of vocabulary (say, moral or modal) does not have as its function 'describing' certain metaphysical features of reality (Price 2010, 2) (this is in line with Carnap's idea that we needn't first have metaphysical justification

---

9. Though 'quasi-realism' is a poor choice of term, since it suggests a contrast with genuine realism. I think, however, that the right reading of this approach is as giving a straightforward, out and out, simple realism about the questioned entities: realism *in the only sense the relevant terms have*. At least in some of his more recent writings, I think Blackburn shares this characterization (see, e.g. his 1993, 57, and his 2005).

for introducing the relevant vocabulary). Instead, the expressivist might identify the function of moral vocabulary as expressing certain mental states (say of approval or disapproval), or of modal vocabulary as making explicit the semantic or conceptual commitments and connections that are already implicit in our use of ordinary empirical vocabulary (Brandom 2008, 99). The expressivist becomes sophisticated when she insists, however, that this is not to deny that there are moral or modal truths, facts, or properties. As Huw Price aptly puts it:

> Quasi-realism begins where expressivism begins, with the thought that the primary function of certain of our (apparent) statements is not that of describing how things are. But it aims to show, nevertheless, how such expressions earn a right to the trappings of descriptive 'statementhood', in particular, the right to be treated as capable of being true and false . . . If successful, quasi-realism explains why the folk practice of making moral claims is in order just as it is, and explains why further any metaphysical inquiry about whether there are *really* moral facts is inevitably missing the point.
>
> *(2011, 9)*

The sophisticated expressivist insists that claims such as 'Child abuse is wrong' or 'Lions are necessarily animals' may be true or false (perhaps by adopting a minimalist approach to truth [see Price 2011, 253–79]), and insists that we can also, by trivial inferences, conclude that there is a property of wrongness possessed by instances of child abuse, or that lions have a certain modal property of being necessarily animals (see my 2013a). Thus, though the connections between these traditions have seldom been drawn out, the most sophisticated (and to my mind most plausible) versions of expressivism about a relevant area of discourse also make use of the kinds of trivial inferences endorsed by people like Schiffer and myself in developing the easy approach to ontology.

While Schiffer's view and the neo-Fregeans' have much in common, there are also some notable differences between them. One perhaps superficial difference is that the neo-Fregeans employ an equivalence principle, Hume's Principle, in reaching their ontological conclusions, whereas Schiffer's pleonastic inferences take the form of $S \to \exists x(Fx)$,[10] only requiring one-way entailments from the uncontroversial premise to the derived claim. This is important as it enables us to formulate easy ontological arguments even where we do not have available an equivalence principle (as we might not in cases where the candidates for S may be diverse and not fully enumerable). Nonetheless, the neo-Fregean only makes use of the right-to-left direction of the equivalence principle ("If the ms and ns are equinumerous, then the number of ns = the number of ms") in reaching the ontological conclusion, so there seems no reason to think that the neo-Fregean relies on there being an equivalence principle rather than a simple one-way entailment.

Second, the derived claim of the neo-Fregean has the form of an identity statement, and it is because it has the structure of an identity statement that Hale and Wright insist that the terms in it must refer, and thus that we are licensed to say that numbers exist. By contrast, Schiffer's derived claims do not have to take the form of an identity statement, and he makes no use of that idea in reaching the ontological conclusion that there are the disputed entities.[11] Instead, the introduced singular term may figure

---

10. More fully and properly, Schiffer says that $S \to \exists x(Fx)$ is a something from nothing f-entailment claim iff "(i) its antecedent is metaphysically possible but doesn't *logically* entail either its consequent or any statement of the form '$\exists x(x=a)$', where 'a' refers to an F, and (ii) the concept of an F is such that if there are Fs, then $S \to \exists x(Fx)$" (2003, 56–57).

11. Schiffer also makes it explicit that pleonastic concepts for Fs may be introduced without there being any nontrivial criterion of identity for Fs. (2003, 63 n. 14)

in other kinds of sentence in the derived claim. For example, the singular propositional term '<that snow is white>' figures in the derived claim "<that snow is white> is true", and the singular event term 'May's birth' appears in the true derived claim "May's birth occurred on a Monday". Both singular terms (as Schiffer insists) seem guaranteed to refer. Thus, from these derived claims it seems we are still licensed to make the inferences to the ontological conclusions that there are propositions and that there are births. In short, a Schifferian can easily accept the neo-Fregean's trivial transitions from 'the cups and saucers are equinumerous' to 'the number of cups = the number of saucers' to 'there is a number'. But it is not so clear whether or not a neo-Fregean would be equally happy to accept all of Schiffer's arguments to ontological conclusions— many of which don't go by way of a true identity statement. I will leave those differences to the side for the present, though they will come back into view later as we consider objections to each view. In any case, Schiffer's pleonastic approach can be seen as a generalization of the neo-Fregean approach in the sense that he can accept their arguments for the disputed entities and capture them in his terms, although it is not clear whether a neo-Fregean would accept all of Schiffer's arguments.[12]

In much the same way, the easy approach to ontology I have been developing and arguing for may be seen as a third route to getting easy answers to ontological questions that generalizes Schiffer's approach. Understood in my terms, we can see the trivial arguments of Schiffer (and the neo-Fregeans) for the

---

12. This hinges on whether neo-Fregeans would be willing to accept existential entailments from derived claims that do not take the form of identity statements. They do make use of the fact that theirs is an identity statement in arguing that we are licensed to infer that the terms in it refer, for they treat identity statements as paradigmatic reference-demanding statements (Hale and Wright 2009, 202). But of course this does not mean that they are the *only* sort of reference-demanding atomic statements.

existence of disputed entities as special cases of the use of the easy approach to existence questions I have defended above. For both neo-Fregeans and Schiffer, we are licensed (given certain conceptual truths) to move from an uncontroversial truth to an ontological conclusion. On my approach, "do Ks exist?" can always be addressed by determining whether the application conditions actually associated with 'K' are fulfilled. But often, given the rules of use for the term in question, the application conditions for 'K' are *guaranteed* to be fulfilled provided that some other sentence not involving 'K' or any co-referring term is true. On the easy approach we can say that the conceptual truths made use of in the trivial arguments are articulations of rules of use for the introduced noun term ('number', 'property', 'event' . . .) that guarantee that the actual application conditions for the introduced noun are fulfilled, provided the uncontroversial claim is true. That is why the truth of the uncontroversial sentence licenses us to infer 'there is a K'.

We can see, in all of these cases, how competent speakers may make use of their conceptual mastery, often combined with empirical knowledge (whether that arrived at by looking around the restaurant, by knowing that snow is white, that May was born on a Monday, or that the cups and saucers are equinumerous) to arrive easily at the conclusions that there are things of the relevant sort. In cases in which we can infer the existence of the relevant entities from a conceptual truth, rather than an empirical truth, we may say that the application conditions for the new term are null: they are guaranteed to be fulfilled simpliciter, given the rules that introduce the concept. Along with inferentialists about meaning, we can speak more generally of the 'introduction rules' for terms or concepts. In some cases, the introduction rules may license applying the term if certain application conditions are fulfilled (or given the truth of an empirical claim which guarantees that those conditions are fulfilled). In other cases, introduction rules may license introducing the term from a conceptual truth (in which case their application conditions are null.)[13] In the former case, speakers may make use of their conceptual mastery and powers of observation (or knowledge that an uncontroversial claim is true) to conclude that things of the relevant sort exist. In the latter case, speakers may make use of their mastery of the rules governing the introduced term to move from knowledge of the uncontroversial conceptual truth to knowledge that the things in question exist.

In short, we can see each of these three positions as relying on less in making easy ontological arguments than the view that came before it. While the classic neo-Fregean position makes use of a true identity statement in arguing that the terms refer, and so that there are the relevant entities, Schiffer does not require a true identity statement. But while he doesn't require that the statement we begin from be an *identity* statement, he does (like the neo-Fregean) start from an uncontroversial true statement (S) (not involving the disputed concept or a coreferential one) to make the trivial inference to the ontological conclusion. By contrast, I do not think we always need a true conceptually distinct statement to use as a premise to be able to answer ontological questions 'easily'. Sometimes we can reach the ontological conclusion easily just by making use of our conceptual competence and empirical skills, without needing to make an inference from a distinct uncontroversial truth.

Generalizing the approach in this way makes it more powerful. While the neo-Fregean or pleonastic approaches were largely introduced to address debates about entities other than concrete objects,

13. Terms such as 'property' and 'proposition' may nonetheless have distinct meanings even if both have null application conditions, given differences in their inferential role—including differences in their introduction rules.

this approach is just as effective at resolving questions about the existence of ordinary concreta as it is at resolving debates about recondite abstract or philosophical entities.[14] The question 'Are there tables?', for example (I have argued [2007a]) may be straightforwardly answered by beginning from a claim that is not a point of controversy between realists and (most) eliminativists:

- Uncontroversial claim: There are particles arranged tablewise.[15]

But the following seems to be a conceptual truth:

- Conceptual truth: If there are particles arranged tablewise, then there is a table.

That is, where there is what eliminativists would call a situation in which particles are arranged tablewise, that seems sufficient to guarantee that the application conditions for the ordinary term 'table' are met. Thus, we can, by trivial inferences move to

- Derived/ontological claim: There is a table.

In this way, ontological debates about the existence of concrete objects may be settled just as 'easily' as debates about disputed

---

14. Despite the focus on numbers, Hale (1988, 11) is explicit in noting that the argument pattern is perfectly general, and may apply to concrete objects as well as other abstract objects.

15. Some table-eliminativists might not accept it: e.g., existence monists (e.g., Horgan and Potrc 2000) hold the world itself to be the only concrete particular, and thus (when speaking in the strictest ontological contexts) would accept neither that there are particles nor that there are tables. Nonetheless, a similar pattern applies to debates between existence monists and those who accept tables: the truth of a claim existence monists would accept ('the world is table-ish hereabouts') seems to guarantee that the application conditions for the ordinary term 'table' are met, and so that there is a table.

abstracta, events, and so on. The rules of use for a noun term may involve basic application conditions, or may be introduced by rules that entitle us to introduce the new term based on inferences from other truths. But in either case, provided those rules are in place and the term is being used (not mentioned), existence questions may be answered straightforwardly, and in many cases given quite obvious positive answers.

Another way in which generalizing the approach in the way I have done makes it more powerful is that it enables us to see how existence questions may easily be answered even in cases in which there is no 'uncontroversial truth' that we can state in terms omitting the concept J (or any coreferring concept) and from which we can make the trivial inference. So if there is no developed 'stuff' language from which we may make trivial inferences to the existence of tables, say, and if even statements about the existence of particles are considered controversial (say, by those who are eliminativist about all 'objects'), then we would be left without an uncontroversial truth from which we can infer the existence of tables. Yet it seems that a competent speaker is no less entitled, using her conceptual competence, to infer 'there is a table' from veridically observing the inside of a restaurant than she is to infer 'there is a property' from knowing the truth of 'Beyoncé's dress is red'. Taking the approach I have recommended enables us to see both ontological conclusions as equally licensed for those who possess the relevant conceptual competence.

Moreover, if we require the truth of an uncontroversial claim as the basis for resolving the ontological dispute, then there is some hazard that more serious minded metaphysicians will take the uncontroversial claim to be the only one which is 'really true' or which properly matches the 'logical structure of the world' and the like (this is a move that it seems Hale and Wright reject in any case [2009]). But if we do not require that we start from an uncontroversial truth (stated in terms that don't involve the concept *J* (or any coreferring concept)), we do not foster any illusion that there is a more basic, more ontologically apt or ontologically privileged way of *describing* the situation. Nor do we encourage the thought that ontological claims expressed using the newly introduced noun should be viewed as anything other than straightforward and literal truths. This of course is in line with Carnapian tolerance: the idea different linguistic frameworks may be useful for different purposes—without commitment to the idea that there is a single best language that most ideally maps the logical structure of reality.

In any case, whichever way it is developed, adopting the easy approach to existence questions has a number of attractions. The first attraction is its ability to lay to rest seemingly endless debates about the existence of entities of various sorts, and to clarify the methodology of metaphysics. Along with this we gain epistemic attractions, for we are able to answer existence questions in ways that cohere with what we want to say in the ordinary business of life, but in answering them we need rely on methods no more mysterious than straightforward empirical and conceptual methods.

There are other epistemic attractions as well. Chief among them is the ability to demystify our knowledge of numbers and other abstracta. As Hale and Wright put it, the view is motivated by its ability to "tackle directly the question how propositional thought about such objects is possible and how it can be knowledgeable" (2009, 178). For given the trivial inferences that take us to claims about abstracta, we can see how speakers may acquire knowledge of these things by knowing the uncontroversial truths and mastering the rules of use for the terms that entitle them to make inferences from those uncontroversial truths to the existence of numbers and the like. We can thus avoid the epistemic problems the traditional Platonist faces in saying how we can 'come into contact with' and thereby come to acquire knowledge of abstracta—since such 'contact' is in no way presupposed for this account of knowledge to work. The view also enables us to accept that there are the relevant entities without the ontological difficulties incurred by Platonists who treat them as explanatory posits (see also my 2007a, especially chapters 9 and 10, and 2009b). Finally, the view is motivated by its ability to give an apt reading of our discourse—by treating the inferences that seem redundant in ordinary English as genuinely trivial. I will return to discuss some of these advantages at the book's close; here I just want to prefigure them. While I will mainly be concerned to examine the consequences of, and defend my version of, an easy approach below, at least some of what I say will be equally relevant to certain other forms of easy ontology.

3.3. FIRST RESULT: SIMPLE REALISM

Making use of the easy approach to ontology leads directly to first-order consequences about what we say exists. Typically, it leads to affirming the existence of the disputed entities. For in most of the disputed cases, uncontested truths may lead us via trivial inferences to conclude that the controversial entities (numbers, propositions, tables, etc.) exist.

But it is often thought that if we can arrive at ontological conclusions via these trivial inferences, the objects we now say exist can't themselves be very substantial: they must be somehow reduced in ontological standing, mere shadows of language, or else the existence claim itself must be reduced in standing from that of more serious existence claims. Schiffer himself often talks this way, speaking of the ontology that results—an ontology of what he calls 'pleonastic' entities—as a kind of 'cheap' ontology (1994, 304), and suggests that the entities we become committed to are 'ontologically shallow' (1994, 304), or 'thin and inconsequential' (2003, 62). In acknowledging their existence, he writes, we are "merely playing along with the language games that introduce these notions"; their existence should be treated in a "suitably deflationary, or minimalist, manner" (1994, 305).[16] Propositions, for example, are mere "shadows of sentences" (1996, 153), and are said to be "not as ontologically and conceptually independent of us as rocks and electrons, . . . there is a sense in which they're products of our linguistic or conceptual practices, a sense in which properties and propositions are mind- or language-created entities" (1996, 153). Hofweber paraphrases Schiffer's view as holding that these are "second-class entities, whose existence is guaranteed merely by talking a certain way" (2007, 5).

I think, however, that we should not suggest that the entities to which we become committed via trivial inferences are in general 'thin and inconsequential', 'ontologically shallow', or that their existence is somehow to be understood in a deflationary manner. Instead, we should simply say that such entities exist—full stop—and adopt a simple realist view of them. Let me explain.

Schiffer's claims that so-called pleonastic entities have a diminished ontological status arise from observations like these:[17]

---

16. This way of speaking has also led some to think that the ontological commitments we get out of the trivial inferences are in some sense merely fictional or pretenseful (as we 'play along with' the relevant language game) (Yablo 2001, 2005). I argued elsewhere (2013b and chapter 5 below) that this is a mistake.

17. There is also a modal clause: the natures of pleonastic entities are determined by our linguistic and conceptual practices, in such a way that there is no more to their natures than is determined by our practices; they have no "hidden nature for empirical investigation to unearth" (2003, 66). But since that requires a great deal more discussion than there is space for, I will leave it to the side here. I discuss modal claims in my (2007b) and (2013a) in a way that makes clear how they may be handled in the same way regardless of whether or not we arrive at reference to the entities via trivial inferences from uncontroversial truths.

1. Epistemology: such entities have a 'diminished epistemo-
    logical status' in that to learn of the existence of properties,
    propositions, or states, one need only be inducted into the
    language games involving these terms; whereas the same is
    not the case for cats, trees or volcanoes (2003, 62).
2. Causality: pleonastic entities are said to be inconsequen-
    tial in the sense that adding the relevant concepts to a prior
    theory merely 'conservatively extends' that theory,[18] and so
    "does nothing to alter that theory's take on the pre-existing
    causal order" (2003, 63).

In each case, Schiffer writes as if there is an important difference between the 'shallowness' of pleonastic entities to which
we may become committed via such trivial inferences, and the
'depth' of 'more robust' natural entities like trees. In the epistemological case, he contrasts pleonastic and non-pleonastic entities
on grounds that learning of the existence of physical entities such
as electrons requires substantive discovery, while to learn of the
existence of propositions, for example, it is necessary and sufficient
simply to adopt the relevant language game that takes us from,
for example, "The apple is red" to "That the apple is red is true"
(Schiffer 1994, 307).

But on my view the contrast here is misleading. For—depending
on what uncontested truths we have to start from—we may be able
to answer questions about the existence of trees no less easily than
questions about the existence of events or properties. If we began
in a metaphysical debate from the uncontested truth that certain
particles were arranged treewise, we could go on to make use of

18. Where, roughly, a theory T' conservatively extends a theory T if T' doesn't have any
consequences that would be statable in the vocabulary of T that aren't already logically
entailed by T (see Schiffer 2003, 54–61, for discussion and refinements).

our conceptual competence that entitles us to accept that if there are particles arranged treewise, there is a tree, and from there infer the existence of trees. The fact that we may come to know of the existence of certain things by undertaking trivial inferences does not show that the entities *themselves* are in any way epistemically diminished or ontologically shallow—or that there is some crucial difference between them and regular old concreta like trees. In each case one may move from knowledge of an uncontested truth that doesn't make any use of the new concept (or any concept supposed to be coreferential with it) to easily acquire knowledge of the existence of the new kind of entity.

Regarding causality, Schiffer again suggests that there is a contrast between concepts like <property> or <proposition>, and concepts like <wishdate>, or presumably like <person>, <volcano>, or <electron>. For, he argues, concepts like <property> and <proposition> are causally inconsequential, given that their addition conservatively extends a theory in the sense that it entails no new causal commitments. As Schiffer puts it, adding them to one's ontology "via legitimate something-from-nothing entailments does nothing to disturb the pre-existing causal order" (2003, 55). One theory that contains another conservatively extends it if (roughly) adding the new vocabulary doesn't logically entail any causal commitments that are stable in the vocabulary of the old theory but not entailed by it.[19] For example, if we take a wishdate to be (by definition) a person who pops into existence whenever someone wishes for a date, then adding the concept of a wishdate to English does not conservatively extend the language. For, from the premise that Jack wished for a date on Friday, it entails that a person appeared in Jack's house on Friday night—stable but false in unextended English. By contrast, once we have a thing-language

19. For the precise final definition, see Schiffer (2003, 57).

that enables us to say that the notebook is red, we may indeed conservatively extend it by adding the notion of a property.

But again I think the suggestion that this gives us a contrast between entities we become committed to by trivial inferences, versus natural entities like trees and volcanoes, is misplaced. The question of whether a given concept is a conservative extension is a *relative* matter: relative to the prior theory accepted. As I have argued, however, we can also use trivial inferences to acquire commitment to trees or volcanoes, if we start (in a metaphysical dispute) from an undisputed claim such as 'there are particles arranged volcanowise'. For (to alter Schiffer 2003, 52) 'to have the practice [of using the term 'volcano'] is to have the *concept* [<volcano>], and *it is a conceptual truth*—a truth knowable a priori via command of the concept—*that the existence of* **volcanoes** is guaranteed whenever there are particles arranged volcanowise'. The concept of <volcano> would not conservatively extend a prior theory that had no grip on exploding lava-filled peaks, but it would conservatively extend a prior theory that made empirical claims couched in the language of particles being arranged volcanowise. And the same could be said for other concepts of concreta. This undermines the claimed contrast, and perhaps more importantly, provides a reminder that the fact that a term conservatively extends a prior theory does not show that the entities referred to by the term are 'inconsequential' in the sense of *lacking* causal powers; it doesn't show anything about the causal or ontological standing of the entities referred to. Instead, (as the original definition also has it) it only shows that the addition of the relevant concept is inconsequential to the theory's *standing empirical commitments*, whatever those may be.

It seems then in general that there are no across-the-board differences to be drawn between entities the existence of which we may infer by making trivial inferences from an uncontroversial truth and those we cannot. Whether we may infer the existence of a given sort of entity via trivial inferences depends to a great extent on what language or theory, and what uncontested truths stated in that language, we have from which we may make the relevant inference. So, for example, it is true enough that <tree> and <table> are not pleonastic concepts in our actual (nonphilosophical) English language, and if we do not have terminology such as 'particles arranged tablewise' we may (depending on what other terms or concepts we have) not be able to trivially infer that tables exist from any uncontested truth statable in that language without the concept <table>. If we add the terminology of n-wise arrangements, however, we may make the trivial inference. But whether we have such terms as 'particles arranged tablewise' in our language cannot make a difference to what ontological standing *tables themselves* have—to whether tables are in any sense 'shallow' entities or not. So we should not be looking for a difference in ontological standing of *entities* that we can versus cannot (or do versus do not) become committed to by trivial inferences. We may be able to distinguish which *concepts* are pleonastic additions to a given language, and which are not, but there seems to be no absolute answer to whether or not the *entities* referred to by a given concept are pleonastic.

None of this is to deny that there may be important epistemic and causal differences between, say, trees and propositions. But the difference to be drawn is not one in the ontological 'shallowness' versus 'depth' of those entities we may/may not infer the existence of through trivial inferences. Instead, the significant contrast seems to be between entities the existence of which we may infer given the truth of an undisputed *empirical truth*, and entities the existence of which we may infer from a *conceptual truth*. The undisputed truth we begin from in making an easy inference may be either an empirical truth (e.g. 'May was born on a Monday') or a conceptual truth. For example, we may move from 'there are dogs or there are not dogs', to 'the property of being a dog is or is not instantiated', to 'the property of being a dog exists' (cf. Schiffer 2003, 66)—and rely on no empirical truth. Similarly, we can move from 'Janice is tall or it's not the case that Janice is tall' to '*That Janice is tall* is or is not true' to infer the existence of the proposition that Janice is tall—again relying on no empirical truth, though we do begin from an uncontroversial true claim—a conceptual truth. Inferences made from a conceptual truth are genuinely something-from-nothing inferences, for the truth of their premises requires nothing of the empirical world. The fact that one may come to legitimately infer the existence of the relevant entities regardless of the empirical facts in the world suggests a reason such entities are often thought of as independent from the empirical world and suggests a deflated way of understanding that intuition (rather than picturing them as inhabiting some separate Platonic heaven).

And that difference—between cases in which we make the trivial inference from an empirical versus a merely conceptual truth—may lead to the sorts of differences Schiffer identifies as holding between 'pleonastic' and 'nonpleonastic' entities. Where the trivial inference is made from an empirical truth, it does require some empirical work to discover the existence of the relevant entities: we must know that some uncontroversial empirical claim that can be fed into the rule is *true* to know that the entities exist (e.g., we must know that some particles are arranged volcanowise to infer the existence of volcanoes). In the latter case, by contrast, no empirical work is required (we may infer that the proposition <that snow is white> exists, regardless of whether or not snow is white).

Regarding causation, we may again suspect that where the existence of the questioned entities must be inferred from an *empirical* truth, the entities may have causal impact but where it may be inferred from a mere conceptual truth, they do not. Event concepts such as <heart attack> are supposed to be pleonastic concepts: we may infer the existence of heart attacks from an empirical truth as follows: from "Smith's heart stopped beating" we are licensed to infer "Smith had a heart attack" and so that there are events (namely of heart attacks). But while <heart attack> may conservatively extend a prior theory that only made reference to hearts and their beating, we should not conclude that heart attacks lack causal efficacy or are causally inconsequential in any other sense. Nonetheless, pure abstracta such as propositions and numbers may plausibly be thought to lack causal efficacy altogether. But even if entities such as numbers, properties, and propositions, the existence of which we may infer from a conceptual truth, entirely lack causal impact, we cannot assume that the same holds true of those entities the existence of which we infer trivially from an empirical truth.

I have argued that we should not attribute a difference in ontological standing to entities on the basis of whether or not we (may) become committed to them via trivial inferences. Whatever differences do arise between particular cases (say, those of trees versus propositions) are better attributed to differences between those cases in which one requires an empirical truth versus merely a conceptual truth to infer their existence. But in any case we should deny that the entities we are committed to (by either of those sorts of inference) are ontologically deflated or exist in some second-class way. The conceptual truths that underwrite the trivial inferences should be seen as articulations of rules of use for the concept in question.[20] We may think of them as if they were rules to

---

20. Carnap similarly emphasizes that it is the rules that introduce the concept or term <property> or <number> that license us to make the trivial inferences to the ontological conclusion (1947/1956, 208–10). Schiffer himself makes a similar point, arguing that we can get knowledge of things like properties that exist independently of a linguistic or conceptual practice merely by engaging in that practice "Because to engage in the practice is to have the concept of a property, and to have the concept of a property is to know a priori the conceptual truths that devolve from that concept" (2003, 62). Neo-Fregeans similarly take equivalence principles such as Hume's Principle to function as implicit definitions of the introduced sortal concept (Hale and Wright 2009, 179).

introduce the new concept to a language that began without any coreferring concept (though of course that is merely as-if, and not to make actual claims about etymology).

If we take seriously the idea that the conceptual truths that enable us to make the trivial something-from-nothing inferences are object-language articulations of rules of use for the sortal term 'N' used in the conclusion, then we should not say anything less than that Ns exist (in the only sense that 'N' has) in the conclusion. As long as the terms <property> or <number> are being used in their standard sense, we may easily answer the existence question in the affirmative—and simply say that these things exist, full stop. And so, properly understood, the easy approach to ontology should not be characterized as leading to the position that the *entities* accepted are deflated or have some 'second-class' status. Easy ontology leads to realism about the questioned entities in affirming that there are properties, propositions, numbers, and so on, *in the only sense these terms have.* As Blackburn aptly puts it for his (misleadingly named) quasi-realist program:

> What then is the mistake in describing such a philosophy as holding that 'we talk as if there are necessities when really *there are none?'* It is the failure to notice that the quasi-realist need allow no sense to what follows the 'as if' *except* one in which it is true.
>
> *(1993, 57)*

(And this in my view shows precisely what is wrong with the name 'quasi-realism' for the position: better to simply call it 'realism'— or, to be a little more precise, 'simple realism' which, as we will see below, may be contrasted with 'explanatory realism'). What we get, in short, is a straightforward, out and out, realism about the entities in question. Once we see the full generality of the view, as applicable to ordinary objects as much as to abstracta, we can see that we shouldn't suppose that whether a term is or is not introduced by trivial inferences makes a difference to the ontological status of what's referred to. What is deflated is not the entities but rather the *ontological debates* about the entities (more on that below). Thus, to be clear, I call the first-order position that results from the easy approach 'simple realism', and the metaontological position that results 'deflationism'.[21]

But although the easy approach typically leads us to realism about disputed philosophical entities, that is not to say that it leaves us accepting the existence of purported objects of absolutely any kind, including such (putative) things as phlogiston and witches. For the application conditions associated with 'witch' and 'phlogiston' turned out not to be met. (And there is no uncontroversial claim from which we may trivially infer the existence of witches—it's not as if we all agree that there are particles arranged witchwise.) Since the application conditions for 'phlogiston' require that a kind of chemical is released during combustion (and no such chemical is released), the application conditions are unfulfilled, and phlogiston doesn't exist. By the same token, if the application of 'witch' to a woman requires that she be endowed with supernatural powers in virtue of making a pact with the devil, in the absence of such powers and/or devil, witches don't exist. So this method of handling existence questions apparently gives us the right results, denying existence just where doing so is the most obviously correct thing to do—where speakers made some *mistake* in thinking that the application conditions associated with their term were fulfilled, although they were not.[22]

21. For further response to the claim that the easy approach to existence questions leaves us accepting the existence of purported objects of absolutely any kind, including such (putative) things as phlogiston and witches, see Schiffer (1996, 152) and my (2009b).
22. Some might be tempted to say: similarly, the application conditions for 'number' require that there be something abstract, but it turns out that nothing is, and so there

But if the easy approach to ontology typically leads to realism about the disputed entities (properties, propositions, numbers, etc.), how does it really differ from traditional Platonist views? Carnap outlines a way of distinguishing his views about relations, properties, propositions, and so on from the Platonist's by noting that he will reject as pseudo-statements, devoid of cognitive content, such classic claims of the Platonist about properties as 'they reside in a super-heavenly place', 'they were in the mind of God before they became manifested in things', and the like (1947/1956, 22). While I have no objection to rejecting such statements, contemporary Platonists seldom use phrases like these. As a result, we need another way of distinguishing our simple realism from Platonism.

So how does the simple realist view that results differ from traditional Platonist views, if both accept that the disputed entities exist? The two will indeed make the same sorts of first-order existence claim; the only difference lies in the motivations for making it, and in what one thinks the benefits are of making it. The motivations for realisms vary, but especially among those post-Quinean metaphysicians who see themselves as involved in providing a best explanatory theory, the motivations typically include the claim that 'positing' the relevant entities provides some 'explanatory' benefit. The Platonist, for example, invokes numbers to help us explain our number talk, its objectivity, its usefulness in science, and the like. The Platonist about properties

are no numbers. But the neo-Fregean (and in general the defender of easy ontology) will deny that that gives a correct reading of how our number terms work: since number terms may be introduced by trivial inferences from a conceptual truth, given that conceptual truth there is no 'risk' that certain additional 'conditions' for the term to apply might not be met. (We infer the existence of an abstract object from the existence of the number; we don't presuppose it as a condition for the number term to refer.) On a related point, see Hale and Wright's (2009, 193) arguments that the view leaves no 'hostages to metaphysical fortune'—there is no risk that it might just 'turn out' that there are no such abstract objects as the abstraction principles require.

holds that the existence of properties may 'explain' what it is that two things may have in common, and so on. But while the simple realist accepts that there are such entities, she does not argue for them by suggesting that they are 'posits' that (like the posits of scientific theories) explain phenomena; instead, she accepts them just on the basis of the trivial arguments, as she takes the existence of the entities in question to be a trivial consequence of the truth of other (uncontroversial) sentences. To mark the difference I will call the first 'simple realism', and the second 'explanatory' realism.

Not only does the simple realist not need to appeal to explanatory power or the like to justify her acceptance of the relevant entities, she *cannot* do so. Any attempt to do so would yield only a dormitive virtue explanation. Consider the classic dormitive virtue explanation from Moliere: Q: 'Why do poppies make us sleepy?' A: 'Because they have the dormitive virtue'. Now, if saying that something has the dormitive virtue is just a fancy way of saying they make us sleepy, it may be perfectly true to say that poppies have the dormitive virtue. The joke lies in the fact, however, that if A is just a fancier way of restating the fact that poppies *do* make us sleepy (one that introduces a new noun term) and so is redundant, it clearly cannot (as it purports to do) provide any *explanation* of the fact that poppies make us sleepy. Put more precisely, and cohesively with the prior observations, if an existence claim is derived by trivial inferences from an uncontroversial claim, it cannot contribute any *more* explanatory power than we got from the uncontroversial claim itself (and it can't explain the truth of the uncontroversial claim). So either 'Poppies make us sleepy' or 'Poppies have the dormitive virtue' may explain other facts—such as 'Why did Dorothy fall asleep after walking through that field?' And similarly, either 'Particles arranged baseballwise hit the window' or 'A baseball hit the window' may explain why the window shattered. But in neither case are we able to explain something new by shifting from the first expression to the second (which contains a new noun term).[23] Similarly again, on the simple realist's view (as contrasted with the explanatory realist view), we can move from 'The house is red' to 'There is a property, redness, that the house has'. But we cannot use the latter to *explain* why the house is red—it is just a redundant way of restating the former (introducing a new noun term for a property). So on the simple realist view, there are the disputed entities all right, but these are not 'posits' that are parts of 'theories', the inclusion of which is justified by their explanatory power. Instead, we can simply see that there are guaranteed to be such things given the truth of an uncontroversial sentence. We have here a genuinely Carnapian alternative to the neo-Quinean paradigm.

And since (unlike the earlier versions developed by Schiffer and neo-Fregeans) this is an across-the-board view, that also means that in general, the easy ontologist cannot embrace any kind of truthmaker theory according to which we *posit* a certain ontology (as opposed to empirically equivalent rival ontologies) in order to *explain* what it is that makes our sentences true.[24] On the deflationary approach, trees or electrons, say, can no more be thought of as 'posits' used to 'explain' what makes a sentence like 'There is a tree in the courtyard' or 'An electron was emitted' true than properties

---

23. Introducing the new nominative vocabulary that enables us to refer to new kinds of objects might, however, pragmatically enhance our ability to formulate explanations, and might in that sense aid in explanation. (Think about the explanatory use for medical researchers in introducing the noun term 'heart attack' rather than just speaking of hearts that stop beating.)

24. This thus follows up on the point made in chapter 2 (in response to Cameron): that we need in no case 'posit' x to serve as the truthmaker for 'x exists'. See also Augustin Rayo's arguments against what he calls the 'metaphysicalist' position that for an atomic sentence to be true there must be a certain kind of correspondence between the logical form of a sentence and the metaphysical structure of reality (2013, 6–11).

can be used to explain what makes 'The house is red' true. This is of course not to deny the equivalence: that 'There is a tree in the courtyard' is true iff there is a tree in the courtyard; it is only to deny that the ontology of trees provides any sort of *explanation* of its truth that an ontology of particles arranged treewise, or other empirically equivalent ontological characterizations, could not. Nor is to deny that other sorts of explanation involving appeal to trees or electrons are perfectly legitimate; for example, we may explain why there are leaves all over the courtyard by saying that there is a tree there suffering from a disease; we may explain why an atom changed its charge by saying that it emitted an electron.[25]

3.4. SECOND RESULT: METAONTOLOGICAL DEFLATIONISM

The easy approach to existence questions I have defended not only leads to a first-order simple realism about most disputed entities; easy ontological approaches of any kind also lead to the controversial metaontological position that something is wrong with many of the hard ontological debates that have been earnestly engaged in over the past fifty years or so. For the approach to answering existence questions is straightforward, utilizing only empirical and conceptual methods, and involves nothing 'epistemically metaphysical' nor any distinctively *philosophical* enterprise of figuring out *what really exists*. Moreover, although on this view the disputed

25. This rejection of a heavyweight sense of truthmaking is of course perfectly coherent with the deflationary approach to truth that was used as a model for the deflationary approach to existence: for on that view, we should not think of truth as a special kind of property possessed by a sentence when it is related in a proper way to those entities in the world that make it true. (See also Horwich's criticisms of truthmaker theory [2010, 299–322].)

existence questions are meaningful and answerable (generally in the positive), they turn out to be answerable so trivially that the 'hard' debates about these issues that have so exercised metaphysicians in recent decades seem misguided and pointless. The easy approach to existence questions, in my view, is in line with Carnap's position that those existence questions that may be sensibly asked (as theoretical questions)—the internal questions—may be answered by empirical or conceptual means.[26] As I have interpreted Carnap's position above, as long as the terms are being *used* with their customary rules of use (thus used in asking internal questions), when we ask the existence question, the answer is straightforward to come by for those who have mastered the use of the relevant terms. We can, moreover, *show* how this makes many existence questions easy to resolve by showing how we can derive the answer to a disputed ontological question by way of trivial inferences from uncontroversial truths. If the terms are *not* being used, the existence question cannot be a meaningful factual question about the disputed topic at all, but at best can be reinterpreted as *mentioning* the term and enquiring about whether or not we should use it (along with the associated linguistic framework) at all. It is this sort of easy approach to ontological questions, not the internal realism of Putnam or quantifier variance of Hirsch, which is the true heir to Carnapian deflationism about ontology.

We thus have a view like that alluded to in chapter 1, on which something is wrong with ontological debates, and "there are no questions that are fit to debate in the manner of the ontologists"

---

26. Thus on my view it is strange to see Hale (1988) feel he must argue against Carnapian deflationism before defending his own arguments for the existence of numbers. (For I think those are totally in line with Carnap's own way of resolving internal existence questions—the only ones he thought had sense.) Yet the difference between Hale and I may be only regarding interpretation of Carnap—not anything substantial. For in discussing Carnap, he aims to argue that "there neither are, nor need be, nor can be other than 'internal' questions" (1988, 9).

(Sider 2009, 386), but which does not say that disputants are talking past each other, each uttering truths in their own language, or engaging in "different—and equally good—ways to talk" (Sider 2009, 386). The questions are not fit to debate because the answers are so straightforward and easy to come by (as long as we are using the terms in question); not because no answer can be found, or because any answer (expressed in its own language) would be as good as any other.

Given the widely shared commitment within metaphysics to the idea that there is room for hard metaphysical debates, the metaontological deflationism that results from adopting the easy approach to ontology is often met with hostility, and a great many objections have been raised against it. In chapters 5–10, I will examine many of these objections one at a time, in hopes of better evaluating the prospects for the easy approach to ontology. But first, it will be useful to locate the view better by comparing it with other broadly skeptical approaches in metaontology.

[4]

OTHER WAYS OF BEING SUSPICIOUS

The easy approach to ontology that I have outlined above is just one manifestation of a more widespread and growing suspicion that something may have gone wrong somewhere in 'hard' ontological debates as they have been conducted in recent years. But what, precisely, is wrong with ontological debates? There are various ways of articulating the suspicion that something has gone wrong. While I hold that ontological disputes are too easily resolved to be worth debating about, some hold that the disputes are merely verbal, others that we can never know the answer, while still others hold that the claims of the ontologists have no truth-value or there is nothing to decide the issue. It may help to both avoid confusion and to locate my view in conceptual space by contrasting it with some other positions that hold something to have gone wrong in recent ontological disputes.

In this chapter I begin by locating the easy approach (and the deflationary metaontological approach that results from it) among other suspicious views. In doing so I hope to make clear how they compare, where they are consistent, and where they diverge. (I will put off until chapter 5 discussion of one prominent alternative: fictionalism, since there is enough to be said about that to warrant its own chapter.) The primary goal of this chapter and the next is to make clear where the easy approach fits among broadly deflation-ary or skeptical views, and to argue that it is a strong and attractive contender among them. In closing this chapter I will briefly discuss the hermeneutic question of how we can understand what is going on in hard ontological debates, if we take the easy ontologist's defla-tionary metaontological attitude.

4.1. DENYING THAT ONTOLOGICAL DISPUTES ARE GENUINE DISPUTES

The most prominent form of skepticism about ontological debates (as I have often mentioned above) comes from those who hold that the meaning of the quantifier may vary in ways that are equally acceptable (there being no difference in 'metaphysical merit' between them, as Hirsch puts it [2011, xii]). On this view, while at least one of the disputants in any debate might be criticized for rep-resenting herself as speaking English (while she is not), we can at least charitably interpret her as speaking a possible language with an alternative quantifier meaning in which what she says is true, and yet does not conflict with what her opponent is saying in a dif-ferent 'ontological language'. In that sense, ontological disputes can be understood as merely verbal disputes.

One goal since the beginning of this book has been to make clear how the easy approach differs from quantifier variance views, and thereby to make it evident that an important challenge to hard metaphysics remains even if the hard metaphysicians can defeat the specter of quantifier variance. As I have argued in chapter 1 above, Carnap's approach differs from the quantifier variance approach in that it doesn't rely on the idea that the meaning of the quantifier (or 'exists') does or could vary in order to show that something is wrong with common ontological debates. His diagnosis of the problem with ontological disputes is quite different. This carries over to the easy approach to ontology that takes off from Carnap's views about how internal questions (the only sensible existence questions) may be answered. On this view, the quantifier may be treated as a formal term with fixed rules of use, so the view is not susceptible to defenses of hard ontology (such as those in Van Inwagen 1998 and 2009) that go by way of defending the notion that the quantifier is a univocal formal term. The differences among the disputants are attributed not to using the quantifier with different meanings, but rather to the fact that one accepts and the other implicitly rejects a new range of noun terms. The eliminativist who says 'there are no numbers' (if interpreted literally, rather than as making a pragmatic suggestion about what linguistic forms to reject) is saying something false. For there is no way to both use the term with its extant rules of use (which permit easy inferences like those above) and have the claim come out as true.

Another important difference between quantifier variance and the easy approach to ontology is that Hirsch requires, as a condition for dissolving apparent disputes, that each side be able to find some charitable way of interpreting the other side, such that (according to the opposite side) their claims are true:

> I would therefore define a verbal dispute as follows: It is a dispute in which, given the correct view of linguistic interpretation, each party will agree that the other party speaks the truth in its own language.
>
> *(2009, 239)*

When we interpret a dispute as merely verbal, on Hirsch's view, we must see it as involving two (or more) 'ontological languages' that are truth-conditionally equivalent in the sense that "for any sentence in one, there is a truth-conditionally equivalent sentence in the other"

(2011, xii). This approach, Hirsch argues, enables us to declare a number of metaphysical debates (e.g., between friends and foes of mereological composition [Hirsch 2002a], or between perdurantists and endurantists [Hirsch 2009, 240]) to be 'merely verbal'. In such cases, he argues, "speakers of either language ought to allow that speakers of the other language assert sentences that have the same characters and hence the same truth-values as the sentences that they themselves assert" (2009, 243).

But there is a snag in applying this strategy broadly. As Hirsch himself points out, it is not at all clear that this approach will work to dissolve disputes, say, between Platonists and nominalists about the existence of numbers, properties, or other abstract objects (2009, 253). For a Platonist may treat a sentence like the following as true:

> There are two [nondenumerably] infinite sets X and Y, whose members are [nondenumerably] infinite sets of angels, satisfying the condition that, for any set X′ in X, there is a set Y′ in Y such that all angels in X′ love all and only angels in Y′, and some angel in Y′ loves some angel in some set X other than X′.
>
> *(2009, 253)*

But it is not clear that nominalists can find any possible sentence in their own language that can enable them to charitably interpret what the Platonists are saying and count it as true.

So the idea of quantifier variance, as developed by Hirsch, is importantly limited, in that it can only be employed to dissolve ontological disputes where we plausibly have truth-conditionally equivalent languages, such that each can interpret everything the other says as saying something true (in her own language).[1] This

---

1. He does, however, consider a distinct route to dissolving debates, based on a 'second degree' of Carnapian tolerance, in his most recent work (forthcoming).

captures the idea that Hirsch takes as a core part of his deflation-ism: that "in an ontological dispute each side can convert to the other side simply by a change of language".

The easy approach to ontology is hostage to no such constraints. This approach gives us a way of expressing the Carnapian idea that differences among ontologists boil down to differences in the lin-guistic framework they accept, without having to rely on the claim that the languages meet Hirsch's 'equivalent languages condition'. We may accept instead the plausible view that introducing some ranges of new terms (e.g., noun terms for numbers, predicates apply-ing to them . . .) may add expressive power to the language—that's part of the pragmatic point of introducing such terms.[2] But then we shouldn't expect everything expressible in the new (Platonist) lan-guage to be translatable into the nominalist's language. And yet the failure of translation doesn't show that there's a dispute here that doesn't boil down to the choice to introduce and accept a new lin-guistic framework—and that if the eliminativist could be brought to drop her linguistic scruples (about adopting the framework—perhaps based in the mistake of thinking one needs ontological justification 'first' to accept the framework), she would speak like a Platonist.[3]

This is a difference that makes a difference, since it suggests that this easy ontological approach to deflating debates may be readily applied to a wider range of debates than quantifier vari-ance while imposing fewer requirements. As a result, the easy approach is a potentially more powerful form of deflationism

2. See Yablo (2005) for an insightful story showing ways in which the language may gain in expressive power with the addition of mathematical vocabulary.
3. Rayo (2013) makes a related point that those who accept that for the number of dino-saurs to be zero *just is* for there to be no dinosaurs have no need to commit themselves to the availability of a paraphrase of mathematical discourse. For more on the pointless-ness of paraphrase projects, see my (2007a, chapter 9).

than quantifier variance views. For it does not require any translation scheme to be available in order to deflate a debate, and so (unlike quantifier variance views) can clearly deflate debates between Platonists and nominalists. It is also not hostage to claims that the quantifier does or could vary in meaning, or susceptible to any of the many arguments that the quantifier is univocal (e.g. in Van Inwagen 2009). Given these advantages, it remains a quite attractive alternative to quantifier variance for those who suspect that something has gone wrong in recent ontological debates.

4.2. DENYING THAT WE CAN KNOW THE ANSWERS

A far gentler form of skepticism about recent ontological debates is expressed in the epistemicist view. On the epistemicist view, ontological questions are legitimate but very, very hard—the problem is that they are so hard that (although there may be answers) often we may lack sufficient grounds for ever knowing what is the correct answer and settling these debates. Karen Bennett (2009) develops this approach, arguing that (although we must proceed on a case by case basis) in at least some prominent debates—such as debates about composition or constitution—there is little justification for taking either side. For neither is obviously simpler (they just trade reductions in ontology for increases in properties or ideology and vice versa), and both face versions of the same major problems. Uriah Kriegel (2013) raises a similar epistemic challenge for revisionary metaphysics by suggesting that often none of the three oft-cited criteria—of empirical adequacy, fit with intuitions, or possession of theoretic virtues—give sufficient justification for adopting one metaphysical theory over another, leaving revisionary metaphysicians with the challenge of articulating what it is that makes some metaphysical theories epistemically preferable to others.

It is easy to see the difference between the epistemicist approach and the easy approach. For those who use the easy approach do not hold that we have little evidence to justify us in choosing one position over another. Instead (for most disputes) the idea is that we have extremely good reasons for embracing the view that there are the relevant objects (numbers, properties, propositions, etc.). The friend of easy ontology will say that what is wrong with the debates is not that we don't have enough evidence to justify us choosing one side over the other, but rather that we have such convincing reasons for thinking that the realist side is correct that there is no room for serious disputes about the subject.[4]

The easy ontologist, however, may nonetheless learn from the epistemicist and take on board some of her results. From the easy ontological point of view, the epistemicist's worries nicely articulate the indeterminacy that results if we take the neo-Quinean approach to existence questions. Thus, we can accept the conditional that *if* you take ontological debates in the neo-Quinean spirit, *then* we typically run into insurmountable epistemic problems. And that in turn can be taken as a plus for the easy approach: that throwing over the neo-Quinean approach entirely enables us to avoid these epistemic barriers, and the uncomfortable position that there is a huge range of deep metaphysical facts that we simply can never know.

---

4. Nonetheless, the realist may feel the need to show where various arguments against the disputed entities go wrong. I aim to do much of this for arguments against ordinary objects in my (2007a).

4.3. DENYING THAT THERE ARE ANSWERS TO KNOW

A stronger form of skepticism does not (merely) deny that we can know the answers to hard ontological questions: it denies that there *are* such answers to be known. David Chalmers develops and defends this view, calling it "ontological anti-realism", understood more precisely as the view that denies that every unproblematic ontological existence assertion has an objective and determinate truth-value (2009, 92). He gives several arguments against heavyweight realism. For example, if we know everything about the properties of two objects and their relations, it seems that we can trivially know everything about them—that there is no further nontrivial truth about whether they have a mereological sum (2009, 103). But he also argues that there are reasons to prefer ontological antirealism over the sort of realism that we get from the easy approach to ontology (Chalmers calls this 'lightweight realism', but of course I prefer to call it 'simple realism', for reasons articulated in chapter 3). Chalmers thinks it is clear that the disputants in typical ontological debates are at least trying to use a 'heavyweight' sense of the quantifier distinct from the sense used in ordinary existence claims (roughly, the sense I have tried to explicate above). While the antirealist agrees with the realist that ontological existence assertions involve a heavyweight quantifier, the antirealist thinks "that the absolute quantifier is *defective*. Either it does not express a concept at all, or if it expresses a concept, that concept is defective, too. In particular, the absolute quantifier does not have a determinate extension" (2009, 102).

There is actually, however, a reading on which lightweight/simple realism and what Chalmers calls 'ontological anti-realism' are compatible.[5] I have tried to explicate the rules for our actual term 'exists' in English. I think this is what has been historically used in philosophical debates, at least until very recently. It is perfectly compatible with this view to think that recent metaphysicians have been (tacitly or explicitly) attempting to introduce a new term, with new rules of use, in which to conduct their debates. If we find that their introduction fails, or that the term introduced is defective in a sense that prevents many of their assertions using the term from having truth-value, then we can hold the following view: existence questions, in their normal sense *and the only sense that they have*, may be answered 'easily', as described above. Of course I have not yet examined whether their introduction fails or the introduced term is defective. (I examine one such attempt to introduce a new Ontologese term in chapter 10 below.) The point for the present is merely that one can be an antirealist about the questions (some serious) ontologists think of themselves as addressing, and a simple realist about those existence questions that are fully meaningful and well formed. This again is a thoroughly Carnapian option, as Carnap held that the only existence questions that are meaningful, not pseudo-questions, are internal existence questions which can be answered straightforwardly by conceptual and perhaps empirical work. Carnap, however, as mentioned above, thought that that *could not* be the sense that the serious existence debaters had in mind, but held that attempts to ask other sorts of existence questions (external questions) result in defective pseudo-questions.

---

5. This is not to deny that there are other points at which Chalmers and I diverge, e.g. in our readings of Carnap, ways of showing that ordinary existence assertions are acceptable while ontological ones are defective, and diagnoses of what has gone wrong in the serious debates. But those details can be left to the side here.

Stephen Yablo (2009) argues on a different basis that in debates, for example, about the existence of numbers, there simply are no facts to know. He develops an interesting and subtle quizzicalist approach to ontological debates (distinct from his earlier fictionalist approach discussed in chapter 5). Yablo argues that many philosophical debates about existence are 'moot' in the sense that there is nothing to determine whether (e.g.) our number terms refer, and indeed that there is 'no fact of the matter' about their existence. He presupposes that the central argument for thinking that our number terms (etc.) refer is that they make distinctive semantic contributions—they contribute to the felt truth/falsehood of a sentence. But (using an interesting and novel analysis of topicality to isolate a sentence's assertive content) he argues at length that sentences may aptly count as true(/false)—if their total *assertive content* is true(/false), even if they have an existence presupposition that fails. So, for example, despite the failure of 'The present king of France' to refer, "The present king of France is sitting in this chair [pointing at an empty chair]" may count as false *on grounds that it has a false implication, independently of its reference failure:* namely that *someone* is sitting in the chair. The assertive content of a sentence, he argues, is the sum total of its analytic implications that are free of the relevant existence presupposition.

By this method he aims to show that we can account for the felt truth of a number sentence such as 'The number of planets is odd' without having to say that there are numbers. For its assertive content (that there is exactly one planet, or exactly three planets, or exactly five planets . . .) is true even if the presupposition of the existence of numbers fails. Thus we can account for why the relevant sentence strikes us as true without positing the existence of numbers (2009, 516–17). (We might still wonder how mathematical claims (e.g. "there is a prime number between 2 and 4") are to be handled: do these have all true entailments (free of the presupposition that there are numbers) that can account for their felt truth?) But if we assume that it is only a difference in semantic influence that can make a difference as to whether or not we say a term refers, and if (as Yablo argues) the assertive content of number sentences remains the same (and the sentences have the same truth value), whether numbers exist or not, then there is nothing to determine whether the number terms refer, and so nothing to determine whether numbers exist (2009, 520–21). That, in brief, is why Yablo holds that ontological debates about the existence of numbers (and many other things) are moot.

Yablo's recent view is thus also quite different from the deflationary view presented here. For on my view, there *is* something to settle the question of whether the disputed terms refer (namely, whether or not the application conditions are fulfilled)—and so the questions, on my view, are not moot but instead easily answerable.

Does this view present any threat to the easy approach? As mentioned above, Yablo's argument presupposes that the only thing to determine whether a term refers is its effects on the meaning and felt truth-value of a sentence (2009, 521). This line of argument might worry neo-Fregeans, as their argument proceeds from the fact that singular terms for numbers figure in true identity statements to concluding that the terms refer—thus taking the appearance of the term in a certain kind of true statement as grounds for saying it refers. If we can take the assertive content of "the number of bagels = 2" to be that there are two bagels, and take the truth of the latter (and other implications free of the presupposition that numbers exist) to account for the felt truth of the identity statement, then we may lose the justification for concluding that number terms refer on grounds of their appearing in an (apparently) true identity statement.

But that argument is powerless against those forms of deflationism that do not rely on the idea that we are justified in concluding that there are numbers (properties, propositions . . .) *because the terms figure in sentences (perhaps of a particular form, e.g., an identity statement) that seem to be true (or false).* As I have discussed in chapter 3, that is not Schiffer's argument and it is not mine. On my view, we have reason to think that the terms refer *because we have reason to think that the application conditions for the terms are fulfilled.* In the cases at issue (for number terms, property terms and the like), the application conditions for the singular terms are *guaranteed* to be fulfilled given the truth of the uncontroversial claim. I never make use of the argument that since the singular terms appear in an apparently true claim (identity claim or whatever) the terms must refer. Instead, as I have made clear above, I think what determines whether a term refers is whether its application conditions are fulfilled.

Moreover, all three deflationary views would reject the idea that there is some presupposition of the derived claim that might fail though the assertive content remains true. For on each of these views, the derived claim is a trivial or analytic *entailment* of the uncontroversial claim. Thus there is simply no need for a 'fail-safe' mechanism; there are no 'extra' commitments in the latter two sentences that are not already implicit in the first, which might fail though the first is true. (The idea that there are such extra commitments [that provoke the need for a fail safe mechanism] is related to the fictionalist idea, discussed in chapter 5, that there is something more that it would take for there to *really* be the relevant entities.) On the easy approach, the existence of numbers is not *presupposed* by claims such as 'the number of planets is odd' but rather entailed by it.

4.4. UNDERSTANDING HARD ONTOLOGY

Deflationists about metaphysical debates are often presented with a challenge: how would you then interpret what the debates in hard ontology are up to? For the disputants are (undisputably) smart people and competent speakers of English, who think of themselves as engaged in robust, nonverbal debates about fundamental matters of existence. Where, precisely, do you think they go wrong, and what sense can you make of these debates (which have seemed, at least to the practitioners, to be sensible and even important)?

It may in certain cases be difficult to determine what the best interpretation of an ontological dispute is—and no deflationist is obliged to give a uniform diagnosis of the problems with all debates, or to give a diagnosis the disputants themselves will accept (of *course* they won't). Where ordinary, rather than technical terms, are in use (and it is those that are primarily in question in this book), this difficulty is compounded by the difficulty of determining what the rules of use for our standard terms are, so that we can determine whether the disputants are straying from them to such an extent that we can no longer regard them as using a customary term at all. Nonetheless, there is one thing we can say if the above is correct. Wherever it seems clear that there are conceptual rules that enable the relevant questions to be answered easily (by empirical observations or trivial entailments from undisputed truths), metaphysicians engaged in debates about whether the relevant objects *really* exist cannot be simply *using* the predicates and quantifier in their usual sense, or else the question could be answered easily along the lines of a Carnapian internal question. But this still leaves open many options about how to understand what they are up to—and in fact there may be no single option that best captures how diverse metaphysicians see their disputes and their claims.

Some have rejected the easy approach to existence questions on allegations that it means we must accuse those who do hard ontology (especially those who reject the relevant entities) of semantic incompetence: of misusing either the sortal terms such as 'number' or 'property', or the quantifier in their statements (or both). For, if they grasped and used the terms properly, they would evidently find the questions easy to answer in the positive. What is the evidence that they are not semantically incompetent? Presumably just that they use the terms perfectly unexceptionably in the business of ordinary life. But this does not preclude the idea that they may misuse the terms—whether intentionally or inadvertently—when they (as they would put it) enter the 'ontology room'. This is one interpretive option.[6]

Nonetheless, we do not need to say that the disputants are semantically incompetent—even when they use the relevant terms in ontological debates. (See also chapter 7 below for more on this.) One option is, with Hirsch, to suggest that the disputants are each speaking a truth in their own idiolect. Even if we don't join Hirsch in attributing them different meanings for the quantifier, one could hold that they are using the disputed sortal term in different senses, and each speaking a truth. But this does not seem terribly plausible, unless one may think of certain eliminativists as implicitly importing new, higher standards for there to be numbers, and so on, than those enshrined in the core rules of use for our terms. (Those who think that for there to be numbers there would have to be something causally efficacious, for example, might be accused of changing the meaning of 'number' in their idiolect in this way, and so of talking past the realists who accept no such requirement.) Of course the eliminativist won't like this assessment—since she thinks that she is denying just what the Platonist is asserting; she doesn't think of herself as changing the subject. However, ontologists might be wrong about whether they are implicitly changing the subject or importing new meanings for the disputed sortals without their being incompetent in the use of ordinary terms.

Carnap's view, as we have seen, was different from both of these: he would have held that nominalists and nihilists, for

6. Thanks to David Ripley and David Kovacs for insisting on (roughly) this point.

example, are most charitably seen as tacitly *rejecting* the noun terms for numbers and mereological sums. This seems an apt charitable (re)interpretation of what may be going on in many of those classic cases in which an eliminativist makes efforts to show how our talk about numbers, say, may be paraphrased in a language that does not use number terms as nouns. On this view, the eliminativist need not be branded as semantically incompetent, but rather can be seen as mistaken about what it is she is doing: she thinks of herself as asking a factual question using a term, when she is better understood as making a pragmatic recommendation about language, mentioning the terms. Then we may see the eliminativist and the realist as seriously disagreeing—though the real place to locate their disagreement is on pragmatic rather than factual grounds.

Another interpretive option—increasingly apt, I think, for recent work—is to see hard ontologists as implicitly (or sometimes explicitly) attempting to introduce their own new terminology (often homophonic with the English): most prominently, attempting to introduce a new 'Ontologese' sense of the quantifier in hopes of preserving hard ontological debates. This is consistent with Chalmers's (2009) view that serious ontologists should be thought of as attempting to ask existence questions using a distinctive 'heavyweight quantifier', distinct from ordinary English terms such as 'exists' and 'there is'. This is a relatively recent development; more traditional neo-Quinean work simply presents itself as speaking in English and offering sometimes surprising views about what really exists, with no suggestion that 'exists' is being used in anything other than its standard English sense.

The best-developed version of an Ontologese proposal is Ted Sider's recent attempt to secure a single distinguished meaning of the quantifier. I will discuss this in some detail in chapter 10 below. But a few general remarks are worth making about the proposed move to what Thomas Hofweber (2009) would call a special 'esoteric' term of art. If we see those who aim to do hard ontology as implicitly or explicitly introducing their own new terminology, a further question arises: do they succeed at introducing a new term, with rules of use functional enough to enable proper disputes to be built around it? Without yet answering this question, we can say this much: if what we have said so far is correct, disputants who think there is something deeper to debate regarding these existence questions cannot be speaking plain English, and are in danger of tacitly changing the subject people originally came to metaphysics to ask about—"What exists?"—using the terms in plain English.

In any case, the defender of the easy approach to existence questions may leave it open what the best understanding is of hard ontology in different cases. The project after all was not the hermeneutic one of charitably interpreting the work of those engaged in hard ontology, but rather the philosophical/conceptual one of figuring out how to properly understand and answer existence questions. And we must be clear what the form of the objection is here. To say, "You say that eliminativists are semantically incompetent (though they are clearly not)" is an objection (one we can answer). But to say "You say that eliminativists are *making a mistake somewhere*, and I don't think that they are" is not an objection. The defender of the easy approach clearly is not saddled with treating those who engage in hard metaphysics as semantically incompetent (flying in the face of evidence of their use of terms in ordinary speech), for there are several other interpretive options available. But the easy ontologist is, of course, committed to treating them as making a mistake somewhere along the line. The best diagnosis of the particular mistake may vary from case to case. And to say that a mistake must have been made somewhere does not commit one to any particular interpretive view about what the source of the mistake is.

[5]

FICTIONALISM VERSUS DEFLATIONISM

Perhaps the most important rival to the easy approach to ontology (at least among roughly skeptical views) is fictionalism. For fictionalism not only presents an alternative that is both well developed and popular, it also has been used in raising one of the most recurrent criticisms of the idea that ontological questions can be answered easily. In this chapter I tackle the fictionalist threat: I will show why that criticism is no threat to the easy approach, and go on to argue that the deflationary package that comes with the easy approach to ontology, overall, gives a preferable route to take for those who suspect that realists and eliminativists in ontological debates are both taking things too seriously.

Fictionalism has most often been wielded in first-order ontological debates, where it has long presented an attractive alternative to both eliminativist and heavyweight realist approaches to ontological questions. On the fictionalist view, the discourse of mathematics, say, should be seen as implicitly fictional, metaphorical, or figurative, and so we needn't answer the existence question at all to go on in good conscience in using the relevant discourse. Thus, we needn't (with the heavy-duty realist) be committed to saying that there really are such objects in order to (contrary to the eliminativist) take the discourse in question to be perfectly acceptable (cf. Kalderon 2005, 3). The language in novels shouldn't be taken as attempting to describe real people and activities, and its acceptability doesn't depend on its truth. Instead, the language in novels is doing something else, such as engaging in a certain kind of pretense (within which it is appropriate to say some things and deny others). Similarly, according to the fictionalist, the discourse in question (whether it is the discourse of mathematics, properties, possible worlds, or the courthouse) needn't be taken to ontologically commit us to the disputed objects. We can preserve our ways of talking about numbers or properties, say, without having to be committal about the existence of numbers or properties.

This leads the fictionalist to the metaontological conclusion that something is wrong with traditional ontological debates: they are pointless and misguided, since they are in effect arguing about something that *doesn't matter.* On the fictionalist view, it doesn't matter whether or not the disputed objects exist, since the discourse doesn't presuppose this and can get along fine without it. On the fictionalist view, hard ontological debates arise from the mistaken assumption that the objects must exist for the discourse to make sense.

In many ways, the fictionalist approach and the easy approach are similar. Both are equally opposed to both traditional Platonism and to traditional nominalism or eliminativism about disputed entities. Both bring to ontological debates a 'no worries' attitude that suggests that we can preserve the discourse in question without saddling ourselves with a heavy-duty ontology (such as Platonism in mathematics). Both reject the assumption that the function of, say, mathematical discourse is to track objects (in the way that biological discourse might be thought to). And they tend to appeal to the same sort of philosopher: someone who suspects the heavy-duty realist of taking the discourse in question too seriously, and suspects the eliminativist of overreacting by rejecting a perfectly functional range of discourse.

Fictionalists are typically divided into two camps. Hermeneutic fictionalists *interpret* the relevant discourse as merely speaking fictionally or figuratively (Yablo 2001, 2005). Revolutionary fictionalists (Field 1980), by contrast, take themselves to be making a proposal: the restrained ontologist may *choose to* speak in a merely fictional or pretending way, regardless of whether the original discourse was doing so (Kalderon 2005, 5–7). I shall focus below on hermeneutic fictionalism, especially as developed by Stephen Yablo (2001, 2005).[1] For it is hermeneutic fictionalism that may be wielded in an argument against the deflationist, by suggesting that the deflationist has misinterpreted the discourse in easy arguments by taking it too seriously. Thus henceforth when I speak simply of 'fictionalism', hermeneutic fictionalism is the view I shall have in mind. Hermeneutic fictionalists typically take the discourse of mathematics to be only making fictional or pretended assertions (claims that are supposed to be true only in the 'fiction of mathematics'), or (in other versions) to be speaking somehow other than literally—that is, figuratively or using simulation. On the hermeneutic fictionalist's view, those who thought that mathematical discourse committed us to numbers were simply taking that discourse too seriously.

---

1. It is important to be clear, however, that what I shall have to say is about fictionalism as a general approach (exemplified by some work of Yablo's), not about Yablo's views (taken to be exemplified by fictionalism). For Yablo has in fact tried out many views on the subject—from treating the statements as engaged in a kind of pretense or make-believe, to treating them as metaphorical or figurative, to his current appeal to the idea of non-catastrophic presupposition failure, as giving us reason for thinking that claims about the existence of numbers are less than fully ontologically committal. I will focus here only on the fictionalist strand of his work (2001, 2005), since what I am interested in is the viability of fictionalism as an approach, and its merits relative to deflationism. On changes in his view, see also his (2005, 110–11, first [unnumbered] note), and note 5 below. I discuss his more recent view, that the relevant debates are moot as there is nothing that can settle them, in chapter 4 above.

Despite all that fictionalism has in common with the easy approach to ontology, the two views are rivals. The views are clearly in conflict, for taking the easy approach leads us to the simple realist view that there are entities of the disputed kind, while the fictionalist does not assert that there are such entities.

Not only do the views conflict: the fictionalist line is wielded in making one of the most frequent attacks on 'easy' arguments in favor of entities of various kinds. For while the inferences that (according to the easy ontologist) take us from undisputed claims to controversial ontological conclusions seem to be clearly acceptable in ordinary English, the fictionalist's response is to deny that the ontological claims we apparently get as outputs from the trivial inferences are to be understood as serious assertions about the disputed topic at all—and so to deny that they really provide answers to ontological questions.[2] As Yablo writes, "the *a priori* approach to existence questions is undermined by doubts about literality" (2000a).

Thus I will address three questions: Does the fictionalist approach undermine the easy approach to existence questions? Do the motivations that fictionalists appeal to to motivate their view over *Platonism* also give reason for preferring it to the deflationary alternative (consisting of the easy approach to existence questions and the simple realism and metaontological deflationism that result)? Most importantly, supposing you were inclined to look for an alternative to traditional Platonism and eliminativism, which of these rival views should you choose?

I will begin by discussing the motives for adopting a fictionalist position. Then I will examine the argument that fictionalists wield

---

2. More precisely, this is the response of the hermeneutic fictionalist. The revolutionary fictionalist would say that they *needn't be* so understood. Another response— Hofweber's dual quantifier approach discussed in chapter 9—denies that what they are asserting is genuinely *existential* in import (Hofweber 2005a, 2005b, 2007).

against the easy approach to ontology. I will argue, however, that the fictionalist's argument does not give any grounds for rejecting this approach but merely begs the question against it. Moreover, I shall argue, close attention to this argument reveals an important problem for fictionalism, and a crucial disanalogy between the disputed discourse (about numbers, about properties) and overtly fictional or make-believe discourse. Finally, I will argue that motivations for fictionalism are served as well or better by adopting the easy approach to ontology and the simple realism it leads to. All in all, then, I will argue that the deflationary package may provide the preferable approach for those who suspect that heavy-duty realists are just taking things too seriously.

5.1. MOTIVES FOR FICTIONALISM

Early versions of fictionalism were motivated primarily by the desire to avoid the perceived ontological excesses of heavy-duty realist views. The advantages early fictionalists sought were ontological: not having to 'posit' the disputed objects to make sense of the discourse. But these were advantages for fictionalist views over heavy-duty realist views, such as Platonism about numbers or properties. I have argued extensively elsewhere (2009b, 2007a) that the kind of simple realism one gets from the easy approach to ontology incurs no such ontological disadvantages, and that those who accept the truth of the undisputed claim do not truly offer a more parsimonious ontology by denying (or avoiding commitment to) the truth of the ontological claim. In chapter 6 I respond to other ontological objections to the simple realism that results from the easy approach, for example that it involves us in some sort of 'magic'. Neo-Fregeans have also shown why the anxious metaphysician's demands that there be some 'guarantee' that there 'really are' the needed entities to refer to are illegitimate (Hale and Wright 2009). If these arguments are correct, the simple realist, like the fictionalist, avoids the ontological problems of heavy-duty realism: where ontological issues are concerned the two views are on a par. Since I discuss them extensively elsewhere, I will leave further discussion of the ontological issues to the side here.

In any case, the most recent and well-developed versions of fictionalism take a different and more interesting approach. As Yablo puts it:

> At one time the rationale for fictionalism was obvious. We had, or thought we had, good philosophical arguments to show that X's did not exist, or could not be known about if they did. X's were obnoxious, so we had to find an interpretation of our talk that didn't leave us committed to them.
>
> That form of argument is dead and gone, it seems to me. It requires very strong premises about the sort of entity that can be known about, or that can plausibly exist; and these premises can always be exposed to ridicule by proposing the numbers themselves as paradigm-case counterexamples.
>
> But there is another possible rationale for fictionalism. Just maybe, it gives the most plausible account of the practice. It is not that X's are intolerable, but that when we examine X-language in a calm and unprejudiced way, it turns out to have a whole lot in common with language that is fictional on its face.
>
> *(Yablo 2001, 87)*

On Yablo's view, the most telling reasons to accept his version of fictionalism do not have to do with avoiding an unwanted ontology, but rather with the ability of fictionalism to 'give the most plausible account of the practice'—that is, of the discourse surrounding our talk of numbers, properties, or other questioned entities. I propose that we take Yablo at his word, accepting that the ontological arguments in favor of fictionalism are 'dead and gone', and that the action lies in assessing which view gives the best account of the discourse.[3] I will argue, however, that although fictionalism may have been well motivated against Platonist competitors in this way, it cannot be so motivated against the easy approach to ontology (and the simple realism which follows), for that gives a better account of the discourse.

5.2. THE FICTIONALIST'S CASE AGAINST EASY ARGUMENTS

Yablo argues for his variety of fictionalism (or figuralism etc.) by emphasizing what discourse about numbers has in common with overtly fictional or make-believe discourse. He also emphasizes the ability of his view to account for some otherwise puzzling features of our discourse about numbers (including such features as impatience, insubstantiality, and indeterminacy—to which I return in section 5.6 below). For now, let us begin by examining what Yablo thinks discourse about numbers has in common with overtly fictional or make-believe discourse, and how this forms the basis for an argument against the easy approach to answering ontological questions.

Yablo (2001, 2005) makes use of Kendall Walton's (1990) work on 'prop oriented' make-believe in making his case that talk of

---

3. Those who would like to revive them are referred to my other work against ontological objections, in my 2007a, 2009b, and chapter 6 below.

numbers has much in common with overt make-believe talk. He expresses the view regarding mathematical objects as follows:

> [Numbers (as they figure in applied mathematics)] are part of a realm that we play along with because the pretense affords a desirable—sometimes irreplaceable—mode of access to certain real-world conditions, viz. the conditions that make a pretense like that appropriate in the relevant game.
>
> *(2005, 98)*

The rules that apparently leave us saying that numbers, properties, possible worlds, and the like exist, Yablo suggests, are analogous to what Walton calls generative principles in games of make-believe, which (in conjunction with props) yield only pretend or simulated assertions.

So, for example, as Walton develops the view, children playing a game of make-believe may adopt the generative principle that stumps are to count as bears (i.e., that we are to pretend that any stump is a bear) (Walton 1990, 40). The stumps are the 'props' in this game, and (combined with the generative principle) may generate make-believe truths, such as that there are five bears in the backyard. Speaking within the game, a player only *pretends* when she says 'Look out, there are five bears!' and does not commit herself to there *really* being five bears. Nonetheless, she does commit herself to the 'real content' of the claim—that is, roughly, what information it communicates about the props (that there are five stumps).

Likewise, on Walton's view, if we say "A woman named 'Anna' died on the train tracks" in the context of discussing *Anna Karenina*, we do not commit ourselves to there really being a woman so-named who died on the tracks. Instead, we only commit ourselves to the real content of the claim: that the relevant book says so, using the novel as a prop in our game of make-believe, in which we employ the generative principle that what the book says counts as true in the make-believe game authorized by the fiction.

So similarly, on Yablo's view, the rules cited by neo-Fregeans are best understood simply as rules for generating make-believe truths within the 'fiction' of mathematics. (Similarly, rules that apparently yield reference to properties, states, possible worlds, and the like are only principles for generating relevant truths in the property-fiction, possible-worlds-fiction, etc.). So, for example:

> The governing fiction [generative principle] of applied arithmetic says that whenever there are some E's, there is an entity their number that measures them cardinality-wise; if there are five E's, this further entity is 5.
>
> *(Yablo 2001, 77)*

And so from the fact that there are five stumps in the backyard, we can (in conjunction with this principle) generate the claim that there is some number—five—of stumps. But this (like the claim about bears) should be taken merely as a *truth within the relevant make-believe*—this time, the fiction of mathematics (Yablo 2001, 77). So those who say things like 'the number of stumps is five' do not commit themselves to there *really* being numbers. They do, however, commit themselves to the 'real content' of the claim, that is, that there are five stumps (Yablo 2001, 77). The idea that those who utter claims in applied mathematics *do* commit themselves to something (the real content of the claim) is crucial to making Yablo's view plausible. For it is that which enables him to preserve the idea that (although its literal content is figurative or pretending) our applied mathematical discourse is important, and enables us to state and commit ourselves to important truths about the world: those expressed in the real content, which *is* asserted.

The fictionalist's idea that the claims about disputed ontological entities shouldn't be taken literally forms the basis for a worrying argument against the easy method of answering ontological questions. For while we wanted to say that easy arguments take us from uncontroversial truths to ontological claims that give us (positive) answers to disputed ontological questions, the fictionalist would block those arguments. If the fictionalist is correct, then the apparent ontological claims we get by applying the rules lack the relevant force to give serious answers to ontological questions. They would instead be merely in the context of a pretense or make-believe, and would not even be intended to provide serious answers to disputed ontological questions. Thus, the fictionalist accuses the simple realist of taking the disputed discourse too seriously by taking it to be making proper existence assertions when it is only simulating or pretending. If this criticism is correct, then it will give us reason to accept fictionalism and reject the easy approach—along with the simple realism to which it leads.

5.3. A PROBLEM FOR THE FICTIONALIST'S ANALOGY

But although Yablo motivates fictionalism by appealing to what he takes to be strong analogies between talk in applied mathematics and in works of fiction, an obvious disanalogy between mathematical and overtly fictional talk immediately suggests itself: those making claims about numbers certainly don't *feel* that they are engaging in mere pretend or make-believe talk. Yablo meets this objection by first trying to point to a great number of places in ordinary discourse where an element of pretense, metaphor, or figurative talk may be involved even if we do not explicitly think of ourselves as merely pretending. He also, in his later work, avoids this by saying that speakers may be engaged in *simulation* rather than make-believe, where "Simulating is being in relevant respects as if one believed, while not believing except possibly per accidens", and where simulating (unlike making believe) need not be an activity "easily brought to consciousness" (2001, 90).

But even if we don't feel that the shift to *simulating* badly undermines the analogy between mathematical and make-believe or figurative discourse, there is a more telling disanalogy that remains. For there is a disanalogy between the rules involving number terms and the generative principles of an overt make-believe game. For it to make sense to say that we *merely* pretend that P, there must be a difference between what we are committed to in *merely pretending that P*, and what we would be committed to in *really asserting that P*; a speaker can *merely pretend* that P only if she is not committed to the truth of P.

In the case of the pretense about bears, we can understand the distinction between what it is to assert that there really are five bears in the backyard, and what it is to *merely pretend* to assert it. For what it is for there to be a bear, for 'bear' to apply, is established by rules for applying the term in various situations, requiring, for example, that there be a creature of a certain sort (perhaps the same sort as those ostended in a sample originally baptized as 'bears', or the like). We can leave the details to the side, because it's pretty clear that however we understand the application conditions for 'bear', these are *not* met merely by the presence of a stump—there is something more (or rather, something else) that it would take for there to *really* be bears. So a speaker who *pretensefully* asserts (in the game of make-believe) that there are five bears, and *really* commits herself only to the real content, there being five stumps, undertakes very different commitments than one who seriously asserts the literal content, that there are five bears. Here it is clear that we can be committed to the truth of the real content (that there are five stumps) without being committed to the truth of the literal content (that there are five bears). Likewise, in the case of obvious works of fiction, we can see the contrast between what it is to merely pretend that a woman was killed on the tracks and asserting it. In the first case we are committed only to the real content (that the book says so), but that is a very different matter than the second case, in which we are committed to there actually being a woman who died.

But it is not so easy to identify a similar contrast that enables us to say we are 'merely pretending' that there are numbers, properties, social objects, or other disputed entities, while committing ourselves only to the real content of the claims. Simon Blackburn makes a similar point when (responding to David Lewis' characterization of his view as a form of fictionalism) he writes:

> ... working in terms of make-believe does not avoid the problem that we have to have a fixed content for what we pretend to be true. If after reading some skeptic we only make-believe that there are colours or values or duties, we still need to know what it is that we are pretending, and that requires knowing the difference between worlds allegedly unlike ours, in which there are colours or values and duties, and worlds including ours in which there are not.
>
> (2005, 326)

So let us see whether such a contrast can be drawn, enabling us to make good on the idea that we are 'merely pretending' that there are the disputed entities, while committing ourselves only to a distinct 'real content' of the claim. I'll begin with the easier case of institutional rules, for example, the rule that if two suitable people knowingly visit the justice of the peace, sincerely say the relevant vows and undertake the relevant paperwork, they come to be married (and so a marriage comes into existence).

Should we say that this is merely a generative principle in a game of make-believe?

Many have wanted to say something along these lines: that talk of corporations or marriages is a mere 'manner of speaking' or 'legal fiction', and Yablo uses talk of 'marital status' as an example of "figurative speech" (2001, 86). Even John Searle, who offers perhaps the best-developed philosophical account of institutional facts, speaks of

> Our sense that there is an element of magic, a conjuring trick, a sleight of hand in the creation of institutional facts out of brute facts.... In our toughest metaphysical moods we want to ask.... Is making certain noises in a ceremony really *getting married?*... Surely when you get down to brass tacks these are not real facts.
>
> *(1995, 45)*

Should we then hold that someone who says 'We are married' is just *pretending* to assert this (while all that is *really* asserted is the 'real content' of the claim: that certain vows and paperwork were undertaken)?

No—all it takes to *really* be married *just is* to have undertaken the proper vows and paperwork in the proper context. To commit oneself to that 'real content' *just is* to commit oneself to the claim that we are married. The only sensible contrast that can be drawn between what it is to *merely pretend to* assert that we are married, versus what it is to *really* assert it, is in terms of whether we are asserting or only pretending to assert *that the vows and paperwork were undertaken.* But then we can't understand the claim "we are married" as really asserting that the vows and paperwork were undertaken (the real content), but not as really committing the utterer to the claim that they are married (the literal content).

This brings to light an important disanalogy between the cases the fictionalist wants to identify as situations in which the speaker is merely pretending, making believe, or simulating, and paradigmatic cases of pretense or make-believe. In the case of works of fiction or children's games of make-believe, there is a clear contrast to be drawn between committing oneself to the real content (the truth about the props) and committing oneself to the literal content: a difference between being committed to stumps versus bears, words on pages versus deaths on train tracks. That difference, however, is not obvious for the fictionalist about disputed ontological entities such as social entities, numbers, events, and properties. Committing oneself to the vows and paperwork being undertaken does seem to commit one to being married. Similarly, to the extent that it sounds redundant in English to say "there are five stumps *and* the number of stumps is five", being committed to the first claim does seem to commit one to the second, and so to there being a number. Similarly, being committed to 'Snow is white' does seem to commit one to accepting 'The proposition that snow is white is true'. But then we cannot (as Yablo wants) take the latter claims, explicitly about numbers or propositions, to be *merely* pretending while the former are committing. Of course there are moves the fictionalist may make in response (I consider these below). Nonetheless, there certainly is not the clear and obvious contrast in these cases that there is in cases of overt make-believe and fiction, between what speakers are committed to in asserting the real versus literal content. This seriously undermines the supposed analogy to genuinely fictional or make-believe discourse that was supposed to motivate modern fictionalism.

It also makes evident an important and unnoticed challenge for the fictionalist approach, wherever it appears in metaphysics: we can claim to *merely pretend, make-believe, or simulate* that there are properties, possible worlds, or even fictional characters, while genuinely asserting only the 'real content' of the corresponding claims only if we can be committed to the real content without being committed to the literal content. So the fictionalist faces the challenge of saying how one may be committed to the real content without being committed to the literal content. I will return to discuss this challenge below.

But first a simpler point can be made: the fictionalist's criticism of the easy approach to ontology does not hold up. Yablo claims that the easy arguments are "undermined by doubts" about whether the conclusions should be taken literally. But it is part and parcel of the easy ontological view that the uncontroversial claim that expresses the real content of the claim trivially or analytically entails the derived claim (the literal content). The rules are supposed to reflect rules of use that could be used to *introduce* the new terms to our vocabulary, just as legal definitions may introduce technical terms for (legal) marriage. According to the easy ontologist, these rules make the move from the uncontroversial claim to the derived claim truly trivial. If that is the case, then a speaker who is committed to the uncontroversial claim (the real content) *is* thereby committed to the derived claim (and to the ontological claim that follows from it)—even if she does not yet possess the new terms and concepts employed in the derived claim. (Just as a speaker who says "Hey, John is an (eligible) unmarried man" is committed to John's being a bachelor, even if she doesn't possess the term 'bachelor'). If, as the easy ontologist insists, these really do reflect rules of use for these terms (rules we master in being inducted into number talk), then *no contrast can be drawn* between what (according to the fictionalist) it takes for a speaker to be committed to the real content of number claims and what it takes for the speaker to be committed to their literal content.[4] If that is the case, we can't *merely pretend* that there

---

4. Fine (2009, 4) similarly suggests that, if straightforward claims about the existence of numbers are "not strict and literal truths, then one is left with no idea either of what a strict and literal truth is, or of what the strict and literal content of these claims might be". Cf. Hirsch (2002b, 110).

are numbers while *really committing ourselves* only to the real content of number claims, any more than we can commit ourselves to vows and paperwork having been properly undertaken while *merely pretending* that we are married.

Similarly, on the easy ontological view the idea that principles such as: 'if an individual x is P, then there is some property P possessed by x' merely generate *make-believe* truths (that it is true in the property-fiction that there is some property), makes no more sense than the idea that the laws for marriage in the state of California only make it *make-believedly* the case that we are married, or even that the principle: 'if there is a man and he is unmarried, then he is a bachelor' just tells us when to *make-believe* that there are bachelors. In short, if (as the easy ontologist insists) these do reflect rules of use for the terms in question, then no sense can be made of the suggestion that the ontological claims we get as output from rules are merely pretending—while we are committed only to the 'real content' expressed in the uncontroversial claim. For if the rules reflect genuine rules of use for our terms (specifying sufficient conditions for the term 'number', 'marriage', or 'property' to apply) then *nothing more is required* for the ontological claim (the literal content) to really be true than for the uncontroversial claim (real content) to be true, and so in committing herself to the 'real content' of the claim a speaker also commits herself to the truth of the ontological claim—in the only sense it has—and cannot be merely pretending.

Thus we can only entertain the possibility that the derived claim is to be taken as *merely pretending*—a suggestion that was supposed to undermine the easy arguments—if we already *presuppose* that the easy ontological view, grounded in the idea that such inferences are indeed trivial, is false. (The neo-Fregean insists that the undisputed claim and derived claim have the same truth-conditions, while Schiffer holds that the latter is a trivial, redundant consequence of the former, and I hold that the first analytically entails the second). The fictionalist's criticism, in short, merely begs the question against easy ontology by assuming that there are no such valid trivial entailments. Thus the easy ontologist should not be at all moved by the fictionalist's argument against them, and one of the most worrying lines against easy ontological arguments is blocked—leaving the view intact.

The fictionalist's argument also cannot be revived by suggesting that while the conclusion might not be merely pretending, it may involve 'simulation'. For if the rules do reflect genuine rules of use for our terms, then the speaker cannot be merely *simulating* belief in numbers (where simulation is "being in relevant respects as if one believed, *while not believing except possibly per accidens*" [2001, 90; italics mine]). If someone believes the undisputed claim that there are three cups on the table, it would be no *accident* that she believes that there is a number (of cups on the table), given that the latter would be a trivial consequence of the former. And if someone believes that May was born on a Monday, it would be no accident that she believes that there are events (e.g., of births). Thus, it doesn't help the fictionalist argue against the easy approach to ontology to suggest that the speaker is merely *simulating* (rather than pretending), even if we take simulation to be compatible with belief.

The chief difference between the fictionalist's and deflationist's readings of the discourse used in 'easy arguments' lies in whether the rules are taken to be generative principles in games of make-believe, or implicit definitions or introduction rules for the terms in question. So far, I have argued that the supposed analogy with generative principles in games of make-believe looks questionable on closer examination. The better analogy seems to be with institutional and legal terms, which are introduced by explicit definitions, and entitle us to make the relevant inferences trivially. But if that is the closer analogy to discourse about numbers, properties, and the like, then it seems thus far that the easy ontologist should be untroubled by the fictionalist's criticisms, and is on the road to offering a better account of the discourse than the fictionalist has given.

5.4. HOW THE FICTIONALIST INCURS A DEBT

But can't the fictionalist deny that the inferences in question really are trivial, or reflect constitutive rules for the meanings of the terms in question, and thereby hold onto the idea that one may really assert the basic claim while only pretending to be committed to the ontological claim? Yes, but only at the cost of (1) abandoning the idea that this can provide any argument against deflationism, and (2) incurring a daunting argumentative debt.

First, as we have seen above, if the fictionalist denies that the inferences in question are trivial, or denies that the derived claim and uncontroversial claim share the same truth-conditions, she clearly begs the question against those who defend an easy approach to existence questions and so doesn't provide any argument that the easy ontologist should be in the least moved by. Thus one of the most worrying lines against easy ontological arguments is blocked.[5]

---

5. One might wonder whether Yablo's more recent (2009) work on fail-safe presupposition failure fares any better. His line of argument there is based on the presupposition that the only thing to determine whether a term refers is its effects on the meaning and felt truth-value of a sentence (2009, 521). (The argument then works by showing how we can preserve the apparent assertive content and truth-value of, say, applied arithmetical sentences regardless of whether number terms refer.) This line of argument might worry the neo-Fregeans, as their argument proceeds from observing that singular terms for numbers figure in true identity statements to concluding that the terms refer—thus taking the appearance of the term in a certain kind of true statement as grounds for saying it refers. If we can take the assertive content of "the number of bagels = 2" to be that there are two bagels, and take the truth of the latter (and other implications free of the presupposition that numbers exist) to account for the felt truth of the identity statement, then we may lose the justification for concluding that number terms refer on grounds of their appearing in an (apparently) true identity statement.

But that argument is powerless against those forms of deflationism that do not rely on the idea that we are justified in concluding that there are numbers (properties,

Moreover, the fictionalist who denies that such inferences are trivial also incurs a daunting argumentative debt. Since he thinks that the ontological claims are *merely pretending*, it seems he must hold that there is *something more it would take* for the ontological claim to be *literally* true than for the undisputed claim to be true, or else we can't make sense of the idea that one can be committed to the real content without being committed to the literal content.[6]

What more could it be supposed to take for the literal content to be literally true, than merely for the real content to be true? There might be some who are tempted to think that more *is* required for there to *really be* numbers, properties, or even marriages and corporations, than can follow via trivial inferences from the truth of the undisputed statement: namely, that there *really is some (new) object/ entity/individual* present.

But as I have mentioned above (chapter 2) and argued elsewhere (2007a, 2009a), there is a problem with this use of generic

propositions. . .) *because the terms figure in sentences (perhaps of a particular form, e.g., an identity statement) that seem to be true (or false).* That is not Schiffer's argument and it is not mine. On my view, we have reason to think that the terms refer *because we have reason to think that the application conditions for the term are fulfilled.* In the cases at issue (for number terms, property terms, and the like) the application conditions for the singular terms are *guaranteed* to be fulfilled given the truth of the uncontroversial claim. I never make use of an argument of the form: since the singular terms appear in an apparently true claim (identity claim or whatever) the terms must refer.

Moreover all three deflationary views would reject the idea that there is some presupposition of the derived claim that might fail though the assertive content remains true. For on each of these views, the derived claim is a trivial or analytic entailment of the uncontroversial claim. Thus there is simply no need for a 'fail-safe' mechanism; there are no 'extra' commitments in the latter two sentences that are not already implicit in the first, which might fail though the first is true.

6. Interestingly, Yablo seems almost to notice this point at one stage, remarking that "'really' is a device for shrugging off pretences. . . [but] I'm not sure what it would *be* to take 'there is a city of Chicago' more literally than I already do" (1998, 259). But he adds in the attached footnote, "I have a slightly better idea of what it would be to commit myself to the literal content of 'the number of As = the number of Bs'" (1998, 259 n. 74). Unfortunately, he does not say what that idea is, and I don't know what it could be, unless it's the common idea (discussed below) that there really is some *object*.

terms like 'object'. For the relevant general sense of 'object' in which it seems to make sense to say that there is a number there only if there is *some object* involves using 'object' in a covering sense, under which we are licensed to make the inference from 'there is an S' (where S is any well-formed sortal term), to conclude that there is an object. As a result, we can't deny that the original inference succeeds on grounds of denying that there is an object. Instead, we can first move from the undisputed claim to the specific ontological claim (there is a number), and then undertake another trivial inference from the specific ontological claim to the generic ontological claim to reach the conclusion that there is an object. No further conditions are required to make that true than to make the undisputed claim and the specific ontological claim true.

Another standard use of 'object' is as a sortal term, typically used to track medium-sized, unified, bounded, and independently mobile lumps of stuff. It may well be that Yablo tacitly has something like this in mind, since he classifies many forms of speech as involving 'metaphor' simply because of the way they use the term 'thing'. So, for example, he takes as examples of nonliteral speech such claims as "Something tells me you're right", "There are some things better left unsaid", "The last thing I want is to", and so on (2000b, 214). Such claims do not, intuitively, have anything non-literal about them, and it seems we can only see them as involving some kind of metaphor or make-believe if we think of the 'thing' here as involving some sortal use of the term that would appeal to a unified lumpish entity whispering 'You are right!' in your ear, and the like. But that seems to involve a misreading of the straightforward placeholder use of 'thing' here, not to reveal an unnoticed element of metaphoricality in what the utterers would take to be perfectly straightforward speech. In any case, clearly anyone who thought that it took the presence of an 'object' in this sortal sense for there to be a number failed to grasp the number concept to begin with.

Other ideas of what more it would take for the literal content to be true seem similarly inappropriate. If one held,, for example, that the literal truth of 'there is a number (of bagels)' would require there to be something beyond the bagels that is *causally efficacious* (something to which one is not committed in just asserting the real content: there are two bagels), one would seem to have missed the point of our number concepts: there seems no reason to think that for there to be numbers there would have to be 'things' (apart from the bagels) that are causally efficacious. In fact, that would seem like quite an odd view of numbers to take. Denying that there are numbers on grounds of denying that there's anything causally efficacious is rather like denying there's a frog here on grounds of denying that there's anything that lights up.

Another possibility is for the fictionalist to defer to the traditional Platonist, saying, "I think it would take whatever *she* thinks it would take for the literal content to be true".[7] But given the difficulties (discussed in chapter 3 above) of pinpointing a difference between the views of the traditional Platonist and the simple realist, the challenge here remains. The simple realist thinks it's enough for the literal content to be true (and for there really to be numbers, also for them to be mind-independent, etc.) that the real content is true; what more does the heavyweight realist think it would take for the literal content to be true? Following the lines of the chapter 3 discussions, some traditional Platonists might suggest that for the literal content to be true, numbers would have to be *explanatory* in some sense the simple realist cannot embrace (and that isn't guaranteed by the truth of

7. Thanks to Gabriele Contessa for this suggestion.

the real content). But the challenge remains of specifying what sort of explanation that would be (presumably not causal), and why we should think that numbers only 'really' exist if they can fulfill such an explanatory role.

5.5. A REPLY FOR THE FICTIONALIST

A different line of reply the fictionalist might try is to say that we can maintain that the conclusions of the 'easy' arguments are merely pretenseful or metaphorical without that requiring us to make any sense of what more it would take for the ontological claim to be literally true. For some terms may *only* have pretending or metaphorical uses, and so the fictionalist may hold that the disputed terms like 'number' and 'property' are *always* just metaphorically or pretensefully used. As a result, we can resist the pressure to say what more it would take for the relevant ontological claims to be literally true (as the terms may simply have no literal use) and avoid the daunting debt.

Yablo acknowledges that "it hardly seems possible to use the words 'number' and '10' more literally than I already do" (2000, 19). However, he suggests, we can make pretenseful use of a term even if there is no literal use with which we can contrast it: one may merely pretend that there is 'gravid liquid' even if this term has no literal use in English (the use may be guided by the idea of what 'gravid' is to mean in a novel's pretense: an ultra-heavy liquid 'the tiniest drop of which weighs many tons' [2000, 20]). Similarly, we can say "She has a lot of smarts" even if there is no literal use of the noun form "smarts" in English enabling us to contrast what it would take for this to be literally true with what it takes for the relevant metaphorical claim to be apt—and so for the real content (that she is smart) to be true.

But in the first case, one *can* say something about what more would be required for "there is gravid liquid in this test tube" to be literally true than for the corresponding real content to be true. Clearly here, too, there is a difference between what one is committed to in asserting the *real content* of the claim (viz., that there are certain sentences on the page of the work of literature that serves as the 'prop' in the relevant game of make-believe) and what one would be committed to in asserting its literal content (that, at the least, requires commitment to the presence of a heavy liquid, not [just] to the presence of words in a work of literature). Even if we can't say exactly what more is required, we can say that it would require that there be a liquid-filled test tube. Here there is mere pretense, but there is also the required difference between the real content one is committed to, and what one would be committed to in seriously asserting the literal content.

What about if we say 'she has a lot of smarts'? Here, Yablo argues, even if the noun form 'smarts' has no literal meaning (but has its metaphorical meaning in the noun form informed by the literal meaning of the adjectival form 'smart'), we can retain the metaphorical content even if we can't say what it would take for it to be literally true that she has a lot of smarts (2000, 20). But in this case, as in the case of discourse about numbers and properties, there does not seem to be a difference between what one commits oneself to in asserting the real content (that she is very smart) and what Yablo would call the literal content (that she has a lot of smarts). Someone committed to saying that she is smart seems committed to saying that she has a lot of smarts—even if he doesn't like to use the colloquialism. But nor does the latter use intuitively seem to be metaphorical, pretending, or anything other than literal. If I say 'she has a lot of smarts', I do not mean to be invoking a metaphor according to which she has little pink chips in her head called 'smarts', and lots of them, but rather simply using a different turn of phrase to say that she's quite smart. Here it seems we lack the needed contrast, but we also lack a mere pretense. Or if you do think it is metaphorical in this way, then we *can* again say something about what more you would commit yourself to in being committed to the literal content (that there are the pink chips) that you aren't committed to in just asserting the real content.

In each case again either the derived claim seems not to be merely pretending or metaphorical, or we *can* make some sense of what more it would take for it to be literally true than for the real content to be true. So, I conclude, to maintain the view that the apparently ontological claims are *merely* pretenseful the fictionalist *does* retain the burden of holding that there is something more that it would take for claims about numbers, properties, and the like to be literally true—some additional conditions that are not guaranteed to be met even if the so-called 'real content' is true. But what?

5.6. THE DEFLATIONARY ALTERNATIVE

I have argued that fictionalism doesn't give us any *reason* for rejecting the deflationary approach, and that it also acquires an unpleasant argumentative debt. Still, some might be attracted to fictionalism on grounds that it can at least provide us with an alternative way of understanding how the disputed discourse can be acceptable without being committed to heavy-duty realism.

The fictionalist does admittedly provide an alternative reading of the rules that can save us from the dreaded ontological commitments, but is it a preferable alternative?

Why might one be attracted to fictionalism? One might be attracted to it on ontological grounds—as a way of avoiding commitment to the disputed objects. But as mentioned in section 5.1 above, while this may be an advantage over Platonism, it is not at all clear that the simple realist view that results from taking the easy approach to ontology, properly understood, has any such ontological difficulties—or that fictionalism can be motivated over it on these grounds. Or one might be attracted to it on epistemic grounds—that the fictionalist avoids making our knowledge of numbers, properties, and the like mysterious, since it does not assert that there are these special abstract entities outside the causal realm that we must somehow get to know. But again (to the extent that it is a problem at all) the epistemic problem is a problem for Platonists, not for those who take the easy approach to ontology. Indeed the whole neo-Fregean program in the philosophy of mathematics was designed with the goal in mind of demystifying our knowledge of mathematics by showing how we can acquire mathematical knowledge by way of undisputed nonmathematical claims and conceptual truths. Yablo of course rejects these ontological and epistemic concerns even as grounds for endorsing fictionalism over Platonism; if anything they are even more clearly irrelevant to deciding between fictionalism and deflationism.

If we thus put ontological and epistemic issues aside, fictionalism gives us a preferable alternative to deflationism only if we have independent reasons for thinking that fictionalism gives a more plausible view of the discourse—giving us good reason for embracing its interpretation of the rules over that given by the deflationist. But I have argued that closer attention to the contrasts between genuine fictional/pretenseful discourse and the case of the rules used by easy ontologists to draw ontological conclusions suggests important disanalogies. These undermine the idea that fictionalism can be motivated over deflationism by its ability to give a better account of the discourse. Indeed, the disanalogies make the hermeneutic fictionalist appear to be offering a rather forced reading of what's 'really going on' in number talk. It also leaves fictionalists in the unappealing position of having to require that something (what?) more be the case for there to *really* be those *objects* than is required for the real content to be true.

The simple realist, of course, faces no such problem—for she does not say that statements about numbers, properties, or marriages are merely pretended, figurative, or simulated assertions. Instead, she maintains that claims that there are prime numbers, or properties possessed by whales but lacked by dolphins, or many marriages that won't last, are literally true in the only sense these terms possess: a sense in part constituted by the rules that govern their use.

The easy ontologist also has a number of advantages over the fictionalist in providing a good account of the discourse. To ordinary speakers, claims like "I ate two bagels and the number of bagels I ate is two" or "The shirt is red and the shirt has the property of redness" do sound redundant. The easy ontologist, unlike the fictionalist, may take them to be as redundant as they sound, and may take the apparent platitudes expressed in the introduction rules to be genuine platitudes reflecting rules of use for our terms. In ordinary English, the derived claim does seem to be just a wordier way of restating the basic claim[8] and so it's a virtue to preserve the idea that these really are trivial entailments reflecting rules of use for the relevant English terms.

Another advantage of the easy ontological approach over the fictionalist is that we may take statements about numbers to be a priori and necessary. Yablo argues that he can account for the *appearance* of a priority and necessity of an arithmetical statement like '2 + 3 = 5', by saying that the real content of claims of arithmetic (all that we care about) express logical truths, and so are a priori and necessary (2001, 90). But we can offer an even better account

---

8. Or, as Hofweber suggests (2005a, 2005b, 2007), a way more suited to highlighting some parts of the information rather than others. See chapter 9 below.

of why arithmetical claims and even claims about the existence of, say, a prime number between 1 and 10, 'strike us' as a priori and necessary: because they are. For, given the easy approach to ontology, claims about the existence of numbers (given the rules of use for the terms involved) may be trivially inferred from basic claims that themselves are conceptual truths. This captures the idea that numbers and the like exist *necessarily* (the same goes for properties and certain other entities). Their existence can be known a priori in that the truth of the ontological claim may be inferred by any competent user of the term (who has mastered the relevant trivial inference) without the need for knowing any empirical truth (since one may begin the inference from an analytic claim). Thus, on the simple realist view that emerges from the easy ontological approach, unlike the fictionalist view, we can take these existence claims to be necessary and a priori at the level of literal content, not just at the level of real content.

Yablo argues that fictionalism is preferable to Platonism given its ability to explain otherwise puzzling features of the discourse, and that may be so. But in each case, the friend of easy ontology can do as well as the fictionalist or better at explaining the relevant feature—so this line of argument provides no advantage for fictionalism over deflationism. Among these features is impatience: that is, the fact that mathematicians and others who use number talk are 'strangely indifferent to the question of their existence' (2001, 89). This, Yablo argues, makes sense if that question really is irrelevant to the claims being made about the world (since all that is relevant is the real content of the claim). While that may be an adequate explanation of impatience, those employing the easy approach can do just as well or better by explaining the impatience of mathematicians and other competent speakers as follows: competent speakers are impatient at the question because the answer (Yes: there are numbers) is so patently obvious to anyone properly initiated into the practice of using our number terms. (Thus there is also a suspicion that those who think there is a real question at issue have gone astray somewhere—for one diagnosis of where, see my 2009a.)

Beyond impatience, Yablo argues that the fictionalist can do better than the Platonist at explaining the apparent 'insubstantiality' of numbers, the fact that they lack a 'hidden and substantial nature', and that their identity relations are often indeterminate (2001, 89).[9] For "this is what you would expect of something conjured up for representational purposes. Why should we have filled out the story further than needed?" (2001, 89). But again the easy ontologist can do as well or better: if we think of the introduction rules as object-language articulations of rules of use for the term being introduced, then it is easy to see how certain indeterminacies may result. Where the rules are open-ended, underspecified, and collectively determined, risks of indeterminacies and vagueness in the corresponding modal features enter in. Suppose, for example, that the rules of baseball say that if the batter arrives at the base first he is safe; if a fielder arrives first he is out. In that case, it is clearly left indeterminate what happens if there is a tie at first base. So similarly, if the introduction rules for a term are left gappy or open-ended, the existence and identity conditions for the corresponding entities may be correspondingly indeterminate. So, for example, are we entitled to infer that there is a property only if a predicate is truly applied—or also if it is falsely applied? (We can move from 'Dobbin is a horse' to 'There is a property of horseness [that Dobbin has]'. Can we also move from 'Dobbin is not a unicorn' to 'There is a property of unicornness [that Dobbin lacks]')? If our rules are not determinate,

9. Indeed the very idea that certain entities lack a hidden and substantial nature was introduced by Stephen Schiffer and Mark Johnston in defense of a deflationary view. While I agree that the natures of the entities in question are determined by the relevant rules of use, however, I would not want to treat the relevant entities as having some sort of distinctive second-class status, for reasons I make clear in chapter 3 above.

then there may be no determinate answer to the question of whether there is a property in such cases. If properties P and Q are everywhere coinstantiated across all possible worlds, does that show that the properties are identical? Again, if the rules of use (this time the coapplication conditions) for our terms are indeterminate, there may be no answer to questions like these (see my 2009a).

The other features Yablo mentions involve the fact that numbers, sets, properties, and the like 'come in handy as representational aids', enabling us to say more about the ordinary concrete world. We may retain Yablo's insight that terms for numbers, properties, and other abstract entities are often introduced as representational aids to help us share information about the concrete world—and yet still hold that the terms so introduced (given their rules of use) do refer. A good account of how the terms are introduced and what function they are introduced to perform is not in tension with the easy ontologist's idea that the terms so introduced do, trivially, come to refer to entities not referred to in the basic claim, making the existence claims true in the only sense that the terms in question have.

5.7. CONCLUSION

Fictionalism has long been one of the most important rivals of the easy approach, and has formed the basis for one of the most crucial criticisms of easy arguments. But the classic attractions of fictionalism arose when it was developed as an (at the time perhaps the *only* plausible) alternative to heavy-duty realism on the one hand, and eliminativism on the other hand. While its original motivations were predominantly ontological and epistemic, more recently it has been motivated on grounds of its ability to offer a superior account of the discourse. And fictionalists have suggested that they can undermine the easy arguments by raising doubts about whether their conclusions were to be taken literally.

I hope that the discussion here has made two things clear: one, the fictionalist does not provide any argument that undermines easy ontological arguments or the positions of simple realism and metaontological deflationism that come with them as part of a deflationary package. Two, fictionalism cannot be motivated over this broadly deflationary approach on grounds of an ability to offer a superior account of the discourse. The analogies supposed to hold between genuine fictional and mathematical discourse are tenuous and easily undermined, and the deflationist seems better able to account for the distinctive features of mathematical discourse. As a result the fan of fictionalism will have to return to more old-fashioned epistemic or ontological motivations. But again, while fictionalism might seem an attractive way to avoid the epistemic problems of traditional Platonism, it can't be motivated over deflationism on epistemic grounds.

Those who are attracted to fictionalism over the deflationary alternative are thus left falling back on the alleged ontological advantages of not having to 'posit' these 'suspect' entities, and at that stage the discussion returns to familiar territory, to which I will turn next (see also my 2007a and 2009a). So it seems that although the rhetoric of fictionalism is often directed against the deflationist's 'easy arguments', at the end of the day the fictionalist's arguments are only persuasive if one implicitly has something like the Platonist view in mind as the opposition—or is keen to avoid 'commitment' to the 'extra objects' at all costs. If those ontological concerns are (as I will argue) aptly put to the side where the deflationist's simple realism is concerned, then it looks as if even that reason for preferring fictionalism evaporates.

The deflationist metaontological picture, of course, faces other objections as well, many of which will be addressed in the remaining chapters. If these difficulties can be avoided or over-come—and the ontological worries aptly kept at bay—it seems that although fictionalism was an attractive alternative to Platonism, on the contemporary stage deflationism may provide a preferable view to fictionalism that is able to preserve its advantages as well or better while avoiding its difficulties.

Indeed on reflection, perhaps a view like the deflationary package developed and defended here is what fictionalists should have been looking for all along as a persuasive and acceptable alternative to heavy-duty Platonism. And while heavyweight realists may be taking the disputed *discourse* too seriously, it may be that they, eliminativists, and fictionalists are all alike in taking the ontological *debates* too seriously, and thinking it would take something more for the ontological claim to be true than simply for the undisputed claim to be true.

DEFENDING EASY
ONTOLOGY

[6]

DO EASY ARGUMENTS
GIVE US PROBLEMATIC
ONTOLOGICAL COMMITMENTS?

I have so far worked to articulate in contemporary terms an easy approach to existence questions that typically leads in turn to a simple realism about disputed entities in ontology, as well as to a deflationary metaontological stance. Such a view attracts a great deal of criticism. For if there is one thing metaphysicians agree on (even while they are vigorously disagreeing about whether properties, propositions, or ordinary objects exist) it is that their questions are matters for serious debate that cannot be answered in the easy way I have suggested above.

Thus, to make the view at all plausible, it is essential to show how it can stand up to the main lines of criticism raised against it. To do this, I turn now to discuss some recurrent criticisms that have either been raised directly against the present view, or are raised against the related neo-Fregean position and might be thought to apply here as well. If it can withstand these attacks, we will have better reason to take it as a serious contender in metaontological debates.

In this chapter I consider objections raised to the first-order simple realist ontological positions that (as I have argued in chapter 3 above) result from metaontological deflationism. The first objection holds that there is no guarantee that there are *enough* objects to vindicate the easy arguments; the second suggests that the objects easy arguments tell us exist may not be the *right* ones to settle the relevant metaphysical disputes. In the two chapters that follow, I consider two objections raised to the sorts of inference that are supposed to lead to the relevant first-order ontological commitments: first, the general objection that there are no analytic or conceptual truths of the kind required for easy arguments to go through, and second, bad company objections to the effect that particular problems may arise with existence-entailing conceptual truths. Thereafter, I will consider two versions of the idea that hard ontological questions might use (or be using) a different quantifier than the one that appears in easy ontological arguments.

6.1. ARE WE OVER-COMMITTED?

The first standard line of objection to the easy approach to ontology is to point out that, although it claims to dissolve traditional ontological debates, it actually leaves us committed to substantive ontological positions (Sider 2009; Sidelle 2008; Schaffer 2009b). So, for example, Alan Sidelle notes that "Thomasson cannot quite get away without doing, or needing to do, the sort of 'serious' metaphysics which she hopes to undermine" (2008, 175). Jonathan Schaffer argues that my approach using analytic entailments leads to a 'permissive' ontology (accepting ordinary objects, mereological sums, and the like) which "far from yielding a deflationary metaontology, is actually in tension with deflationism and instead requires a permissivist approach" (2009b, 156). Moreover, Ted Sider writes that my approach "would not make all the ontological questions go away," noting that we could still ask, for example whether, granting that there are some particles arranged personwise, there are some persons in addition (2009, 419).

It is certainly true that even if one accepts my approach, ontological questions remain, and one remains committed to certain ontological positions. But this only shows the need to clarify the sense in which this approach is and is not deflationary. As noted earlier, it is not deflationary in the sense of suggesting that ontological questions are moot or have no answers. Provided the questions are well-formed[1] (and leaving problems of vagueness and indeterminacy aside), there typically are right answers to existence questions. (The answer to Sider's is yes, although I'd rather drop the misleading addition of 'in addition'.) The view is, however, deflationary in holding that these answers are easy to come by via conceptual and empirical enquiry, and that the philosopher's share of work is on the side of conceptual analysis. It is also deflationary in the sense that it suggests that something is wrong with protracted metaphysical debates about whether things of the disputed sorts exist. It was to avoid this kind of confusion that I took pains to point out in chapter 3 that the view gives us a deflationary *metaontological* approach, but a simple realism in answer to most first-order ontological questions.

So yes, the view also does lead me to take straightforward positions on many first-order ontological debates (generally positive positions, that there are the relevant entities). That, however, is not in tension with deflationism once we see what is meant by the sense of 'deflationism' in question, and bear in mind the distinction between a metaontological and first-order ontological position.

The observation that my metaontological approach leads to certain first-order ontological positions, however, may be turned

---

1. Of course some prominent ontologists' questions, e.g. about whether there is some 'object' or 'thing' in a certain situation, or how many there are—using a neutral sense of 'thing'—I have argued (2007a) are not well formed.

into an objection by arguing that the first-order ontological views to which one becomes committed by adopting the deflationary metaontological approach are problematic. The central source of the alleged problem is that the easy method leaves us with a plentitudinous ontology.[2] For, as I have argued above, we can make easy arguments for the existence of most common-sense things speakers assume to exist (persons, chairs, mortgages, symphonies . . .). We can also introduce new or technical terms in ways that permit easy arguments for the existence of their referents, enabling us to make easy arguments for the existence of mereological sums, Van Inwagen's gollyswoggles (which exist if a piece of clay is squished in a particular shape), Hirsch's incars (which are guaranteed to exist whenever a car is in a garage), and so on (cf. my 2007a, 183–85).

This might be thought to be problematic on various grounds: that accepting such entities flouts the demand for parsimony in ontology, leads us into other problems such as violations of prohibitions against colocation, doubling-up of properties, and so on, or even (by accepting the existence of gollyswoggles, sums, and the like) itself violates common sense. I have dealt with all of these objections in *Ordinary Objects* (2007a), so I won't rehash them here.[3]

It may, however, be worth mentioning a point in favor of plentitudinous ontologies. As Phillip Bricker (forthcoming) has argued, it seems implausible to think that the pragmatic theoretic virtues

2. Eklund (2006b, 325–26) similarly argues that generalizing the neo-Fregean approach commits one to what he calls a 'maximalist' ontology. (Note though that his argument only applies directly to the neo-Fregean view, and his way of defining the 'maximalist' position is not one I endorse, though his 'maximalism' is obviously closely related to the plentitudinous ontology that comes with the easy approach.) Hale and Wright (2009) dispute the charge that the neo-Fregean is committed to maximalism in Eklund's sense.

3. Eklund raises another objection to plentitudinous ontologies: that they are apt to be contradictory, as the conceptual truths may entail the existence of incompatible objects (2006a). This is a development of the 'bad company' objection discussed in chapter 8 below.

could give us grounds for thinking that a theory is true. To think they do would tend to make our theory parochial, as the pragmatic grounds seem to give us reason only to think that the theory is useful to *us*, to creatures with our needs, desires, or cognitive limitations. Metaphysical theories (far more than scientific theories) rely on appeals to these pragmatic virtues to justify choosing one over the other. If pragmatic virtues are all we have to favor one over another and these give us no nonparochial grounds for thinking the theory is true (Bricker argues), we do better to accept all of the entities described in all of the metaphysical theories—at least to the extent that the theories are or can be made coherent, understandable, and so forth. We can then treat the pragmatic virtues as giving us reason for talking about some entities rather than others, but not for saying that some exist rather than others. Avoiding the parochialism that comes with choosing one set of entities over another gives us a good reason to be happy with embracing the plentitudinous ontology we get as a result of the easy approach to ontology.[4]

6.2. WHY EASY ARGUMENTS REQUIRE NO MAGIC

But there is a deeper and more general objection to answering onto-logical questions via the easy approach that I do want to discuss here. The idea is this: the truths that underwrite the easy inferences are fundamentally *linguistic or conceptual* principles (reflecting rules for use of our terms or concepts); entities are objects in the

---

4. Bricker only applies this principle to theories about what he calls 'metaphysical entities'—that is, the abstract and modal. While I agree that empirical considerations are centrally relevant in asking questions about the existence of concreta, I also think that where we have empirically equivalent theories about the existence of diverse concreta, the same considerations apply.

world. So (the objection goes) how can linguistic principles guarantee the existence of real entities? Thus, for example, Stephen Yablo writes of attempts to prove the existence of abstracta from a priori or empirically obvious premises, that such "arguments are put forward with a palpable sense of daring, as though a rabbit were about to be pulled out of a hat" (Yablo 2000b, 197),[5] adding, "Our feeling of hocus-pocus about the 'easy' proof of numbers (etc.) is really very strong and has got to be respected" (Yablo 2000b, 199). The rhetoric of magic is ubiquitous on the critics' side. Matti Eklund writes of the neo-Fregean program that it "may seem uncomfortably like trying to pull a rabbit out of a hat. Can so much really be had for so little?" (2006a, 97). Karen Bennett (2009, 50–57) similarly argues against Hirsch by trying to show that he must be committed to the idea that there are certain *analytic* principles that entitle the realist to move from an undisputed claim to the disputed ontological claim. And so, she says, "it . . . would appear that Hirsch is committed to the claim that [the linking principle's] purported analyticity entails that meaning alone is enough *to conjure up the existence of tables*" (2009, 56, italics mine).[6] She quickly dismisses the suggestion on grounds that it "amounts to saying that *we can define things into existence.* But surely an analytic claim cannot be existence-entailing in this way; surely the existence of a new object cannot follow *by meaning alone.* Who knew ontological arguments were so easy?" (2009, 56). Well, of course, neo-Fregeans at least believed that they were quite easy—but the position is here and elsewhere dismissed as one

---

5. A point echoed by Eklund (2006a, 97).
6. Even David Chalmers—who laudably does not invoke the rhetoric of magic—treats as an important consideration against lightweight realism the view that "no existence claim is trivially true. . . and [the claim that there is an object with certain properties] is never trivially or analytically entailed by a sentence that does not make a corresponding existence claim" (2009, 79).

implausibly committed to the idea that we may "have the power to define things into existence" (Bennett 2009, 56–57).[7]

The basic worry underlying the objection is this: if these linguistic principles aren't magically *creating* the entities whose existence they supposedly entail, what ensures that the world 'lives up to' the promises of the linguistic principles? As I have tried to make clear elsewhere (2007, chapter 3), however, this line of objection is based on misunderstanding the easy ontologist's approach. The trivial inferences entitle us to infer that objects of a certain kind exist, but they do not *create* the disputed objects, or in any way call them into existence. The conceptual truths may indeed introduce a new noun term such as 'proposition', 'property', 'event', or 'number': but what is introduced (or 'defined into existence') is just the *term* or concept. The *entities* the existence of which we can infer are not created by this conceptual or terminological introduction. Instead, they typically exist quite independently of our language and concepts. (I say 'typically' since social and cultural entities may depend in various ways on language and/or concepts.) It is just that, given the rules for the term introduced, the application conditions for the introduced term are guaranteed to be fulfilled provided the uncontroversial claim is true, entitling us to infer the existence of the newly named kind of thing.

The 'magic' objection tends to arise again, however, as follows: you say that we may trivially infer the existence of numbers, tables, or properties from the truth of uncontroversial premises. But if there are numbers, tables, or properties, there must be the relevant *objects*. So what ensures that there are all the *objects* there

---

7. Bennett here is not directly addressing the neo-Fregean position, but rather arguing that Hirsch is tacitly committed to it—and then dismissing the position on the grounds above.

would have to be if the linguistic principles were legitimate? (cf. Hale/Wright 2001, 12ff).

Those who would raise this as an objection, however, have failed to see the thoroughgoing nature of the easy approach. The skeptical question is: are there enough objects to live up to the promises of the linguistic principles? (cf. Field 1984; Sider 2007, 3). So, for example, if we have a principle that says that if there are particles arranged tablewise, there is a table—what ensures that there is this (additional) object there? If we have a principle that says that if the relevant paperwork is filed, a corporation is created, what ensures that there is such an object as a corporation in the world that 'pops' into existence when we file the relevant paperwork?

The easy ontologist's first response, of course, is to ask: what would it take for there to be enough objects—for there to be an object where there are particles arranged tablewise or when paperwork is properly filed? This question, too, has to be asked *using* language, and as always, my strategy in answering it will be to try to determine the application conditions for the substantive term involved—in this case, 'object'—and then see if they are fulfilled. Now this is a tricky matter, for as discussed in chapter 2 above and elsewhere (my 2009 and 2007a), the English word 'object' apparently has several uses. If 'object' is being used as a sortal (perhaps in something like Carey's [2009] sense), which has application conditions of its own that may be evaluated without appeal to whether or not there is a table or a corporation (or referent of any other sortal term) there, then either those application conditions are met in the relevant situation (with the particles arranged tablewise, with the paperwork signed) or they are not. If they are, the challenge is met, for there is after all an object there. Suppose they are not met—suppose (what I find doubtful) that the application conditions for 'object' used as a sortal in the relevant way require a quantity of physical stuff unified in certain ways that particles arranged tablewise are not, or (more plausibly) involve conditions not required for the application conditions of 'corporation' to be fulfilled. In that case, we might have reason to deny that there are *objects* in the relevant situations, but we still wouldn't have reason to deny that there are *tables* or *corporations*—so this line would at most suggest that tables or corporations do not count as 'objects' in this sortal sense of 'object'. (This is a line of reply few serious metaphysicians will make use of, as most insist that they are not simply denying, e.g., that tables are objects [cf. Van Inwagen 1990]).

Suppose instead that 'object' is being used in its 'covering' sense, in which it is guaranteed to apply if any genuine sortal term applies (we may think of 'object' itself as being governed by a rule of use that entitles us to make a trivial inference from any claim of the form 'there is an S', where S is a sortal term, to conclude that there is an object). In that case, we can again answer the question of whether there is a relevant object in the situation, and do so in the positive. For we can again make a trivial inference from the claim that there is a table or a corporation, to the claim that there is an object.

How else might 'object' be used in asking whether there really are enough *objects* in the world to make good on the promises of the existence-entailing principles? If 'object' is not being used with any application conditions at all (neither independent of those for other sortals, nor derivative in a 'covering' use), then—given the deflationary approach to existence questions—the question is simply ill-formed and unanswerable. For if a term lacks application conditions, we cannot (in the object language) evaluate claims about whether or not the corresponding entities exist.

So in short if we address the question 'Are there enough objects there?' by way of asking about the application conditions for 'object', the objection quickly dissolves: either the answer is yes, or the answer is no but is irrelevant to the question of whether there are the disputed entities, or the question is ill-formed and unanswerable. Raising it as an objection requires assuming that the question 'Are there enough objects there?' may be answered in a way that does *not* proceed by determining the application conditions for the terms in *that* question, and whether or not they are fulfilled. But that of course is just what I deny. Accordingly, while the above line of thought might articulate the serious ontologists' way of feeling ill at ease with the easy ontological approach, it does not provide an objection to it, but merely begs the question against it.

In fact, on the easy ontologist's view, we can say why we have no reason to worry that there might not be enough 'objects' to live up to the principles: the conceptual truths that underwrite the trivial inferences are analytic principles that ensure that sometimes it takes no more for a novel term to apply than for certain other conditions to hold (or than it takes for the truth-conditions of the undisputed sentence to be fulfilled).[8] On this view, since it takes no more for 'table' to apply than for there to be particles arranged tablewise, it requires no metaphysical magic, no 'popping into existence' for there to be a table provided there are particles arranged tablewise (and given that there is a table, there is guaranteed to be an object in the covering sense of 'object'). In metaphysics as elsewhere, the only way to pull a rabbit out of a hat is if it's already there.[9]

8. This, of course, will raise objections from those suspicious of analytic or conceptual truths; I respond to some of those objections elsewhere (2007a, chapter 2), and others in this volume (chapter 7 below).

9. With thanks to Michael Beaney for this excellent phrase. See also Hale/Wright (2009), who emphasize that the disputed abstraction principles are conceptual truths, and so do not leave any hostages to metaphysical fortune. As they argue, the demand for 'independent reassurance' that the relevant entities exist is misplaced, as it is part and parcel of the neo-Fregean view that the initial and primary means of reference to the disputed entities (numbers, properties, etc.) is via the relevant abstraction principles, and it is not at all clear how the critic can make sense of the idea of what such 'independent reassurance' is supposed to consist in. Rayo (2013, 22) similarly denies that there is a 'gap' that needs to be plugged to be assured that, given that there are no dinosaurs, we can conclude that the number of dinosaurs is zero.

PROBLEMATIC ONTOLOGICAL COMMITMENTS?

6.3. DO WE GET THE OBJECTS
WE WANTED?

Another important challenge raised for the easy approach to ontology is roughly the idea that, even if we do not worry that there may not be *enough* objects to make good on the promises of the easy arguments, we may have reason to doubt that we get *the right* objects to settle the relevant ontological disputes. Simon Evnine (forthcoming) raises a version of this objection as the problem of "too much content".

In brief, the worry is this: on my view, application conditions form part of the rules of use for a sortal term, and their satisfaction is supposed to be sufficient to guarantee that an entity of the kind exists. But even supposing one accepts that an entity is guaranteed to exist, how can we be sure it has the relevant features to be of the right type—the type we were arguing about all along? Perhaps (it is thought) the entities we can get via trivial inferences are simply too 'thin', too 'lightweight' to be the entities we had interest in, or they may lack features that are essential to the disputed entities in question. I hope that my earlier (chapter 3) comments against the idea that the resulting entities are ontologically deflated will help put off the first sort of worry, but let us focus on the second.

We can get the worry into sharper focus by using some examples. Evnine's favored example is that of mereological fusions (sums). On my view, it is sufficient for there to be a mereological fusion (of A and B) that A exist, and that B exist: it is a trivial matter to infer the existence of fusions if there are any other things at all. But, there were certain things supposed to be true of fusions, according to classical extensional mereology. The fusion of A and B is also supposed to have A and B as parts (and to have no part distinct from both). Classical extensional mereology is not *just* supposed to be telling us that there are things, call them fusions, that exist just when some other things exist. It is telling us that when some things exist, something else exists *which has them as parts.*

(Forthcoming)

Moreover, according to classical extensional mereology there is exactly *one* fusion of any two things. Yet it seems that neither of these features can be guaranteed just by the principle that entitles us to infer that there is a fusion of A and B, provided that A exists and B exists. Thus, Evnine argues, easy ontological arguments can't be thought to settle the classical metaphysical debate about fusions, *as the serious metaphysicians discuss them.* And in general, he argues, there will be other features that disputed entities are supposed to have—but even if easy arguments may entail the existence of certain entities, they cannot guarantee that they have any of the other features associated with them, and so cannot ensure that the objects we get are the objects serious ontologists were debating about. Here he introduces what we may call 'Evnine's constraint':

> If the definition of a concept includes conditions for the application of a concept or for the existence of things falling under it, then nothing else can belong to the concept, and hence there is nothing in virtue of which any other properties might belong to entities falling under the concept.

(Forthcoming)

As a result, he argues, the entities that easy arguments might be thought to guarantee the existence of are just too minimal, too full of 'nothingness', to resolve the disputed ontological questions.

The key to responding to this line of worry is to make clear that application conditions are, on my view, not the only rules of use for the relevant sortal terms. It is a basic part of my view (developed in my 2007a) that, in addition to application conditions, for a term to be a sortal term (or name) at all, it must also come associated with coapplication conditions: conditions determining when the term may be reapplied in a way that will entitle us to say it's applied "to one and the same S"—thus establishing identity conditions for Ss (if any there be). (There also is no requirement that these two aspects be the *only* core rules governing the use of the term—I say more about this below).

Bringing in the coapplication conditions enables us to solve one side of Evnine's problem for fusions: uniqueness. For that is ensured by the identity conditions for fusions: Fusion x = Fusion y iff x and y share the same parts. These identity conditions, on my view, are just object-language correlates of the coapplication conditions for the term, in this case reflecting the rule that 'Fusion F' (a name for a fusion) is to be reapplied where and only where we have exactly the same parts. So the question "What guarantees that the fusion is unique?" can be answered on my view. While we can't "stipulate, by definition, that no other entities of a given type exist" in the sense of, say, stipulating that there are no other mice in my attic, it is a core part of my view that we *can* stipulate coapplication conditions for our terms, yielding identity conditions for the things, if any, that fall under them. And these can guarantee that if there are fusions X, Y, Z . . . each of which has as parts A and B (and nothing else), then X = Y = Z; that is, there is only one fusion. (For more on coapplication conditions and their reflection in identity conditions, see my 2007a, chapter 3, and 2007b).

To be fair, Evnine does not just ignore the issue of coapplication conditions. At the end of the paper he considers their relevance and argues that they cannot help but instead are "a source of further problems". For, he argues, the 'application' in 'coapplication' must be used in a different sense from that in 'application conditions'. As I discussed in chapter 2, the application conditions for a basic sortal term "S" should not be stated in such a way that they include the requirement "there is an S" or "an S exists". Evnine calls this 'bare application'. But, he argues, the 'application' in 'coapplication conditions' cannot be like that "since we are after conditions in which a concept applies *to the same thing* on two different occasions," whereas in 'bare application' we must not begin by presupposing that there is some thing to which the concept applies (forthcoming). As a result, he argues, coapplication conditions cannot be simply combined with application conditions as requisites for things of the relevant sort to exist; nor can fulfillment of the application conditions alone ensure that there are things of the sort under (ontological) discussion.

But I think this line of objection rests on a false dichotomy: presuming that either the coapplication conditions must be built in with the application conditions as requirements for things of the relevant sort to exist, or they must apply afterwards—once we can say (given the fulfillment of the application conditions) that there are things of the relevant sort. In fact, coapplication conditions play a rather different role, on my view: they help determine *what sort of thing* our terms refer to, if they in fact refer at all, and so also help determine what sort of thing we are asking about when we ask the existence question in the first place. Coapplication conditions are among the rules of use for a well-formed sortal term. It is not that we can say first that a term applies to something, and then investigate what sort of thing it applies to. Instead, we can only properly pose the existence question at all if we have a sortal term. But a sortal term already has two types of rules of use: some of which (application conditions) tell us the conditions under which there is something of the kind, and others of which (coapplication conditions) fix the most basic identity conditions for the things the term is to refer to (should it refer at all). Thus it is not a matter of first answering the existence question (using a term only defined in terms of its application conditions) and then asking whether the entity is thereby guaranteed to have certain further characteristics. If our terms came only with application conditions, perhaps Evnine would be correct, and we could make no other inferences about the entities the terms refer to. But that is not so for the central cases in question: proper sortal terms (as I have often insisted) must come with application conditions and coapplication conditions, and may also come with other constitutive rules of use, for example, relating their use to that of other terms. It is the presence of these other rules in constituting what it is our term means, even when it is used in the existence question, that can ensure that the things referred to (if any) have other features. For example, as I have argued elsewhere (2007b) modal features of objects, such as their identity conditions, are reflections of the constitutive rules of use (in this case, the coapplication conditions) for the sortal terms we use.

Moreover, just as application conditions for Ss are constrained to not appeal to the existence of Ss, there are similar constraints on how we may state coapplication conditions. Coapplication conditions fix under what conditions we can legitimately say 'This is the same S as that', and so the coapplication conditions for a term 'S' cannot be stated in terms that say: "The sortal term S coapplies to x and y provided that x = y". Rather, the coapplication conditions (if stated) would have to be stated in terms that do not appeal to identities and distinctnesses in objects referred to. Instead, they must appeal to preservation of features such as spatiotemporal continuity or (for those sortals that are not semantically basic) to identities of things of other (more basic) sorts. Coapplication conditions for a genuine sortal term "S" do not presuppose and appeal to facts about the identity conditions for Ss; rather, *they establish what we are talking about in talking about Ss at all and establish what it means to say 'this is the same S as that' and what the truth-conditions are for that claim.* So understood, coapplication conditions avoid the problem Evnine suggests, and may be appealed to in explaining how it is guaranteed that many of our terms, if they succeed in referring at all, refer to entities with the basic modal features commonly attributed to them.

Moreover, a sortal term needn't be governed by just these two sorts of rules. For example, as I have often emphasized, there may also be constitutive interrelations in the rules of use for different terms, for example, such that the application of one term guarantees the application of another. Terms may be interdefined and introduced in large clusters with rules governing their interrelations, and this again enables us to infer other truths about the entities for which our terms are introduced.

We can see this most clearly with institutional terms ('husband', 'wife', 'spouse', 'marriage', 'divorce' . . .) and terms used in games ('pitcher', 'hitter', 'hit', 'strike', 'out', 'base', 'inning' . . .). Suppose a term like 'strike' (plausibly, an accidental sortal applied to the swing) is introduced by giving the following 'application condition': "If a hitter swings at a ball and misses, then that swing counts as a strike". Now we may introduce a further rule, introducing a new noun term 'out' (which is not just an accidental sortal applying to a preexisting entity, but rather introduces a term for a new sort of entity): "If a hitter gets three strikes, then that makes an out", and "If members of a team make three outs, then their turn at bat for that inning is over".[10] Together, these give us an existence condition for outs (in the context of a game of baseball, one way an out is guaranteed to be made is if three strikes occur) combined with

---

10. Baseball aficionados will object that these are not the complete and exact rules. I know, but please permit me this simplification for expository purposes, or things will become unnecessarily complicated and long-winded.

another essential truth about outs: that three of them bring an end to a team's turn at bat (for that inning).

Recall Evnine's constraint—"If the definition of a concept includes conditions for the application of a concept or for the existence of things falling under it, then nothing else can belong to the concept" (forthcoming). If that constraint were apt, then here we would have to say: "Okay, I give it to you that there may be an out in such a circumstance, but *what guarantees that three of them will end a team's turn at bat?*" It is, I think, plain to see that in this case, it is misguided to ask for some further guarantee that three outs lead to a change in which team is at bat—as if we were asking for a guarantee that three bricks under the wheels would stop the cart from rolling. 'Strike' and 'out' and 'turn at bat during an inning' are conceptually related terms, and given their rules of use (including inference rules from 'has made three strikes (in a single turn at bat)' to 'is out', and from 'has made three outs' to 'is no longer at bat for this inning'), the one guarantees the other; we need look for no further 'fugitive facts' available for empirical or deep metaphysical discovery to guarantee the link.

Can we apply this lesson to handle the other question originally raised by Evnine: what 'guarantees' that a fusion of A and B has A and B as parts (and nothing distinct from both as parts)? "Part" is not a clear and stable term—and it is not a sortal term at all. Moreover, as David Sanford has shown extensively (1993), the use we make of 'part' in ordinary English (as when we talk about how many parts a lawnmower has) is not at all the use employed in classical extensional mereology. The mereologist is stipulatively introducing a technical notion of 'part' that is to be conceptually related to 'fusion' in certain specified ways, and (in the object language) is clarifying the interrelations that follow from this in the definitions and axioms of classical extensional mereology. She is not 'postulating' that a certain antecedently discovered relation named by an ordinary English word happens to hold of things 'posited' by her theory. The relations specified go something like this: where we have A and B, say that there is a 'fusion' of A and B, and call A and B the 'parts' of that fusion.

Consider the parallel: Where we have a man M and a woman W who have fulfilled the stated criteria and appear before the justice of the peace and say these vows, say that a 'marriage' comes into effect, and call M and W the 'parties to that marriage'. *But what guarantees that M and W are the parties to the marriage— and not, say, that M's mother and W's grandfather, or the first two random people to walk by the courthouse, are?* Again, silly question: this is definitional of the relations among the concepts in question.

Evnine considers the possibility that terms like 'fusion' and 'part' are simultaneously defined, but writes:

> The problem with this response . . . is that it has the effect of turning the theory of CEM [classical extensional mereology] into an uninterpreted calculus. There would be no point at which the theory itself would make any claims about the world.
>
> *(forthcoming)*

But it doesn't follow from the fact that the rules of use for terms may be interrelated that none connect to the world.[11] Again, this is easy to see in our terms for social and institutional entities. We can start with ordinary terms, connected in part ostensively to

---

11. Moreover, I am not at all sure that this is really a problem for truly classical mereology, considered as a 'calculus of individuals' proposed by Lesniewski, and as an alternative to set theory, rather than considered (with Lewis) as a piece of 'metaphysics' involving certain 'metaphysical posits'. (It is entirely consistent for the deflationary ontologist to accept the first and reject the second.)

the world: this man, this woman, and then introduce a system of related terms on top of them: husband, wife, marriage, divorce ... Or start with a sand-filled sack; introduce the term 'home plate' (in part using ostensive reference to the sack), and go on to introduce interrelated terms like 'hit', 'run', 'strike', 'out', and so forth on the basis of that and similar terms. The fact that terms are conceptually interrelated does not entail that they are *merely* conceptually interrelated, or that they cannot be used to make claims about the world.

Now granted, I have not laid out all of the linguistic rules in question—I have only given a few examples of how our terms may come with interrelated rules. Nonetheless, the basic strategy is clear: once we make evident the various rules of use for the terms in question, we can make it clear that not only are we justified in making an existence claim for entities of that kind, but also that the entities referred to are guaranteed to have many of the identity conditions, persistence conditions, and other features supposed to characterize them. Showing this of course must be done on a case-by-case basis (depending on which features are thought to be crucial for which disputed entities), but I hope that I have at least made the direction of reply clear, and made it clear that it would be premature to judge that entities the existence of which we may infer through these trivial inferences could not have any other characteristic features.[12]

---

12. Evnine's other main case in point is chairs: he argues that even if trivial inferences might guarantee the existence of chairs, they cannot guarantee that such 'chairs' would be constituted by their wood, have the same weight and location as the wood, etc. See my (2013b) for discussion of how many of the features of a constitution view may in fact be explained in deflationary terms, as reflections of interrelations among rules of use for the various terms involved.

6.4. CONCLUSION

I have argued thus far that a better understanding of the easy
approach to existence questions, developed in the way I have suggested, makes it clear how to put to rest worries that there might
not 'be enough objects' to make good on the promises of the trivial
inferences, or that these might not be the objects serious metaphysicians were concerned with. I have also responded to criticisms
that it commits us to an unacceptably plentitudinous ontology, or
requires some sort of magic. Once it is more fully understood, we
can see that the easy approach developed here is not easily assailed
from these angles. But we still must address a further series of objections. If, even after reviewing those objections, the view remains
unassailed, its initial attractions will remain untarnished, and we
can retain the hope that well-formed ontological questions really
are easy to answer.

[7]

DO DOUBTS ABOUT CONCEPTUAL TRUTHS UNDERMINE EASY ARGUMENTS?

Above I have addressed objections to the ontological conclusions that we seem to get from easy ontological arguments. But a separate range of objections comes not from ontological concerns, but rather from objections to the inferences themselves. The easy approach to ontology relies on the idea that competent speakers may begin from knowing an undisputed truth and from there, by making use only of their linguistic/conceptual mastery and trivial reasoning, are entitled to reach ontological conclusions that there are new entities not referred to in the undisputed truth. These inferences, however, apparently rely on there being certain conceptual truths to take us from the undisputed claim to the derived claim and ontological claim.[1]

---

1. The same terminology is not always used: while neo-Fregeans speak of conceptual truths, I have generally said that the undisputed claim 'analytically entails' the onto-logical claim, while Schiffer speaks of the relevant inference as 'trivial' and the onto-logical claim as 'redundant' or 'pleonastic' with respect to the first. But for simplicity I will speak of conceptual or analytic truths above.

But over the past sixty years or more there has been steady and prevalent suspicion of the idea that there are any analytic or conceptual truths. The best-known objections to analyticity of course come from Quine (1951/1976). Elsewhere, I and others have responded extensively to Quine's criticisms of the notion of analyticity.[2] Given that, I will leave Quine's arguments to the side here, to focus instead on an important recent line of criticism of analyticity that is independent of Quine's and that has been very influential:[3] Timothy Williamson's recent (2007) criticisms of the notion of analyticity. I will argue, however, that his criticisms of the idea that there are analytic truths does nothing to undermine the trivial arguments that easy ontology relies on.

7.1. WHY EASY ONTOLOGY NEEDS CONCEPTUAL TRUTHS

It is important first to be clear about exactly what sort of commitment to conceptual truths is required to make good on the easy approach to existence questions. First, defenders of the easy approach to ontology hold that existence questions may be easily answered by those who have mastered the rules governing the concepts employed, and who know the truth of the undisputed claim. So, those who know the truth of

- The apple is red

2. I address Quine's objections in 2007a, chapter 2, but many others have done so in various ways as well; see, for example, Strawson and Grice (1956), Boghossian (1997), and Russell (2008).
3. Harman (1999) also criticizes the very idea of analyticity, but along lines largely reminiscent of Quine's. Thus I will also leave that to one side here.

and have mastered our nominative use of property talk (as well as the other terms involved) are entitled to infer

- The apple has the property of being red

and

- There is a property.

Moreover, they may do so from the armchair, without the need for any further information or empirical investigation. So what we need is a view on which *mastery* of relevant linguistic/conceptual rules governing the terms/concepts employed in the inference, plus knowledge of an undisputed truth, *licenses* or *entitles* one to make the relevant inference using those terms, without the need for any further investigation.

If speakers are entitled to make the inference to the ontological claim based only on their linguistic/conceptual mastery combined with their knowledge of the undisputed truth, then they may indeed answer disputed ontological questions easily. But a bit more than this is required: the defender of the easy approach to ontology wants to hold not merely that speakers are *entitled to* accept the ontological conclusion on that basis alone. She also wants to be in a position to say that those who do not do so—who deny the ontological claim or suspend judgment until deeper inquiries into metaphysics are completed—are open to rebuke. This is the core of what is required for the easy approach to be defensible.

One can connect this to a somewhat more traditional notion of analytic or conceptual truths as follows. Competent speakers who have mastered the relevant rules of use for our terms and rules of reasoning are entitled to simply make the inference in question. But one might, on analysis, notice that the validity of the inference relies on there being a certain conceptual truth: a conditional that can take us from the uncontroversial truth to the derived claim, for example:

* If x is P, then x has the property of being P.

Thus the validity of the easy inferences might be seen as relying on there being such conceptual truths as these to underwrite the inference. Let us be clear at the start, however: competent speakers need never explicitly consider such general conditional claims in order to be licensed to make the inference. The conceptual truth may be seen as an object-language articulation of a rule of use (in this case, an introduction rule for nominative property talk) that competent speakers have mastered, but speakers need not explicitly consider the relevant conceptual truth at all.

Nonetheless, * has all the appearances of being a conceptual truth, and it seems there must be such conceptual truths for the easy inferences to be legitimate. Moreover, it seems that competent speakers who consider the conceptual truth and are capable of the relevant kind of generalization and abstraction would be entitled to accept the conceptual truth on that basis alone, without need for further investigation.[4]

So, it seems in sum that the defender of easy ontological arguments is committed to the idea that speakers who master the relevant linguistic/conceptual rules are entitled to accept the explicit expression of the conditional conceptual truth, and those who also know the

---

4. Does this mean that the conceptual truth is known a priori? That depends, of course, on one's conception of the a priori. I would like to leave those issues to one side, and will make no use of the terminology here. What is crucial for my purposes is that competent speakers be licensed (based on their competence) to accept the inference and (if they consider it explicitly) to accept the conceptual truth that may be seen as underwriting it (though this is just an object-language expression of a rule they have mastered).

undisputed truth are entitled to make the inference and come to the existential conclusion. Yet these ideas might seem to be threatened by arguments against there being analytic truths. Let us turn to examine the most recent and powerful such arguments, and what their bearing might be on the tenability of easy ontological arguments.[5]

There is also a broader issue at stake here: Williamson uses his rejection of analyticity as part of a general argument that no metaphysical (or other) knowledge may be gained by conceptual competence (2007, 77). I hold that metaphysical knowledge may be gained in this way, as we may sometimes reach ontological conclusions through conceptual competence alone (when we may make the inference from an undisputed conceptual truth) and sometimes by adding conceptual competence to our empirical knowledge.[6] Thus I owe a response to his arguments in order to defend both the idea that we may give easy arguments for existence claims, and the idea that we may sometimes gain metaphysical knowledge on the basis of our conceptual competence.

7.2. WILLIAMSON'S ATTACK ON ANALYTICITY

Recent discussions of analyticity typically distinguish between metaphysical and epistemic conceptions of analyticity. Paul

---

5. It is also worth noting that, while a defense of conceptual truth is needed to defend the easy arguments for ontological conclusions, it is by no means required simply in order to avoid hard ontology. For in rejecting the idea that there are questions that are epistemically metaphysical we reject the idea that there are ontological questions that cannot be answered by a combination of conceptual and empirical means—but that doesn't mean holding (against Quine) that there is a strict division between these.

6. I also hold that certain forms of metaphysical modal knowledge may be arrived at through conceptual competence (2007b, 2012, 2013a), though that is not a thesis defended in this book. (A separate book with a fuller defense of this view of modality is in preparation.)

Boghossian distinguishes them as follows. In the metaphysical sense, a statement is analytic provided it owes its truth-value completely to its meaning, and not at all to 'the facts' (1997, 334). By contrast, a statement is epistemically analytic provided that grasp of its meaning alone suffices for justified belief in its truth (1997, 334). He goes on to argue that Quine succeeds in discrediting the metaphysical notion of analyticity, but not the epistemic sense (1997, 335).

Williamson attacks (separately) both the metaphysical and epistemic conceptions of analyticity. The sense of 'analyticity' the easy ontologist needs most directly is clearly something closer to what Boghossian calls the 'epistemic sense'. For what we need is the claim about how speakers become entitled to answer the ontological question (and to endorse the conceptual truth)—though I shall shortly suggest some crucial changes from Boghossian's formulation. In any case, it will be useful to begin by looking at Williamson's (2007) criticisms of an epistemic conception of analyticity (2007).[7]

Williamson suggests that the epistemic conception of analyticity should be understood as follows:

> A sentence s is analytic just in case, necessarily, whoever understands s assents to it.
>
> *(2007, 73–74)*

He adds to this the following clarifications. First, this concerns only the sentence *with its current meaning* "for of course if the phonetically individuated sentence had meant something different, someone might easily have understood it and refused to assent" (2007, 74). Second,

---

7. Sider (2012) does not give a general argument against analyticity, but does argue that the easy ontologist may embrace the analyticities she needs only at the cost of adopting an epistemically metaphysical stand she should reject. I return to discuss this line of objection in chapter 10 below.

the assent should be taken as a disposition to assent (mentally)—not an actual (verbal or mental) expression of assent (2007, 74). He goes on to argue that this proposed understanding-assent link fails in some of the most obvious cases of purported analytic truths (and that various related proposals fail), and thus that there are no epistemically analytic truths. This leads him to the broader conclusion that nothing is epistemically available "simply on the basis of linguistic and conceptual competence" (2007, 77).

His criticisms of the idea that there are claims that are epistemically analytic all take the following form: find someone who is apparently semantically competent with the relevant terms, and yet who is not disposed to assent to it because of radically false (factual) beliefs and/or embracing deviant logical principles. If we can find such speakers, we must admit that they understand the relevant sentence without being disposed to assent to it, and so conclude that the proposed understanding-assent link fails, and thus that the candidate sentence is not epistemically analytic.

Williamson's two central examples revolve around a clear central case of a (purportedly) analytic claim: 'Every vixen is a vixen', which he imagines as being rejected by two competent speakers of English, Peter and Stephen. Both Peter and Stephen are said to be native speakers of English, who learned English in the normal way, and normally would be considered perfectly competent (their deviances only show up in particular circumstances). So both, Williamson insists, "by ordinary standards . . . understand ['every vixen is a vixen'] perfectly well" (2007, 90). Yet they are not disposed to assent to it. Peter holds the logical view that universally quantified statements are existentially committing—so the statement is only true if there is at least one vixen. Yet he also holds a conspiracy theory that there are no vixens at all. As a result, he denies the truth of 'Every vixen is a vixen' (2007, 86–87). By contrast, Stephen holds that, for vague terms V, statements of the form 'x is a V' are neither true nor false in borderline cases. He also holds that 'vixen' is vague, for there are some evolutionary ancestors of modern foxes that are borderline cases, and so 'x is a vixen' is lacking in truth-value for some substitution instances. He also accepts the following truth-conditions for conditionals in his three-valued logic: a conditional is true just in case either the antecedent is false or the consequent is true, false just in case its antecedent is true and consequent is false, and otherwise neither true nor false. Given all of that, Stephen holds that 'x is a vixen → x is a vixen' is neither true nor false for some substitution instances, as a result of which 'every vixen is a vixen' is also lacking in truth-value. Thus he also refuses to assent to 'Every vixen is a vixen' (2007, 87–88). As a result, Williamson concludes, even for a purportedly analytic sentence as clear and uncontroversial as 'every vixen is a vixen', the purported understanding-assent link fails, giving us reason to deny that there are any epistemically analytic sentences.

7.3. HOW EASY INFERENCES SURVIVE

Before we can even begin to evaluate the bearing of Williamson's criticisms on the conception of analyticity presupposed by the easy approach to ontology, we need to bridge some crucial gaps. For the conception of analyticity criticized by Williamson is not the same as what is needed by those who accept easy ontological arguments. The view is not that someone's *understanding* the claim entails that she has a *disposition to assent to it*, but rather that *mastery* of the relevant linguistic/conceptual rules governing the expressions used *entitles* one to make the relevant inference using those expressions and embrace the ontological conclusion—and that rejecting it would leave one *open to rebuke*. If we focus on the linking conceptual truth rather than the inference, we can express this as saying that mastery of the relevant linguistic/conceptual rules entitles one to accept the conceptual truth (without the need for any further investigation), and that rejecting it would be a mistake. What the easy ontologist needs is clearly a *normative* claim, about what competent speakers are *entitled* to conclude (and what would be a mistake)—not a descriptive one about what competent speakers *will be* disposed to assent to. The bare fact that some apparently competent speakers do not assent and are not disposed to assent is neither here nor there with respect to the normative issue (to think that it is would be to fall into the old mistakes of psychologism).

At the end of his original discussion of the issue (in his 2003) Williamson explicitly notes that his arguments do not apply to a normativist version of inferentialism that treats possessing a concept not as entailing that speakers are *disposed to* assent to certain statements, but rather that they *ought to* assent:

> One response to the failure of accepting given patterns of infer-
> ence to be necessary for having a concept might be that the
> required conditions are normative rather than psychological. For
> instance, one understands → if one *ought* to use it in reasoning by
> conditional proof and modus ponens, whether or not one actu-
> ally so reasons. Deviant logicians are not counterexamples to that
> proposal.
>
> *(2003, 291)*[8]

8. Against this proposal, Williamson says only that we are left wanting some deeper explanation of why one ought to reason in this way—or an explanation "of how one can be
obliged to reason according to those rules" (2003, 291). This of course is a request for a
much longer story than can be given here, but it is by no means a hopeless project. There
seem to be two separate questions here: how can an individual be obliged to reason
according to certain rules, and why ought we (collectively) to have those rules rather
than any others. On the first, the right approach seems to be that one can be so obliged
by presenting oneself as a participant in the relevant public norm-governed practice
(just as one can be obliged to follow the rules of soccer by joining the soccer game).
The question of why we ought to adopt certain rules (or norms) rather than any others
is far more difficult. One might look to the work of inferentialist logicians (Beall and

It is a similar normativist view that is at issue here: that speakers who master the relevant conceptual/linguistic rules are entitled to make the relevant inference, and to accept the conceptual truth (and are open to reproach if they refuse to).

Since the question at issue is not, whether Stephen and Peter are *disposed to* assent to 'every vixen is a vixen', but rather, whether they are *entitled to* accept it, given their mastery of the rules governing the concepts employed, this gives us a quick route to disposing of Williamson's worries. Suppose for the moment (as Williamson repeatedly insists), that Peter and Stephen *are* using the terms 'vixen', 'every', and 'is' in the standard way as terms of the public English language, and (as competent speakers) have mastered their use. Are they entitled to endorse the claim 'all vixens are vixens'? In refusing to do so, are they making a mistake that leaves them open to rebuke? It certainly seems that the answer to these questions is 'yes'. Whether or not they actually assent to the claim, or even are disposed to assent to it, is not at issue. The point is rather that, if they are using the standard English expressions they are *entitled* to assent to it, and open to rebuke if they do not. And if that's the case, then Williamson's examples do nothing to undermine the ideas required by easy arguments: that those who have mastered the relevant terms and use them (in their standard senses) are entitled to accept the relevant conceptual truth and (provided they know the truth of the unconditional claim) to make the inference to the ontological claim.

Yet some might be unconvinced by this quick route. For they might see Williamson's examples as capable of also undermining the idea that Peter's and Stephen's mere mastery of the relevant concepts and expressions entitles them to accept 'every vixen is a

Restall 2013, Ripley 2013) for a way of understanding certain basic norms regarding acceptance and rejection as constitutive norms for thought, and thus as non-optional. And we might look for a pragmatic justification for adopting other (less basic) norms or rules.

vixen' (when those terms are being used in their standard senses) and leaves them open to reproach if they do not. They might have the intuition that Peter and Stephen aren't making a mistake that leaves them open to reproach; perhaps the thought is that *given their other commitments*, including Peter's empirical belief that there are no vixens, and the pet theories each has about the functioning of logical terms involved (the universal quantifier in Peter's case, the conditional—under conditions of vagueness—in Stephen's), they are not making a mistake in drawing the conclusions they do. *Given the rules each is working with*, (one might say) each is reasoning well and not open to rebuke on those grounds. Rephrasing Williamson's point in normative terms, one might then suggest that their mastery of the expressions alone does *not* entitle them to accept that every vixen is a vixen—instead, that hinges on what other factual and metalinguistic views they accept. Given their peripheral factual and metalinguistic views, one might hold, although they master standard use of the expressions and use them in the standard way, they are right to refuse to assent to 'every vixen is a vixen' and not open to rebuke for refusing—so we can't after all treat that sentence as a conceptual truth in the sense required. (And if *that* sentence is not a conceptual truth, one might think, nothing is—and so there are not the conceptual truths relied on by easy arguments.)

But is it true that Peter and Stephen have mastered use of the expressions and use them in the standard English way—and nonetheless are entitled to refuse to assent to 'every vixen is a vixen'? Williamson insists that Peter and Stephen are competent speakers who have mastered use of the standard English terms, and I am prepared to grant him that much.[9] What I think is more open to

9. Some might be inclined to reject Williamson's claim that they are semantically competent, taking their deviations to be evidence that—despite the fact that they learned the terms in the usual way and would normally 'pass'—they have foresworn that basic acquired competence in favor of adopting pet theories, e.g., about the way universally

question is whether they are using those expressions in their standard English (and standard logical) sense when they refuse to assent to 'every vixen is a vixen'.[10] Williamson insists that, owing to the public determination of meaning, when they refuse to assent to 'every vixen is a vixen', they are using these terms in their standard, publicly determined senses. They intend to do so (they are "not making [a] unilateral declaration of linguistic independence" but rather use the words "as words of the public language" [2007, 89]). Of course, as Williamson allows, one may intend to use words with their normal public senses but fail "in cases of sufficiently gross and extensive error". But he denies that the errors in the cases of Peter and Stephen are extreme enough to defeat their intention to use the terms with their public senses. They are *using* terms in their standard public senses, he insists; it's just that they make mistakes in their semantic *theories* in which they articulate the truth-conditions for statements involving 'every' (2007, 89). (Peter of course also goes wrong in his factual view that there are no foxes.) But, Williamson insists, "Giving an incorrect theory of the meaning of a word is not the same as using the word with an idiosyncratic sense—linguists who work on the semantics of natural languages often do the former without doing the latter" (2007, 89). The mistakes Peter and Stephen make, Williamson holds, are just *factual* mistakes: they

quantified claims work. If we take them to have foresworn their competence, then of course Williamson's examples do nothing to undermine the analytic entailments the easy ontological inferences rely on. There is something to be said for this line of thought, but I am prepared to grant Williamson that Stephen and Peter are semantically competent in his sense (that they learned the terms in the usual way, would normally not be caught out. . .).

10. I add this caveat since there might be a case to be made that the rules of use for the common English term 'every' are indeterminate enough to make Peter's and Stephen's claims plausible interpretations. The sense in which one thinks it clearly analytic that 'every vixen is a vixen', however, presupposes the standard first-order logical sense of the term 'every'. And of course, claims are only analytic within a language (say that of first-order logic), keeping the senses of the terms in question fixed.

'manifest only some deviant patterns of belief' (2007, 91). And so the point (translated into our normative terms) would be that mastery of the relevant expressions alone (which they have) does not entitle one to draw any conclusions without collateral factual beliefs—so there aren't any conceptual truths understood as claims we are entitled to assent to just using our reasoning abilities and mastery of the relevant concepts.

But it doesn't seem plausible to think that Peter and Stephen are merely making mistakes in their semantic theories for English— taking these as factual proposals for understanding how our actual terms work. They do not seem to be offering a theory of the truth-conditions for English expressions involving 'every' in the same sense that a linguist would. Being the intelligent people they are, if that were what they aimed to do, they would notice that their 'theories' don't fit the data of English usage very well. They would also notice that when they follow these theories and refuse to accept that every vixen is a vixen, other competent speakers look bewildered or correct them. Yet they persist just the same. If we take them to be offering a theory of how the English expression works, they must know that their 'theory' leads to a poor fit with usage. But—unlike real linguists—they don't seem to care.

This gives us good reason to deny that what they are doing is making a *factual* mistake while attempting to devise a theory about how our English term 'every' actually works. I don't think Peter and Stephen are simply making *mistakes* either in their way of using the term 'every' or in their semantic theories about how the English term works. Instead, each thinks he has special reason to think that term *should* follow the rules he articulates instead; each is offering a revisionary semantic theory (not a faulty descriptive one). Perhaps Peter thinks this is the *best* treatment of universally quantified claims where there is nothing of the sort described, or Stephen thinks this is the best treatment of vagueness and of conditionals on a three-valued logic. And 'best' in each case presumably means best in terms of forming part of the best logical theory overall—with greater clarity, precision, avoidance of difficulties, or what have you (the best on pragmatic grounds?)—not best in terms of most closely mapping ordinary use (given the significant deviations).

Moreover (*pace* Williamson 2007, 90) those revisionary semantic theories seem to lead Peter and Stephen to use the term 'every' in a way that deviates from the standard English sense—for example, leading them to reject the claim that every vixen is a vixen. (It's not that they start from some independent intuition that this claim is not true and then get to the relevant semantic theory; it's that their revisionary semantic/logical theories lead them to this conclusion). If they are not using terms in their standard sense, however, then although they *represent themselves as speaking (unmodified) English*, they are implicitly (through their own use) changing the rules governing certain key English expressions. Maybe they think they have good reasons for these changes. Perhaps they even do.

But regardless, they then are not using the terms in their standard English sense. And when we say this we are not accusing them of semantic incompetence. Rather, they think they have some special insight that entitles them to give a revisionary semantic theory and modify the rules of the expressions, while representing themselves as speaking the same way as everyone else. This isn't semantic incompetence. It's semantic chutzpah.

In short, Peter and Stephen go wrong not in 'holding deviant patterns of belief' (apart, of course from 'there are no foxes'), but rather for representing themselves as uttering truths in standard English when they are implicitly changing the rules on the basis of adopting a revisionary semantics. If they are implicitly changing some of the rules for the expressions (most plausibly, 'every') in the purported conceptual truth, then that does nothing to undermine the idea that those who have *mastered* the (actual) rules of use for the terms used in the claim are *entitled* to accept the claim (and that refusing to do so would constitute a mistake).

Williamson himself accepts that a condition on the understanding-assent link he criticizes should be that it concerns only the term *with its current meaning* (2007, 74). But plausibly the meaning of a term is tied to its (actual) constitutive rules of use— and so a change in constitutive rules of use constitutes a change in meaning. On this view, if Peter and Stephen are implicitly changing the rules, then they are implicitly changing the meanings of the terms involved, and so using other (homophonic, and closely related) terms. If so, then even if they are entitled to reject 'every vixen is a vixen' based on their revisionary construal of the rules governing key expressions, this does not undermine the idea that (given the *actual* rules of use for the terms involved in the English sentence) the claim is a conceptual truth, in the sense that those who have mastered the use of the actual terms involved are entitled to accept it, without any further investigation.[11]

Consider some parallel cases, where competent participants in a practice come to unilaterally alter some of the standard rules for what they take to be very good reasons based on their special insights. Consider Magdalena, who is a competent speaker of English, but believes that given the Glory of God, the name of God should always be emphasized in importance by placing it at the end of a sentence. Thus she does not accept 'God is good' as

11. Williamson considers and rejects a superficially similar proposal: that whoever understands the sentence 'Every vixen is a vixen' and assents to it on that basis does so with justification (this is a version of his AJI', modified to avoid his too quick objection) (2007, 130–33). He rejects this on grounds that actual assent would (in fact) require exercise of cognitive and logical capacities that "are not semantic or conceptual in any relevant sense", and so wouldn't be based just on understanding (2007, 131). Again, sticking to the strictly normative claim about what they are *entitled to* accept (rather than what anyone actually *does* accept and on the basis of what capacities they possess) avoids this problem.

a well-formed sentence, instead, she only accepts "is good, God". Does this have the least tendency to show that 'God is good' is not grammatical in English, or that competent speakers are not licensed to accept this as grammatical and reject Magdalena's expression as ungrammatical? Certainly not. She counts as competent given Williamson's criteria: she, too, has learned English in the usual way and not forgotten it, and would get by in most standard conversations. We can understand what she is doing and needn't treat her as irrational, of course, once we understand her background motives. And we wouldn't react to her as we would to a speaker of a foreign tongue who is just learning English and is simply confused about the grammar. Nonetheless, her attempt to change the rules for idiosyncratic reasons does nothing to undermine the idea that the grammatical rules of English license speakers who have mastered them to accept the first sentence as grammatical and reject Magdalena's as ungrammatical.

Or consider Cheryl, a competent—indeed first-rate—player of NCAA basketball, who (it so happens) is also a philosophy major. After a compelling metaphysics class, she comes to believe that time is unreal, and rejects the authority of the shot clock. Is she still basketball competent? Well, sure, she has learned basketball in the usual way, acquired the necessary skills, and has mastered and followed the rules for years (though she now comes to reject the authority of one of them). Nonetheless, are her teammates entitled to implore her to shoot the ball *now* when the shot clock is down to three seconds? Certainly. Are they entitled to rebuke her when she does not? Absolutely. For she is still playing the public game of NCAA basketball, regardless of her private reasons for rejecting some of its rules. Those public rules remain in place, and preserve the usual entitlements and demands. The fact that some competent practitioners may (for global reasons of their own) come to reject or attempt to alter certain of the rules in place does not change what the public rules are or what entitlements and requirements follow from them.

The upshot is that Williamson's clever examples of deviant speakers do nothing to undermine the trivial inferences that the easy approach to ontology relies on. Those who have mastered the constitutive linguistic/conceptual rules are *entitled* to make the inference from the undisputed claim without further investigation, as well as to rebuke those who refuse to make the inference. Nor does it undermine the idea that there is a conceptual truth underwriting the inference, which (provided they are still using those very terms) competent speakers are entitled to accept without further investigation (and are open to rebuke if they refuse to accept it).

A final general point is worth mentioning. If we think of Williamson's arguments as providing the basis for seriously undermining easy ontological arguments (by undermining the idea that a speaker's linguistic/conceptual mastery and trivial reasoning may entitle her to reach new conclusions or accept something as a conceptual truth), they would equally undermine the idea that competent speakers' mastery of linguistic/conceptual rules may *ever* entitle them to make inferences using those terms (perhaps on the basis of prior knowledge).

But this would pretty clearly be proving too much. For consider how radical it would really be to reject the idea that competent speakers who have mastered the relevant linguistic and conceptual rules may sometimes be entitled to accept new claims and make new inferences on that basis alone—without the need for any further investigation. If we deny this, we deny that we are ever entitled to simply reason from some things we know to accept other conclusions. Thus we would be unable to expand our knowledge by reasoning; every claim would have to be separately considered and evaluated. If we deny this, we seem to deny the possibility of acquiring new knowledge deductively, and even to deny that we are ever entitled to accept a paraphrase or translation of a claim we already accept—even if they seem to all competent speakers completely redundant, each again would require separate evaluation. This is a radical thesis indeed. Of course there may be specific reasons to worry about the particular inferences used in easy ontological arguments—such as worries that arise in virtue of these inferences being 'ontologically ampliative' or that arise based on thinking that the quantifier is being used in two different senses. I address these concerns in the chapters that follow. But these are not Williamson's worries. If his rejection of analyticity causes problems for easy ontological arguments, it equally well causes problems for all attempts to expand our knowledge by simply making use of conceptual mastery and our reasoning abilities. Yet rejecting all of this would, in the eyes of all but the most radical, be rejecting far too much.

7.4. CAVEATS AND CONCLUSIONS

I have argued that we can preserve the claims the easy ontologist needs: that those who accept the undisputed claim and have mastered the relevant constitutive semantic/conceptual rules are entitled to make the inference and accept the ontological conclusion it leads to on that basis alone (and may on the same basis be entitled to accept certain conceptual truths). This of course relies on the idea that our terms (and concepts) *have* constitutive rules.

One thing I should be upfront about, however, is that it is not always perfectly clear what precisely the constitutive rules are that govern any particular natural language expression. Indeed discerning these may be difficult work for the linguist or metaphysician. Many of our natural language terms, including some of the logical terms at work in Williamson's examples, may be indeterminate regarding some of their rules. Does the English term 'every' used in 'every x is a y' require that there be xs for such sentences to be true or not? English may be indeterminate about this, leaving Peter's interpretation looking perfectly reasonable for one who has mastered the use of the English term. But of course, in this philosophical context the discussion presupposes as a background the truth-conditions linked to the universal quantifier in standard first-order logic (for it is given those that we think of 'every vixen is a vixen' as an analytic truth). In any case, on the conception of analyticity at issue, what is analytic is always so *relative to a system of rules for the relevant expressions mastered by speakers*—whenever those rules change, we must be open to the thought that what is analytic (in the altered language) may have changed. So if there are two (or more) alternative precisifications of the rules of a natural language term, different claims may be analytic under these different precisifications and it may simply be indeterminate whether certain claims that involve the natural language term are analytic (or are expressions of conceptual truths). Nonetheless, the fact that the rules may be vague or indeterminate for certain natural language expressions does not undermine the idea that there *are* such rules.

Williamson notes that the two core principles behind his argument against analyticity are epistemological holism and semantic deference. He uses the holism claim to bolster the idea that, despite their deviations from standard uses of the key terms, Stephen and Peter may "compensate" for their unorthodoxy on one point by their 'orthodoxy' on others, and so overall their "usage of the key terms is not beyond the pale of social acceptability" (2007, 91), entitling them to be considered competent speakers. The deference claim, in turn, he uses to justify saying that—despite their deviations—they are nonetheless using the key terms in their standard public senses. We can be noncommittal about whether we should see semantic deference as sufficient to ensure that they are using the terms in their standard public senses: if they are using the terms in their standard public senses, then (given the attached rules of use) they are entitled to accept 'every vixen is a vixen' and other competent speakers are entitled to rebuke them for refusing. If they are not using the terms in their standard senses (but rather using revised rules), then even if they are entitled to reject 'every vixen is a vixen' in their idiolect, that tells us nothing about whether the standard English claim is a conceptual truth.

An underlying difference between Williamson's view and mine, however, concerns the holism point. For on the view I am defending, there are certain core constitutive rules of use for our expressions that must be in place (and normatively binding on speakers) if those very terms are to be used at all, just as there are core constitutive rules that must be in place if a given game (chess, soccer) is to be played at all. That of course does not mean that we can't choose to alter those rules for some purpose, or in response to certain empirical discoveries—only that we must be clear that that's what we are doing (and remember that that will then alter the analytic truths statable using the changed term).

As an analog to defend holism, Williamson notes that the rules of a casual game of beach soccer may be far more open and indeterminate than the rules of FIFA soccer. That much we may and should accept. But, *pace* Williamson (2011), we should not conclude "There is no rule R of beach soccer such that, necessarily, one is competent in beach soccer only if one assents to R". Put in properly normative terms, the claim would be that there is no rule R of beach soccer such that one who violates R is subject to rebuke. But, as one incompetent in all forms of soccer (and thus often rebuked), I can tell you that that is clearly wrong. If I pick up the ball with my hands and run around with it in the water, I am subject to rebuke: I am violating a constitutive rule of anything that counts as soccer. If I begin singing rather than running or kicking, and declare myself the winner on grounds of my greater melodiousness than my companions, I may be rebuked as not playing beach soccer at all. If my companions join me in my swimming and throwing the ball, or my singing, we have all ceased to play beach soccer. There are constitutive rules even for an informal game like beach soccer—rules that may not always be *followed*, not even by competent players, but that nonetheless must be *in force, binding* on players for them to be playing that very game at all. Of course there may be alternate acceptable precisifications of some of the rules such as the boundaries of the field, whether an offside rule is in force, and so on, which may lead it to be sometimes indeterminate whether the other team is entitled to throw the ball in from the sidelines or to take a free kick. But that does not mean that there are no constitutive rules at all.

So similarly, the fact that the constitutive rules for natural language terms (including some logical terms) may be open-ended, in places indeterminate, open to alternative precisifications, and the like does not undermine the idea that there are some constitutive rules, the mastery of which entitles speakers to make certain inferences and accept certain claims (and rebuke those who deny them). Where it is indeterminate what the rules of a natural language expression are, we should be hesitant to endorse inferences (or purportedly analytic claims) that rely on a particular precisification of the rules. But that is a problem for particular inferences made, or claims accepted, not for the very idea that speakers may be entitled to make inferences or endorse claims based on their mastery of the relevant rules.

In practice, the inferences easy arguments in ontology typically rely on are not cases in which the rules seem indeterminate or open-ended. That is precisely why the inferences seem so trivial, indeed (in the apt description of Schiffer), redundant. It does seem plausible that a rule of ordinary property talk entitles us to make the inference from "x is P" to "x has the property of being P", and from "There are five books on the table" to "The number of books on the table is five". This of course is not to deny that there may be indeterminacies in other areas, for example, in whether we are entitled to make the inference from "x is not P" to "There is a property of being P that x lacks". In such cases, we may doubt and argue about the particular case in question or debate the merits of different ways of precisifying the informal rules of English. But none of that casts doubt on the idea that in general, where the rules are central and clear, easy inferences may lead us to ontological conclusions.

One final caveat is in order. Accepting that our terms and concepts have constitutive rules does not preclude the idea that we may (collectively) choose to change these rules, perhaps even for very good pragmatic reasons, for example to avoid indeterminacies or potential inconsistencies, to enable us to formulate theories that are better able to track changes in the world or that simplify our predictions, and so on. So the view defended here is in harmony with a certain kind of holism that takes everything to be potentially revisable (cf. my 2007a, 37). It only requires us to be upfront about what we are doing here: choosing to revise the rules for good pragmatic reasons, not discovering that what seemed like conceptual truths or valid trivial inferences in the old system really weren't.

[8]

ARE EASY ARGUMENTS
THREATENED BY THE BAD
COMPANY OBJECTION?

Easy ontological arguments rely on there being conceptual truths, and so far I have merely defended the general idea that there are conceptual truths against Williamson's prominent arguments that there are none (or, more precisely, no analytic truths). But even those who accept that there are *some* valid trivial inferences and conceptual truths often balk at the particular form these inferences take in easy ontological arguments. Karen Bennett (2009) notes that all participants in the serious metaphysical debates deny that such principles are analytic, taking this as evidence against their being analytic. But while it may be true that the disputants deny that these principles are analytic, that does not undermine the present critique of the disputes. Instead, the point may be precisely that that is where disputants on both sides of metaphysical debates jointly go wrong (much as the compatibilist maintains that libertarians and hard determinists jointly go wrong in taking our concept of freedom to be more demanding than it in fact is).

Nonetheless, the particular conceptual truths used in easy ontological arguments do raise distinct cause for concern. For these have a peculiar feature that inferences like 'John is a bachelor, so

John is male' do not: the easy ontologist's inferences are *existence entailing* in the sense that we begin from an undisputed claim that makes no mention of Fs (or any coextensive concept) and end with a claim that there are Fs, a new kind of entity not previously mentioned. They are, in the words of David Chalmers (2009, 96), 'ontologically ampliative' inferences.

I have looked at some objections to this feature above, namely, those that suggest that it would take 'magic' to ensure the existence of new entities, or that such trivial arguments could not guarantee the existence of the entities we originally cared about. But I have not yet dealt with the most enduring and troubling objection to existence-entailing trivial inferences: the 'bad company' objection. The bad company objection was originally raised against the neo-Fregean approach to mathematical objects and, as we will see, it takes some work and translation to see if and how this line of objection might apply to the form of easy ontology defended here. Nonetheless, a problem along these lines can be raised for the easy approach. Here I discuss how to handle it and what its broader significance might be.

The original idea (developed in Boolos 1990 and Heck 1992) was this. Neo-Fregeans (as we have seen) argue for the existence of numbers by making use of an abstraction principle, Hume's Principle, which takes the form

HP: The number of *n*s = the number of *m*s iff the *n*s and the *m*s are equinumerous.

This principle (which, in its own right, seems perfectly acceptable and to lead to no contradictions) then is supposed to entitle us to move from simple claims of equinumerosity (say of concrete objects) to infer that two numbers are identical, and from there to infer the existence of numbers.

But abstraction principles that take the same form—a biconditional connecting an identity statement on the left to an equivalence relation on the right—notoriously lead to trouble: in the worse case to contradiction. So, for example, Frege accepted not only Hume's Principle but also Basic Law V (for the special case of concepts F and G):

Basic Law V: $\varepsilon F = \varepsilon G$ iff $\forall x(Fx$ iff $Gx)$

That is, the extension of F equals the extension of G just in case, for all x, x falls under F just in case x also falls under G. This principle has the same form as Hume's Principle, and tells us how to introduce talk of extensions by giving identity conditions for extensions such that we can say that the extensions of two concepts are the same just in case they apply to all and only the same entities. However, Russell notoriously showed that Basic Law V, if combined with Frege's Comprehension Principle for Concepts (which asserts that there is a concept corresponding to every condition on objects that can be expressed in the language), and the Existence of Extensions principle (which asserts that every concept has an extension) leads to contradiction.

The original example to show the problem is this: take the description "an object x that is the extension of a concept which x doesn't fall under". Given the Comprehension Principle for Concepts, there must be a concept corresponding to this description. Call that concept C:

C: being an object x that is the extension of a concept which x doesn't fall under.

Given the Existence of Extensions principle, C must have an extension. Some concepts seem to be in their own extensions (e.g., the concept of *a concept* seems to belong in its own extension); others do not (e.g., the concept of *a cat* is not a cat and so does not belong in its own extension). So let us ask: does the extension of C fall under C or not? Using Basic Law V, we can prove that the extension of C falls under the concept C if and only if it does not, leaving us in paradox.[1]

The idea of 'bad company' then is that principles that the neo-Fregean uses, such as Hume's Principle, keep 'bad company' with superficially similar but demonstrably problematic principles such as Basic Law V. Other problematic abstraction principles (again, with the same superficial form) have been identified as well (see Linnebo 2009a for a useful overview), leaving Hume's Principle with more bad companions. The critic thus suggests that the bad company objection leaves the neo-Fregean with a crucial challenge: give a principled way of distinguishing those abstraction principles that are acceptable from those that are not, in a way that will enable her to justify the idea that that distinction is theoretically well-motivated, not just an ad hoc attempt to screen out problematic cases (see Eklund 2009a).

The bad company problem for neo-Fregeans has been much discussed. A great deal of discussion has revolved around the question of whether various sorts of restrictions on abstraction principles may be given that can both avoid the problematic abstraction principles and yet still preserve a logic strong enough to serve the neo-Fregean's logicist goal of showing how logic alone may lead us to mathematical knowledge, and enable us to derive key parts of arithmetic or set theory.[2] I will not enter these debates here—for the goal here is not to defend neo-Fregeanism per se (still less to

---

1. For the full formal proof, see appendix to Zalta 2014.
2. See the various essays in the special issue of *Synthese* devoted to the bad company problem (Linnebo 2009c) for a good introduction to the recent literature.

defend the neo-Fregean's logicism), but rather to defend the idea that we may easily answer a variety of ontological questions by means of trivial inferences.

As I made clear in chapter 3 above, there are crucial differences between the neo-Fregean's approach and mine (and Schiffer's). The most crucial difference is that whereas the neo-Fregean employs abstraction principles that take the form of bi-conditionals, I (along with Schiffer) am committed only to there being one-way entailments that take us legitimately from uncontroversial truths (stated in terms that don't use the term 'K' or any co-extensive with it) to claims about the existence of Ks. It is worth noting that even the most notorious bad company objection to the (neo-)Fregean does not apply to this model. For we encounter no problems if we adopt the right-to-left direction of Basic Law V, taken alone:

RtL BLV: $\forall x(Fx \text{ iff } Gx) \rightarrow \varepsilon F = \varepsilon G$

(if for all x, Fx iff Gx, then the extension of F is identical to the extension of G), unlike if we adopt the biconditional (Zalta 2014). Yet it does seem to be all we need to infer the existence of extensions from a claim that made no use of the concept. So clearly some of the classic problems—and classic constraints on a solution—do not arise for the form of easy ontology defended here. Nonetheless, a similar objection may be raised that does require a response. I turn to that next.

8.1. THE BAD COMPANY CHALLENGE FOR THE EASY APPROACH

Since the easy approach to ontology defended here makes use of trivial entailments that rely on conditionals that are conceptual truths, the bad company argument may be reformulated to apply specifically to this approach. Here it arises as the problem that similar existence-entailing conditionals may get us into trouble, leading again to the challenge (this time for the defender of the easy approach) to say what it is that distinguishes the good existence-entailing conditionals from the bad ones—and to do so in a way that is well motivated.

As I have argued above, we may think of the existence-entailing conditionals that the easy approach relies on as object-language expressions of rules introducing the term/concept to our language, and thereby extending the language (without altering our empirical commitments). Here are some examples of existence-entailing conditionals we would like to preserve the legitimacy of:

a. If a concrete object x is P, then x has the property of being P (and so there is a property).
b. If x was born at t, then x's birth occurred at t (and so there is a birth).
c. If snow is white, then the proposition that snow is white is true (and so there is a proposition).
d. If an author uses a name fictionally in writing a story, then there is a fictional character.
e. If x and y say the proper vows in the right context, then a marriage comes to exist.

To raise a form of the bad company objection against this approach requires finding existence-entailing conditionals that lead to trouble, though they have the same structure as those above (and are also plausibly seen as object-language expressions of rules introducing the term or concept to our language).

One classic example of an apparently problematic existence-entailing conditional arises in ontological proofs for the existence of God, which might be thought to proceed from a conditional such as

1. If the concept of *God* includes perfection, then God exists (and so there is a God) (see Field 1984).

Yet few these days would accept that conditional as the basis for an argument for the existence of God. Other easy cases to find are cases in which the offending conditional leads to an obvious empirical falsehood. Stephen Schiffer discusses one such example, namely the concept of a 'wishdate' understood as "a person whose existence supervenes on someone's wishing for a date, every such wish bringing into existence a person to date" (2003, 53). Thus one might propose the following existence entailing conditional for wishdates:

2. If x wishes for a date, then x gets a wishdate (and so there is a wishdate).

In other cases, purported existence-entailing conditionals may even lead to contradiction:

3. If there is a description, then there is a property corresponding to the description.

This principle can lead to contradiction if we consider the description: "being a property that doesn't apply to itself." If we use the conditional to conclude that there is such a property, then we may ask whether it applies to itself or not—and find that if we assume it does, it does not, and vice versa. (The restriction to concreta in (a) avoids this, as it would be a category mistake to think a concretum either applies or doesn't apply to itself.)

In other cases, entities introduced by such easy methods may not lead to contradiction individually, but rather collectively. To adapt an example from Matti Eklund (2006a, 112), suppose we introduce the concepts *xheart* and *xliver* as follows:

4. If there is a heart and there are no xlivers, then there is an xheart.
5. If there is a liver and there are no xhearts, then there is an xliver.[3]

Each conditional alone seems to lead to the conclusion that there are the new entities (xhearts, xlivers), yet the two cannot coexist.

With these examples in hand, we can state more clearly what is needed in order for the defender of easy ontology to respond to the relevant form of bad company objection. What we need is a principled way in which to rule in existence-entailing conditionals like (a)–(e) above (and others like them) as conceptual truths, while ruling out conditionals (1)–(5) (and others like them) as illegitimate.

8.2. AVOIDING BAD COMPANY

When are existence-entailing conditionals legitimate? In brief, when they may be seen as object-language reflections of rules of use that could successfully and minimally introduce new terms or concepts to a (previously) more restricted language. By 'minimally introducing' I mean introducing in such a way that we do not incur any new empirical commitments that might turn out to fail—the idea being that the

---

3. I have put the case in somewhat different terms than Eklund in order to make it apply clearly to the easy approach under discussion (his was directed at the neo-Fregean, on his own maximalist interpretation of neo-Fregeanism).

relevant principles are *merely* extending our linguistic or conceptual scheme, not reporting new empirical discoveries or hypotheses (as we might when introducing terms for newly discovered biological entities or newly hypothesized astronomical entities). I will argue that the problematic (purported) existence-entailing conditionals (1)–(5) cannot be seen as object-language expressions of a rule of use that successfully and minimally introduces the relevant term or concept, while (a)–(e) can.[4]

A first way of drawing this distinction makes use of the form of easy ontology I have defended here. On my view, as explained in chapter 3 above, the conditionals (a)–(e) are legitimate precisely because, given the rules of use for the introduced noun term, the application conditions for that term are guaranteed to be fulfilled provided that the antecedent is true (and in some cases, even if it isn't); that is what makes it legitimate to introduce the new term, and what makes it a minimal introduction relative to the prior theory. The difference between existence-entailing conditionals (a)–(e) versus conditionals (1) and (2) is precisely that, in the latter cases, there are application conditions for the introduced noun terms that are not guaranteed to be met merely by the truth of the antecedent. So, for example, a wishdate is supposed to be a *person* to date. But the application conditions for 'person' require far more of the world than that someone (else) have a wish for a date. God (on the traditional conception presupposed) is supposed to be an all-powerful, all-good being capable of creating the world and intervening in it.[5] But that includes application conditions (e.g., for a

---

4. In fact, (1) does not even look like an attempt to introduce the term or concept 'God', since the concept of <God> appears in the antecedent (in what could only be thought to be a partial explication of the concept at best). I will not put weight on this, however, as we may identify other problems with taking any of (1)–(5) to be object-language expressions of rules of use that could successfully introduce a new term or concept.

5. As Evnine (forthcoming) notes, (2) also violates the requirement that the application conditions for the new term not require that things of the same substance-sort exist. That is, a wishdate is supposed to be a person (so, we might say 'wishdate' would be an accidental sortal, not a substance sortal); but we infer their existence only from some

causally potent being) that are not guaranteed to be fulfilled merely by the existence of a concept (of any kind). Cases (3)–(5) seem to misstate the application conditions for the introduced term altogether. In case (3) we have a purportedly analytically sufficient condition for the existence of a property—but this is a condition quite different from that defended by those who favor the easy approach (which would state it rather in the form of (a) above). That some people can misstate and misidentify the application conditions for our terms (and thereby come to misstate in the object language the introduction rules for the relevant concept) should not lead us to deny that, where we have correctly identified the relevant conditions and made proper object-language expressions of the rules, the conditionals are perfectly acceptable. What about cases (4) and (5)? In these cases, if that is all we have to go on, then we do not seem to gain any clear grasp of the application conditions for the introduced terms whatsoever given the circular way in which they are introduced. Thus we are not licensed to infer that the application conditions for 'xheart' are guaranteed to be fulfilled given the truth of the antecedent, for we do not know what it takes for there to be xlivers.

The above line of reply relies on my particular application conditions approach to existence questions—but that is by no means universally shared by those who accept certain easy arguments for the existence of certain kinds of entity. Thus it is worth giving a more general line of response to bad company-style objections to easy arguments that does not appeal to application conditions, but nonetheless gives us reason for holding that (a)–(e) can, while (1)–(5) cannot, be seen as object-language articulations of rules that successfully and minimally introduce the new term or concept to the language. I turn now to do that.

(other) person having a wish for a date, so the existence of persons (as a substance sort) is presupposed, in contrast with the usual inferences that are supposed to entitle us to make claims about the existence of a new (substance-)sort of thing.

Recall that for Carnap we could introduce 'a system of new ways of speaking, subject to new rules' (1950/1956, 206) to bring nominative talk of properties, numbers, and so on into the language and to license us to quantify over such things. Think of the acceptable existence-entailing conditionals as object-language expressions of introduction rules for the new noun terms. The idea is that these conditionals aim to introduce new, usable terms to a language (to be used for some purpose), and *only* to expand the language (not to change our empirical predictions or commitments). If we think of them in this way, we can get non–ad hoc grounds for thinking that there are constraints on the sorts of conditionals that are acceptable.

Let us introduce the concept of a (sortal) term that is 'minimally introduced' with respect to some prior language L. Then we can lay down certain conditions for new sortal terms to be minimally introduced to the unextended language L:[6]

1. The term(s) must be introduced via a conditional that gives sufficient conditions for its(/their) application, stated using the extant terms of L and/or other minimally introduced terms. (Note that this permits that we may simultaneously introduce interrelated terms, as with the various terms of baseball and other games, or for corporations, stock, and shareholders, or other social and institutional entities. But it requires that to do so there must be sufficient conditions for all of them statable in terms of L or other minimally introduced terms.)

2. Introducing that term must not analytically entail anything statable in unextended L that was not already analytically entailed by truths stated in L. (This is a version of the familiar conservativeness requirement, demanding that the new

---

6. This in certain ways parallels the suggestion in Linnebo (2009b) that the neo-Fregean require that concepts be introduced by way of a 'well-founded process'.

concepts not give us new commitments about the previously recognized ontology—for we aim with introducing these terms not to gain or express new empirical knowledge but only to make use of new concepts/terms. It also rules out introducing a term by rules that would lead to inconsistency, and thus entail everything.)[7]

3. The term must also be associated with sufficient coapplication conditions to enable us to make judgments of identity and distinctness for things of the kind (if any) named. (This is part of what it takes for the new term to be a *sortal* term. Notice that for the term to be usable in this way, the coapplication conditions must be consistent. It does not require, however, that the coapplication conditions be completely free of vagueness such that in any possible situation we can make a judgment of identity or distinctness for things of the kind.)

Together, these conditions rule out all of the bad examples (of problematic existence-entailing conditionals) while leaving intact those that the easy approach to ontology relies on. Condition (1) rules out Eklund's xheart/xliver cases, as the terms are clearly not introduced in terms of previously well-introduced sortals. Condition (2) rules out the problematic cases of God and wishdates. For the claim of the existence of God entails, for example, that there is always someone who has the power to help me in times of need (or who is the original cause of the universe, or who causally intervenes with miracles, etc.). But while this is statable in the unextended language, it is not

---

7. The 'unextended language' L is the language prior to adding the new term/concept, and not quantifying over things of sorts for which there is no concept in the prior language. This condition follows (roughly and more informally) Schiffer (2003). For fuller discussion see his (2003, 54–57). For discussion of the conservativeness requirement, see also Hale and Wright (2001, 133) and Linnebo (2009a, 325).

analytically entailed by truths accepted in that unextended language. Similarly, the problematic existence-entailing conditional about wishdates analytically entails, for example, that a new person come into existence when I make a wish for a date. Again, this is a conclusion statable in the unextended language (which included the term 'person'), but not analytically entailed by truths statable in the unextended language (indeed, it is ruled out by empirical truths stated in the unextended language, e.g. that Fred wished for a date last Friday but no one appeared).

Another sort of problematic inference is occasionally raised as placing the conditionals used in easy arguments in bad company. It might be thought that if conditionals (a)–(e) above are in good standing, then the following conditional should be, too:

> If he did it for her sake, then there is a sake for which he did it (and so there are sakes).

But this would us with a silly ontology of sakes and like 'entities'. But condition (3) rules out silly inferences like these, since the term 'sake' is not associated with coapplication conditions that enable speakers to make judgments of identity and distinctness of sakes.[8]

Not only do these requirements rule out the objectionable conditionals while retaining those the easy ontologist relies on, it is also easy to make the case that the requirements are not at all ad

---

8. Simon Evnine has suggested to me that perhaps 'sake' *is* associated with coapplication conditions: if x is a sake and y is a sake, then x = y just in case the person whose sake x is and the person whose sake y is are the same person. He also suggests that given that the term is associated with such conditions, I should accept the existence of sakes. For, he says, given my other views, "silliness is hardly a reason for being against something" (personal communication). Fair enough, I concede: if 'sake' is sufficiently associated with coapplication conditions, one may accept the existence of sakes. In any case, condition (3) may rule out other unwanted cases.

hoc conditions brought in to save the easy arguments. Instead, each of the criteria (1)–(3) above is justified given the goal of (merely) extending the language to include new sortal terms that will be usable.

Criterion 1: Requires an order of introduction: we cannot understand the term(s) to be introduced unless we already understand the terms used in its(/their) introduction.

Criterion 2: Makes sense, given that the point is to expand our language, not to revise any of our empirical beliefs (or to express new empirical discoveries). We want merely to introduce a new linguistic form, not to alter our empirical knowledge (and certainly not to introduce any contradictions that would commit us to everything).

Criterion 3: Is required for the term introduced to be a sortal term.

So far, it seems like we have the tools we need to rule out the bad (purported) existence-entailing conditionals while leaving the desirable ones intact. Moreover, we can draw the line in a way that is justified given the view of what the conditionals are (object-language expressions of introduction rules for new sortal terms), so we need not fear accusations that these are merely ad hoc restrictions.

If we can make this work, we can retain hope that it may not be 'bad, bad company, till the day I die'.

Nonetheless, it is certainly conceivable that some clever examples may be devised of problematic existence-entailing conditionals that will require that further constraints be stated. The above is not presented as a definitive solution, but at least a good sign that a justified way may be found in which we can make the needed distinction between acceptable and unacceptable existence-entailing conditionals by appealing to the needs and purposes for which we might seek to expand our language by introducing new terms (or what Carnap would have thought of as additions to a linguistic framework).

In any case, it is worth stepping back from the details of counter-examples and constraints to look more broadly at what the import of bad company-style objections really is for the easy approach to ontology. For it is less than is commonly supposed.

8.3. THE LIMITED IMPACT OF BAD COMPANY OBJECTIONS

Let us then close by examining in broader strokes what the impact of bad company objections is supposed to be, and what our attitude towards them should be—something the generality of the easy approach defended here can shed new light on.

Bad company objections raise important challenges for the deflationist to refine her view by saying what constraints existence-entailing conditionals must meet, but they do little to undermine the approach as a whole. The deflationist allows that we may introduce new terms that have sufficient conditions for application that are guaranteed to be met if other statements in the (unextended) language are true. And while bad company objections remind us that there may be constraints on what rules are (individually or jointly) permissible, they do not undermine the idea that there may be—and indeed in most cases there are—terms that are successfully introduced via such rules (expressible in the form of conceptual truths). Indeed, as Hale and Wright have argued (2009, 192), even if we don't have a full and definitive (or for that matter, any) statement of the requirements for existence-entailing conditionals (or rather, for what they treat as implicit definitions), we are entitled to assume that our implicit definitions are fine and to use them in acquiring knowledge, unless shown otherwise. As they write, "Explanations which seem to work well enough should surely be regarded as innocent until proven guilty" (2001, 282), and again, "Implicit definition is *default* legitimate practice—although, again, subject to defeat in particular cases" (2009, 192). The person who uses the relevant terms, makes the easy inferences, and claims that the corresponding entities exist is not obliged to justify her claim by working out exactly what the requisite conditions are and demonstrating that they are met by the term used, any more than the inquirer who uses perception to gain knowledge of the empirical world is obliged to first show that her eyes and ears are working properly before claiming she knows that there is a chair before her. We can have first-order knowledge that there are properties, propositions, or the other entities accepted on grounds of easy arguments even without having a justification of the claim that the inferences used are nonproblematic (in the form of a set of criteria for distinguishing legitimate from illegitimate existence-entailing conditionals and showing that they are met). So while a statement of the requirements for legitimate existence-entailing conditionals is desirable, from the point of view of defending the easy ontological approach against bad company-style objections, we should not think that we couldn't make easy arguments and legitimately accept their conclusions until we have a definitive statement of those requirements.

This point is reinforced when we note, with the deflationist, just how ubiquitous such existence-entailing rules are. We find them not only in introducing reference to the refined abstracta of mathematics, but also in introducing reference to such pedestrian entities as mortgages, corporations, churches, contracts, and the like. Although there may be cases in which problems can be shown to arise with the relevant rules, this does not seem to give us the least reason to doubt that many of these rules are perfectly well-functioning, and that there are mortgages, corporations, and the like.

A helpful comparison comes from considering games. The constitutive rules of a game include rules that, combined with empirical facts, tell us under what conditions there are, for example, touchdowns, fouls, and the like. The rules of some games are demonstrably inconsistent. For example, as Ted Cohen (1990) has pointed out, the rules of baseball are subtly inconsistent. But the fact that some games have rules that are inconsistent casts no doubt on the idea that many games may have consistent rules—rules that (combined with empirical facts) entail that there were, for example, three touchdowns scored by the Seahawks in the fourth quarter or seven fouls committed by Manchester United. Nor then should the problems that can arise for superficially similar rules be taken to undermine the general idea that there may be well-formed rules that entail the existence of entities of new sorts given the truth of sentences that appealed to no such things, and that existence questions may often be answered simply by appealing to the basic truths and making use of a well-formed rule.

The comparison with games is doubly useful, since it's not even clear that the subtle inconsistencies of the rules of baseball show that there are none of the entities the existence of which would be entailed by the rules of *that* game—no pitchers, base hits, home runs, and so forth—despite the fact that the rules are inconsistent. Instead, such difficulties might raise interpretive questions. We might require the principle of charity to reinterpret baseball discourse in a way that minimally revises it to avoid the contradictions while retaining the vast majority of its rules intact, including rules that tell us under what conditions there are hits, runs, errors, and the like.

This brings us to a second general point about bad company-style objections to easy arguments for the existence of entities of various sorts. The standard objections to accepting existence-entailing conditionals involve attempts to stipulatively define newly introduced technical terms (e.g., 'wishdate', 'xheart') that turn out to be problematic in some way. Bad company objections remind us that we shouldn't accept just any purported existence-entailing conditionals that claim to introduce a new term 'K'; we need to add in constraints on how 'K' is introduced (and I have argued above that the relevant constraints are *pragmatically* justified by appeal to the purposes of expanding the language).

But what we were interested in initially was the answer to the question 'What exists?'—or rather, more specifically, to answering questions stated in English about whether numbers, tables, properties, and the like exist. The ontological questions we're most interested in involve extant terms of a living language, and so we have to *figure out* what the application conditions for our natural language terms are and what rules of use govern their introduction. And this requires (sometimes very tricky) interpretation—it's not just a matter of stipulating some new definition, or even reading out the explicit definitions in the baseball rulebook. The constraints governing interpretation might ensure that—for the living terms of a natural language—any plausible interpretation of the rules of use for our terms will ensure that the rules on the whole meet the relevant constraints, for we aim to interpret our terms as having consistent rules of use, as introduced in ways that make them understandable and usable, and so on. And so, in answering normal existence questions, we might not need to separately examine whether these conditions are met, provided we do our interpretation well.

Thus we should be suspicious of the idea that bad company objections give us reason to doubt the legitimacy of the easy arguments for the existence of objects of various sorts, where those involve using ordinary terms of English (or another natural language). We're very unlikely to turn up inconsistencies, failures of harmony, and the like in the rules of use for ordinary terms if we do our interpretive work well. For interpretive constraints such as charity might by and large prevent us from ascribing to the terms of a language such problematic rules as would characteristically undermine the claim of its terms to be well introduced.

If the foregoing is correct, then we needn't worry that there is no plausible line of reply to bad company-style objections, or that (even if we don't yet have a perfect reply) we must give up our claims to know the existence of disputed entities by undertaking easy arguments for existence. The easy approach to ontology thus remains on the table, even in the face of these concerns.

[9]

DO EASY ARGUMENTS FAIL
TO ANSWER ONTOLOGICAL
QUESTIONS?

So far I have considered objections to the easy approach to ontology based on either ontological worries or worries about the conceptual truths the easy arguments rely on. But there is another line of resistance to easy ontological arguments. While the inferences that (according to the easy ontologist) take us from undisputed claims to controversial ontological conclusions seem to be clearly acceptable in ordinary English, one standard response is to deny that the ontological claims we apparently get as output really provide easy answers to ontological questions.[1] Thomas Hofweber (2005a, 2005b, 2007) argues that there are two different uses of the quantifier: an internal use and an external use. The former, he argues, is at work in the output of the easy inferences, but only the latter 'external' use involves making a genuine existence claim. Thus, Hofweber argues, as the apparently ontological claims employ a

---

1. A separate but similar suggestion is the fictionalist's view (discussed in chapter 5 above) that the ontological claims we get via the easy inferences are not serious claims of existence for the simple reason that they are not *assertions* of their literal content at all, but instead involve some sort of make-believe, pretending, or figurative use of language.

merely internal use of the quantifier without ontological import, they do not provide answers to ontological questions.

In this chapter I will address Hofweber's argument. I will argue that the metaontological deflationist may take on board his most important linguistic insights without denying that the terms introduced by easy arguments really refer, or that we are entitled to draw ontological conclusions from these arguments. Indeed, I will argue, the easy approach to ontology, which can accommodate the relevant linguistic insights without being committed to two uses of the quantifier, is preferable overall.

9.1. HOFWEBER'S SOLUTION TO THE PUZZLE ABOUT ONTOLOGY

In a series of subtle and careful papers (2005a, 2005b, 2007), Thomas Hofweber has drawn out an important challenge that it seems would apply to the present deflationary metaontological view as much as to the neo-Fregean and Schifferian views that are his direct target. The objection is directed against those views that would accept 'easy' arguments for the existence of disputed entities, which proceed from undisputed claims by way of what appear to be obvious or even trivial inferences.

As we have seen in chapter 3, deflationists of all of these stripes accept 'easy' arguments for the existence of various disputed entities that proceed from an undisputed premise (e.g., The cups and saucers are equinumerous) to a claim (e.g., The number of cups = the number of saucers) that makes use of a new noun term (e.g., 'number') which seems guaranteed to refer. But if it does, we can make a trivial move from the new claim to an ontological conclusion (that there are numbers)—apparently settling a deep ontological dispute through a very easy, obvious argument.

Hofweber treats it as a puzzle that these easy arguments with (apparently) existential conclusions seem valid, although metaphysicians treat disputes about whether numbers and the like really exist as subjects for deep and serious debate. "How could it be that the substantial ontological questions have an immediate trivial answer?" (2007, 1).

In brief, Hofweber's solution to the puzzle is this: the uncontroversial claim and the new claim do have the same truth-conditions; that is why the inference is valid and indeed trivial. But that doesn't mean that the ontological question is so easily answered. For, he argues, the new noun terms that are introduced in the derived claim (but which did not appear as nouns in the undisputed claim) do not really have the function of referring. And as a result, we must take the quantifier in the apparently ontological conclusion to be one that does not involve us in a real ontological conclusion.

The core of his argument rests on an interesting and plausible account of the function of derived claims. If the undisputed claim has the same truth-conditions as the derived claim (e.g., "The cups and saucers are equinumerous" and "The number of cups = the number of saucers"; "The shirt is red" and "The shirt has the property of redness"), then one might ask: why would we have both expressions in our language? Hofweber provides an interesting answer: the derived expressions, which introduce new noun terms (number, property) serve a distinctive linguistic function: they initiate a '*focus effect*', highlighting a part of the information contained in the original sentence that would be suitable to answering certain questions, while preserving the truth-conditions of the original claim (2005a, 266–67). So, for example, I might say, 'The number of bagels I ate is two' to emphasize quantity, in response, for example, to accusations that I'd consumed more than half of the bagels purchased. While in conversation such shifts of focus are often carried by intonation ('I ate *two* bagels'), we can also (especially in more formal or written contexts) make these shifts by way of the structural changes in the sentence brought about by the introduction rules. It is these structural changes that grammatically necessitate bringing in new noun terms—noun terms that the realist takes to refer to the disputed entities (numbers, properties).

This is an entirely plausible and enlightening view about at least one function such trivial transformations may serve. But what is it supposed to tell us about ontology? Hofweber assumes that it gives us reason to think that apparently singular terms like 'the number of bagels I ate' *do not have the function of referring to entities at all*—for they serve the distinct function of initiating a focus effect by syntactically shifting the position of the number term from that of a determiner ('I ate *two* bagels') to the end of an apparent identity statement ('The number of bagels I ate is *two*'). As Hofweber writes:

> That structural focus arises from extraction and movement shows that it is the same word 'four', with the same semantic function, in both:
>
> - (2) Jupiter has four moons.
>
> And
>
> - (5) The number of moons of Jupiter is four
>
> In (5), however, 'four' is moved from its canonical syntactic position into an unusual position for the purpose of achieving structural focus. And this solves the puzzle. We don't get something from nothing. (2) and (5) have the same referring or denotational terms. There is no new referring term coming out of nowhere in (5). 'Four' is merely moved into a special syntactic position in order to achieve structural focus.
>
> *(2007, 23–24)*

It is because Hofweber thinks that the derived claims do not involve any new referring terms that he thinks we must take the quantifier employed in the apparently ontological conclusion to be something other than the traditional ontologically committing quantifier. For if it were a full-strength quantifier, and if (as he holds) the term 'the number of moons of Jupiter' does not refer, then the inference from "the number of moons of Jupiter is four" to "There is a number" (which looks trivial and valid), would not be so.

To explain the validity of the trivial inferences, he argues that there are two different readings available for the quantifier, and at work in ordinary speech; the quantifier is 'polysemic'. On the first, 'internal' or 'inferential role' reading of the quantifier, the quantifier serves simply as a 'placeholder' for forgotten or more specific information, enabling us to move from "F(... t ...)", for any singular term 't', to 'F(... something ...)', *regardless of whether 't' refers* (2005a, 272). So this is roughly a substitutional use of the quantifier, and enables the quantifier inference from 'Two is the number of bagels I ate' to 'There is a number' to be valid even if (as he argues) 'two' does not refer.

Hofweber contrasts this 'internal' reading of the quantifier with the 'external/domain conditions' reading, suitable to claims like "Something ate my cheese", on which the sentence is true "if there is an object out there in reality that is such that . . ." (2005a, 271). Only the external reading is existentially committing, Hofweber argues, and it is not in use in the quantified claims that derive from the relevant rules. Thus the apparent existence claims we get from the introduction rules need not be taken ontologically seriously. Making proper existential claims requires using the quantifier with the external/domain conditions reading.

By this method, Hofweber proposes to get an entirely satisfactory solution to the puzzle with which he began. We can see why the trivial arguments are valid, and yet also see why they do not answer the metaphysician's serious ontological questions: they employ a different, not ontologically committing, sense of the quantifier.

9.2. FOCUS AND ONTOLOGY

Let me begin by making clear where I agree and where I disagree with Hofweber; then I shall go on to justify these views. I think that Hofweber's suggestion about the (or a) function that at least many derived claims serve in language is both insightful and plausible. But I do not think that this tells us anything about whether the introduced noun terms refer. Moreover, I think that the idea that a merely 'inferential role' use of the quantifier is at work in these easy arguments is undermotivated and wrongheaded, and that there are problems with making sense of his idea of an 'external' use of the quantifier as he presents it in these papers.

First, on the relevance of focus effect. Hofweber aims to argue from the idea that introduced noun terms like 'the property of being red', 'the number four', or 'the proposition that snow is white' appear in sentences that introduce a focus effect, to the conclusion that the terms do not even have the function of referring, that they are not referential or denoting terms. One problem with this he is well aware of: even if that is their function in the simple uses of these noun terms he deals with, it is not at all clear that that analysis carries over to give us an argument that the terms do not refer in other contexts (e.g., when we say 'The number five is odd' or 'Being red is a property') (2007, 29). To maintain the view that these introduced noun terms never refer, one would have to have a good story to tell about these more complicated cases. Hofweber indeed begins this project elsewhere (2005b, 2006).

But instead of worrying about those cases in which the introduced noun terms figure in more complicated constructions, I wish to raise a more basic problem. Why should we think that the fact that these noun terms are introduced into constructions with a structural focus effect undermines the idea that the terms so introduced refer? The idea that such constructions introduce a focus effect may not be in competition with the noun terms in it (also) referring.

Certainly in general, the fact that a term figures in a statement with a structural focus effect does not interfere with the idea that the term may refer—whether the terms in a sentence refer (or have the function of referring) and what aspect of information the structure of the sentence focuses attention on seem to be two separate issues. So, for example, we achieve a focus effect by moving from 'I saw John' to '(It was) John I saw', or from 'John likes Mary' to 'It is Mary that John likes', but in neither case does the appearance of the relevant term in a new syntactic position give us any reason to think the term 'John' or 'Mary' doesn't have the function of referring. So its being present in a sentence with focus effect, on its own, cannot give us any reason for doubting that the relevant terms have the function of referring.

There is, however, one important difference between the derived claims and the above sentences with focus effect: in the derived claims, there is a new noun term that was not there at all in the undisputed claim (and nor was there a coreferring noun); in these cases the sentence with a focus effect *introduces* a new noun term. Do we have special reason to think that noun terms *introduced through inferences* that result in focus effect don't have the function of referring?

What would those special reasons be? At places Hofweber seems to suggest that the fact that the undisputed claim and the derived claim have the same *truth-conditions* gives us reason to deny that there are any new referring terms in the derived claim. So, for example, he writes that his discussion of focus effect shows that

> A particular part of a sentence can be extracted into singular-term position for a structural focus effect, but this does not have to affect the truth conditional interpretation of the sentence.
>
> *(2007, 18)*

But of course this is not at issue with the neo-Fregean, or the other deflationary metaontological positions on the table. We all agree that the uncontroversial claim and the derived claim have the same truth-conditions—that indeed is part of the point, and is something often appealed to in showing why the easy arguments work.

Is there some reason to think that the fact that the original sentence and the derived sentence share the same truth-conditions undermines the idea that the newly introduced terms refer (or even have the function of referring)? Sometimes Hofweber seems to suggest this, lumping issues of sameness of truth-conditions and reference/semantic function together, for example when he writes that his observations about focus effect show

> that a simple view of the relationship between syntactic form and truth conditional semantics is mistaken . . . . What part of a sentence has syntactically a special position should not directly lead one to conclude that this part has a special semantic or truth conditional function.
>
> *(2007, 18)*

But it would be a poor argument against the neo-Fregean position to simply assume that sentences with the same truth-conditions cannot have different referring terms. For the very idea of that position is that a new sentence with the same truth-conditions as the undisputed claim may introduce a means of referring to entities not referred to in the undisputed claim. If Hofweber is tacitly relying on the premise that sentences with different referring terms would have to have different truth-conditions then he is simply denying what the neo-Fregean affirms and begging the question against them.

Moreover, even if one did hold that sentences with the same truth-conditions must refer to all and only the same objects, it is not clear why we should think that both the sentence 'Jupiter has four moons' and 'The number of Jupiter's moons is four' *fail* to refer to a number, rather than thinking that the former sentence (with 'four' in the determiner position) tacitly refers to a number all along (with the nominalization just making this explicit).[2]

So, Hofweber still needs to give us some general grounds for thinking that noun terms that are *introduced* via trivial inferences that can initiate focus effects (from instances in which they appear in other parts of speech in the undisputed claim—or in which no coreferring term appears at all) do not have the function of referring.

Some might be tempted to suggest that the problem in these cases is with the fact that the new noun term is introduced via the rules that result in focus effect. But would it be a good principle to accept that wherever a new noun term appears as a result of introduction rules, the introduced term doesn't have the function of referring? There are several reasons to resist this idea. First, we may acquire other new noun terms through similar introduction rules—especially terms for social and cultural objects. So, we are also licensed to move from "Form 6250 was properly filed and the fee paid in the name of 'Altco Corporation' " to "Altco corporation was formed", or from similar statements about the activities of individuals to claims about the existence of a new county, marriage, or driver's license. But we naturally take all of these to be referring terms. There are those of course who would also deny that these are referring terms, and attempt to paraphrase sentences apparently referring to them,

---

2. Thanks to Uriah Kriegel for making this point. See also my (2007a, 167) for a similar argument.

but it is notoriously difficult to paraphrase all we want to say 'about' such entities without using the introduced nouns.

Could one say that the reason for denying that the number terms refer is that these are (in a sense) not new terms: the term 'two' may appear in 'I ate two bagels', and it clearly doesn't refer there, so that gives us reason to think that it also doesn't refer in 'Two is the number of bagels I ate'? The determiner use of 'two', however, is not the same as the noun use: they come with different rules, and we do have a new *noun* introduced. Moreover, in almost all of these cases we do begin (in the uncontroversial claim) with a cognate term in a different part of speech: we might move from 'Incorporation paperwork was filed' to 'Altco corporation was formed' or from 'Neill and Lissie got married' to 'The marriage of Neill and Lissie began today'. It seems a fairly arbitrary matter whether the very same letters and sounds are used in the noun form as in the nonnoun form, or if slight changes are made to signal the shift. (Indeed, in some cases, it is optional whether or not to change the form of the original word: we may begin from "The shirt is red" to infer either "The shirt has the property *redness*" or "The shirt has the property of being *red*"). And we could make similar inferences even if we started with slightly different numerical terms: shifting from 'I sang *Bohemian Rhapsody* twice' to 'I sang *Bohemian Rhapsody* two times' to 'Two is the number of times I sang *Bohemian Rhapsody*'. But surely it shouldn't make a difference to whether or not we think that the noun form 'two' refers whether we have originally made the inference from the determiner use of 'two' or from 'twice'. So whether or not the new noun term is identical to the original term (of another part of speech) in phonetics or spelling does not seem to be relevant to whether the introduced noun term refers or not.

There is a deeper reason for resisting the general principle that noun terms introduced by rules like these do not have the function of referring. Languages may be constructed in various ways, and there is a fair amount of arbitrariness in what terms we start with, and what is derived. There could well be a group of beings who (perhaps having finer-grained vision than we possess, and able to see the fundamental particles that make up ordinary objects) have terms only for ways in which the fundamental particles (or waves) are arranged—they speak a language like Van Inwagenese. And so they speak primarily to ways in which the particles are arranged, saying, for example, 'The particles are arranged chairwise', 'Other particles are arranged tablewise', with 'chairwise' and 'tablewise' serving as adverbs. It would be easy enough for them, from that basis, to introduce new noun terms. They might begin with a simple nominalization, taking them from "There are particles arranged chairwise" to "There is a chairwise arrangement of particles". The latter plausibly even introduces a focus effect: directing the focus to the way in which the particles are arranged rather than to what it is that has been arranged. From there it is a short step to introduce a term 'chair' by the rule that we may infer from 'there is a chair-wise arrangement of particles' to 'there is a chair'.[3] Now in this case we have moved from a sentence in which 'chair' did not appear as a noun term (although a related term played an adverbial role) to one that places focus on the sort of arrangement formed by the particles, and in which we have a new noun term 'chair'.

Should we now deny that 'chair' has the function of referring because it is a noun term introduced by trivial inferences from

3. This is not to say that the term 'chair', so introduced, just refers to the same thing as 'particles arranged chairwise' does: first there is the difficulty that the former term aims to refer to a single object, the latter to refer plurally to many particles. Even if we overcome this by using the term 'collection of particles arranged chairwise', they presumably do not corefer on account of different identity conditions involved in each case. The point is rather that we may introduce a term 'chair' in this way, just as we could introduce 'statue' by the rule: if clay is intentionally modified by an artist intending to produce a three dimensional representation of someone, then a statue is produced. (In both cases, it is important to note that we have merely a one-way entailment, not an if and only if claim.)

statements in which the correlative term 'chairwise' originally had an adverbial use? Not obviously. But if not, then we must abandon the general principle that noun terms lack the function of referring if they are derived via trivial inferences from claims in which the correlative term was some other part of speech. If we do wish to deny that the introduced noun term 'chair' has the function of referring, and so to deny that we should 'posit' chairs as 'objects out there in reality', on grounds that the noun is introduced via trivial inferences like these, then we seem to make ontology unhappily contingent on language. For if we took that view, then what things there really are would have to parallel what terms happen to appear originally as (underived) nouns in our language. If we spoke a different language, say a fundamentally feature-placing language or Van Inwagenese, and later introduced noun terms, we would come to very different conclusions about what 'objects' 'really exist' 'out there in reality'—denying, say, that chairs do 'really' exist 'out there in reality' (whereas, given our current objectual language we accept that chairs 'really' exist 'out there in reality'). What objects we accept as 'out there in reality' shouldn't hinge in this way on what terms happen to be basic versus derived in our language.

The deflationary metaontological view doesn't leave us with any such language-relativity for ontology: whether the (well-formed) noun terms appear as the basic terms of a language or as terms introduced via other parts of speech, they refer just in case the actual application conditions for those terms are fulfilled. On the metaontologically deflationary view, in the case of 'chair' and 'number' alike, these conditions are fulfilled regardless of which language we are speaking. As long as those very terms, governed by those very rules, are used in asking the existence question, we get the same answer: yes there are chairs; yes there are numbers (and perhaps, if we are wise, we drop the 'really' and 'out there in reality' as misleadingly suggesting that some deeper metaphysical conditions are required and have been fulfilled). This is a particularly interesting result, since deflationary views are often (wrongly) accused of making ontology dependent on language. (I have elsewhere [2007, chapter 3] argued that that is a mistake: they only make what we *say about* ontology hinge on what language we accept—but that is simply trivial). But in this context we can clearly see that it is the *opposing* view that leaves ontological claims about what 'objects are out there in reality' dependent on features about what terms happen to be basic versus derived in our language.

A metaontological deflationist can easily take on board Hofweber's insight that the relevant inferences serve the function of bringing different information into conversational focus, but interpret this as a matter of the shifts in syntax serving to direct attention to different aspects of information that lead the sentence to refer to different things than the original did (while, however, preserving the truth-conditions of the original statement). We can thus incorporate Hofweber's view that new noun terms are often introduced to put a 'focus' on new parts of information, but hold that in so doing we get sentences with new singular terms that are guaranteed to refer to entities not referred to by any singular terms of the original sentence—just as when we shift focus with a camera, we may bring into prominence *other objects that were in the scene all along* (but perhaps not noticed).[4] It may well be, as Hofweber says, that the singular terms arrived at via trivial inferences "are the result of movement and extraction that places particular parts of the syntactic material of the sentence in special positions" (2005a, 267) but that is not in competition with the idea that those terms refer.

---

4. Indeed, Katherine Hawley (2007, 16) describes the neo-Fregean view as holding that, where there is a single fact that includes both a pair of parallel lines and identical directions, "Which of these entities we 'see' depends upon the perspective from which we consider the fact; it is the shift between perspectives which involves recarving or reconceptualizing the fact".

It is also salutary, I think, for a deflationist to take on board Hofweber's observation that there may be a difference in function between nouns like 'Mary' or 'chair', which are introduced to track observable entities, and nouns like 'property', 'proposition', and 'number'. The deflationist is the friend, not the foe, of acknowledging functional pluralism about language. The deflationist's claim is emphatically not that such terms are introduced to track preidentified entities (or entities singled out through ostension), but rather that, once introduced, they enable us to acquire reference to abstract entities (see Hale and Wright 2009, 202). Thus, the deflationist acknowledges that noun terms referring to numbers and propositions may indeed have rather different functions than noun terms referring to people and frogs, though this does not interfere with the idea that terms of both sorts refer. If anything, Hofweber's argument would seem to provide grist against a heavyweight realist who took noun terms like 'property' and 'number' to aim at functioning like 'proton' and 'weasel'—not against the deflationist. Yet it is the deflationist, who employs easy arguments for numbers, properties, and other entities, who is the target of Hofweber's argument.

We can draw a general lesson here. Hofweber's argument, like Yablo's, gives us a story about how the relevant discourse might come to be introduced to serve functions (introducing focus, serving as a representational aid) rather different from the function of, say, names of people or terms for newly discovered biological species (which we might think of as introduced to track independently identified entities). This might help debunk a kind of naive Platonism that thinks of number terms and property terms on analogy with terms for students or species. But it is in complete harmony with the deflationary project, which begins by noting the different purposes different elements of discourse may serve, and the different rules of use our terms accordingly follow, while nonetheless allowing that the terms so introduced function perfectly well, and refer in the only sense these terms have. The deflationist, unlike the Platonist, is in a position to absorb and make use of these functional analyses of the discourse, without incurring the disadvantages these views have (in suggesting that there are two kinds of quantification, or that there is something more that it would take for the literal content to be true). Thus in the case of both Hofweber's two-quantifier view and Yablo's fictionalist view, the deflationist may absorb their advantages while shedding their disadvantages.

With that in mind, we can take on Hofweber's analysis of one function of at least many of the claims that introduce the new noun terms to our language, without giving up the claim that the terms so introduced are guaranteed to refer—indeed to refer to entities not referred to by any terms of the undisputed claim, despite the fact that the two have the same truth-conditions.

9.3. WAYS TO READ THE QUANTIFIER

It is because he thinks that the introduced singular terms do not refer that Hofweber is compelled to think that there is a special use of the quantifier in the apparently ontological claim in the conclusion of an easy argument—for otherwise the move from 'Two is the number of bagels I ate' to 'There is a number' would not be valid (2005a, 267). Hofweber argues that (despite appearances) the apparently 'ontological' conclusions we get out of the deflationist's easy arguments are not really *about existence*, and so are not ontologically committing: "The trivial inferences to quantified statements do not answer ontological questions" (2005a, 276).

But as we have seen above, there is no reason to think that if the introduction rules initiate a shift in focus, the terms they introduce are nonreferring. As a result there is no need, indeed no motivation, for thinking that the quantifier used in the apparently ontological claims has a noncommitting 'inferential role' meaning irrelevant to answering existence questions. We may once again take the deflationist's easy arguments at face value as giving us conclusions that employ a standard use of the quantifier that answers ontological questions.

Yet I think it is still worth examining Hofweber's idea that the quantifier is polysemic, so that we can better weigh up the alternative views of the situation: Hofweber's polysemy versus the deflationary metaontological position that remains intact. Hofweber tries to make the case that even in ordinary language there are two meanings of the quantifier, so that positing them here is not an ad hoc maneuver to avoid an ontological conclusion. (And in my view this aim to stay within ordinary language, rather than shifting to a specialized language like Ontologese, is a virtue of his work.) The first is an inferential role meaning that he argues is at work in the deflationist's 'easy arguments', while the second is an external or 'domain conditions' meaning at work in genuine ontological claims. I will argue, however, that we have reason to reject the idea that a merely inferential role use of the quantifier is at work in the conclusions of the easy arguments, and that we have trouble making sense of Hofweber's external 'domain conditions' reading of the quantifier. In place of these two, I suggest we return to a view on which there is a single meaning of the quantifier at work in standard existence claims: the straightforward meaning explicated in chapter 2 above.

The inferential role reading of the quantifier, Hofweber argues, is introduced into ordinary speech where the quantifier plays a placeholder role for forgotten or incomplete information (2005a, 272). On this use, we are entitled to move from "Fred admires Sherlock Holmes" to "There is someone whom Fred admires". In such cases (as the example makes clear) "it doesn't matter . . . whether or not the person admired is real and exists . . . . The quantifier has to be a placeholder no matter what the original term was, whether or not it referred to some entity, failed to refer, or had some completely different function" (2005a, 272). The inferential role of the quantifier simply licenses us to move from the sentence with the name to the quantified sentence, regardless of whether or not the name refers. As a result we are always entitled to infer from "F(...t...)" to "F(...something...)" (2005a, 272) without that involving us in any ontological conclusions.

But those familiar with the fiction literature will immediately notice something funny about the case. The case Hofweber uses involves moving from "Fred admires Sherlock Holmes" to "There is someone whom Fred admires". The fact that we can make this inference regardless of whether or not the term 'Sherlock Holmes' refers is supposed to give us reason for thinking that there is an inferential role use of the quantifier that is not ontologically committal. But 'admires' famously brings in an intensional context, enabling both the original claim and the quantified claim derived from it to be true regardless of whether or not the name refers. Of course explanations vary of how sentences in intensional contexts can be true even when their singular terms fail to refer. But the point is that it seems to be the *presence of the intensional verb* that accounts for the apparent validity of the inference; the fact that this inference is valid regardless of whether 'Sherlock Holmes' refers (and that it doesn't involve us in any ontological conclusion) seems to be fully accounted for without positing any specially noncommitting use of the quantifier. The evidence Hofweber marshals for thinking there is a noncommitting inferential role use of the quantifier (which he then hypothesizes is at work in the final inference in the deflationist's easy ontological arguments) is better explained as coming from the use of an intensional verb than as demonstrating that there is a distinct inferential role use of the quantifier on which "the inference from 'F(t)' to 'F(something)' is always and trivially valid, no matter what 't' is" (2005a, 274).

In the easy ontological arguments, of course, no intensional verb is present. So we cannot use that to justify saying that the conclusion is not to be taken as ontologically committal. But we also have been left without an argument that there is a distinctive inferential role use of the quantifier—still less that it is at work in the easy arguments.

Moreover, there does seem to be a crucial difference between the cases of inferring from

1. Holmes is a man who lives at 221B Baker Street

to

1*. There is a man who lives at 221B Baker Street

and inferring from

2. The number of planets is four

to

2*. There is a number

or from

3. The property of being blue is possessed by Janet's shirt

to

3*. There is a property of being blue.

1* strikes us as false, even if 1 strikes us as true. But in the case of 2 and 2*, 3 and 3*, the original and starred claims seem equally true. It is not hard to see why: in the case of 1 to 1*, we have reason to think that the application conditions for 'man' are not met at that address (in fact there isn't even that address, but let's leave that complication aside). That is why we hesitate to endorse 1*, and find some other explanation of the failure of the inference (namely, that 1 should be read as implicitly in the context of a story or pretense operator—but if we also read 1* as in the scope of such an operator then it is acceptable). In the case of the inferences from 2 to 2* or 3 to 3* however, we have no such hesitation. And that, I would hypothesize, is because given the rules of these terms, the application conditions for the relevant introduced noun terms are guaranteed to be met, so we can treat the quantified claim in these cases as literally true (where we cannot for 1*). I conclude that there is no noncommittal inferential role use of the quantifier at work in the deflationist's easy arguments, and that as a result Hofweber has not given us reason to think that the easy ontological arguments do not yield ontological conclusions.

The deflationary metaontologist may take the quantified claims that result from trivial inferences to be perfectly standard existence claims. On the view I have argued for in chapter 2 above, for example, there is a single use of the quantifier in claims such as 'there are numbers' and 'there is a mouse [that ate my cheese]'; quantified claims of the form 'there is some K' (where 'K' is a well-formed sortal) are true just in case the actual application conditions associated with 'K' are met. The application conditions for 'number' are of course met more easily than those for 'mouse', but that is a consequence of the rules of use for the relevant sortal terms, not of differences in the use of the quantifier. This gives us a simpler view of the quantifier that, if the above is correct, is in no conflict with the interesting linguistic data Hofweber is to be credited with bringing to light.

If the above is correct, then Hofweber's interesting and influential arguments do not provide any reasons for rejecting the deflationary metaontological approach or for denying that the apparently ontological claims we can get by way of trivial inferences from uncontroversial truths are assertions about existence—giving us a simple first-order realism about the disputed entities.

Yet discomfort will remain among those inclined to take recent ontological debates more seriously. Surely, they might say, there must be more to it than this. Serious ontologists may still hope to distinguish two senses of quantification: a 'lightweight' sense at work in the deflationist's easy arguments, and a more heavy-duty sense of the quantifier suited for proper ontological debates. Thus even if they are persuaded to give up the idea that the easy arguments involve only an inferential role use of the quantifier, they may still hold that doing *serious* ontology requires a more stringently committing sort of quantification than my reading of quantified claims of the form 'There is a K' (where 'K' is a well-formed sortal) as true provided the actual application conditions of 'K' are met. Thus, for example, many serious ontologists would accept that the application conditions for our standard English term 'chair' or 'event' are fulfilled, but deny that this settles the issue of whether or not there 'is such an object out there in reality' in each case. That is, they may be inclined to say that even if the ontological conclusions of trivial inferences are true using a deflated understanding of quantificational statements (like mine), to do ontology we need to also accept a more robust notion of quantification—perhaps along the lines of Hofweber's 'external' reading of the quantifier.[5] (It might be noted that Hofweber himself is no friend of what he calls 'esoteric' metaphysics—metaphysics that involves 'distinctive

---

5. I discuss one prominent attempt to define a more robust notion of quantification—Ted Sider's Ontologese quantifier—in chapter 10 below.

metaphysical terminology' [2009, 267]. Yet for his work to provide any criticism of, or alternative to, the easy approach, there must be some sense of the quantifier at work in ontological debates that is more 'heavy duty' than the deflationist's, or else the existence questions could be settled in the manner I have suggested above. Room remains for argument, of course, about who has the best account of how the standard English quantifier works.)

But can we make sense of this more heavy-duty external reading of the quantifier? Hofweber himself does little to say what's involved in the external reading of the quantifier, except to say that the truth of externally quantified claims requires that 'there is an *object out there in reality* that is such that . . .' (2005a, 271). But can we understand the external reading of the quantifier in a way that both makes sense and contrasts it with the trivial understanding of the above quantified claims?

It is quite challenging to do this. For, as discussed above, the standard uses of 'object' involve treating it either as a sortal term of its own (in which case, on the deflationary metaontological view, we address the question by considering what the application conditions are for 'object' and seeing whether they are fulfilled), or treating it as a covering term, guaranteed to apply if any first-order sortal applies. But if this is the way of understanding 'object', then a so-called 'externally' quantified existence claim is guaranteed to be true as long as a quantified claim like 'There is a number' is—even if this was arrived at via trivial inferences licensed by introduction rules. But then we can't contrast the 'trivial' quantified claims that appear to commit us to numbers and the like with 'serious' externally quantified claims (which don't), for the latter are guaranteed to be true if the former are.

How else can we understand 'object' in Hofweber's explication of the externally quantified existence claims as holding true 'if there is an object out there in reality' (2005a, 271)? I have argued elsewhere (2009a) that if 'object' doesn't have application conditions of its own when used in explicating 'external' quantification, and isn't being used in a covering sense, these so-called externally quantified claims are not well-formed and not truth-evaluable at all and we can't recover some 'deeper' use of the quantifier in this way. (See also section 2.3 above.)

Hofweber (correspondence) has suggested that he does not mean the appeal to there being an 'object out there in reality' to be a way of trying to *define* the external reading of the quantifier, only to 'trigger' that reading in those who already understand it. But the crucial metaontological question is whether there is a meaningful 'external' use of the quantifier there to be triggered, which is separate from the use according to which there is a K just in case the application conditions actually associated with 'K' are fulfilled— standards that existence claims using singular terms we derive from inferences licensed by introduction rules can easily meet.

This of course does not rule out the idea that some other sort of sense might be made of a more heavyweight or ontologically significant sense of the quantifier as it is used in ontological debates. I will consider one prominent attempt in chapter 10 below. The move here again has been a defensive one: to show that the critic's attempts fail to show that the outputs of trivial inferences are not serious existence assertions, and that these prominent criticisms do nothing to undermine the tenability of the deflationary metaontological approach developed and defended here.

But again the lessons we can draw from the above discussion are not purely defensive. For, while I have done nothing to argue *against* a two-quantifier view like Hofweber's, the arguments above do impose a serious debt on those who defend the two-quantifier view: making sense of what the special extra 'external' sense of the quantifier is supposed to be. The easy approach emerges not only unassailed, but also with some visible attractions in comparison with its two-quantifier competitor. It gives a simpler reading of the statements in question, requires that we posit only one use of the quantifier, and is under no pressure to make sense of this 'external' sense of quantification—having no need to say what more is really needed for an externally quantified claim to be true.[6]

6. Many thanks to Thomas Hofweber for helpful comments on an earlier version of this chapter.

[10]

CAN HARD ONTOLOGICAL QUESTIONS BE REVIVED IN ONTOLOGESE?

I began this book by arguing that recent debates in metaontology leave an appealing view, which we can trace back to Carnap, relatively untouched and unexamined: the easy approach to ontology. I have gone on to show one way to develop a deflationary metaontological approach along these lines, and to argue that it is a viable alternative to neo-Quinean mainstream metaphysics. I have also argued that, despite the barrage of criticisms raised against it, the approach survives just fine.

One important feature of this approach is that it makes (well-formed) existence questions straightforwardly answerable by empirical and/or conceptual means. It thus does not leave room for any special 'epistemically metaphysical' existence questions, as Sider calls them: questions about what exists that "resist direct empirical methods but are nevertheless not answerable by conceptual analysis" (2011, 187). It also thus leaves no distinctive room for metaphysics in answering existence questions. (Except of course to the extent that metaphysics may be distinctively involved in certain aspects of conceptual work.) To neutral observers, this should be seen as an advantage, as it saves us from the need to clarify the methods of metaphysics and gives us straightforward ways to resolve debates about existence, while leaving everyday nonphilosophical debates about existence intact and giving us the intuitively 'right' answers to ordinary existence questions. Although fans of the easy approach remain in the minority, it has become increasingly common even for serious metaphysicians to accept that existence questions, asked in ordinary English, may be answered easily in much the way that the easy approach suggests (Fine 2009, 158; Schaffer 2009a, 357; Cameron 2010). But a crucial line of reply remains to be discussed: even if existence questions, asked in English, may be easily answered in the way suggested by deflationists, the ontologist may simply express the existence questions she cares about in another language—one perhaps more suitable for serious metaphysical debates: Ontologese. This move to Ontologese has been increasingly popular among serious metaphysicians, and is explicitly suggested by Dorr (2005, 248–54) and also endorsed by Cameron (2010) and Sider (2009, 2011) among others.

10.1. EXISTENCE QUESTIONS IN ONTOLOGESE

The idea that there is a distinctive language of Ontologese in terms of which metaphysical debates can be assured of being nontrivial and substantive is given its best and fullest development in Sider's *Writing the Book of the World* (2011). Sider presents the move to Ontologese as 'Plan B' for the metaphysician. Suppose it should turn out that the English quantifier varies in meaning (as Hirsch would have it). Or suppose that the meaning of the English quantifier is such that we can answer questions like 'Are there tables?' trivially, even if all that exists *fundamentally* are subatomic particles. In case of such eventualities, Sider argues, those who aim to practice hard ontology may introduce a fundamental quantifier—one distinct from the English quantifier and which can be used to ask substantive existence questions (2011, 171). Ontologese, as Sider envisions it, is a language "whose quantifiers are *stipulated* to carve at the joints . . . . Ontologese quantifiers are to have meanings that carve at the joints, but are otherwise as similar as possible (in inferential role, for instance, as well as in extension), and similar enough, to the meanings of ordinary quantifiers" (2011, 172).[1]

To understand what is meant here, one must understand what Sider means by 'carving at the joints'. The idea that some properties, relations, or features are more 'natural' than others is a familiar one, developed by David Lewis (1983, 1984). Lewis also uses the idea to help relieve the indeterminacy of reference, for those natural features of the world (with natural joints between them) may serve as 'reference magnets' to 'attract' the reference of our terms and disambiguate reference. The best interpretation of a language will be one that assigns natural properties and relations to predicates as much as possible (while still taking into account constraints imposed by use). So, on this view, 'fish' refers (and always did refer) to fish and not to fish and marine mammals because (perhaps inter alia) there is a natural 'joint' in the world separating fish from mammals. The type *fish* is a *natural* kind that can attract the reference of our term, making it refer only to those entities that share the relevant similarities, which group together as part of the world's structure into biological kinds.

One important consequence of this view is that it entails that speakers may be wrong about what their terms refer to: on this view, 'fish' does not (and never did) refer to dolphins, regardless of whether competent speakers (prior to or innocent of modern biology) might have called dolphins 'fish'. As Sider summarizes it, on

---

1. Cameron (2010) also endorses this idea.

this view—"reference is not determined merely by us" (2011, 27). For although our patterns of use of a term (in particular which sentences we count as being true) play some role in determining reference, the *naturalness* of the candidate properties and relations to be referred to also plays a role that may potentially trump use. "Natural properties and relations are 'intrinsically eligible meanings'; they are 'reference magnets'" (Sider 2011, 27).

The idea that some terms, particularly natural kind terms, aim to carve nature at the joints is familiar. But what is bold and innovative in Sider's work is that this idea of the joint-carvingness of terms, and the corresponding structure of the world, may be extended beyond natural kind terms—indeed beyond predicative terms altogether to also apply to other parts of speech. The work of metaphysics, he argues, lies largely in discerning which notions carve perfectly at the joints (2011, 5), and thus also in discerning what the world is most fundamentally like—in discerning the world's structure. "Our conception of structure, therefore, must allow us to ask, of expressions in any grammatical category, whether they carve at the joints" (2011, 8). "Just as Lewis and Armstrong ask which predicates get at the world's structure, we can also ask which function symbols, predicate modifiers, sentence operators, variable binders, and so on, get at the world's structure" (2011, 85).

It is this generalizing move that enables Sider to suggest that even logical terms such as the quantifier may have natural meanings that carve the world at its *logical* joints. Since this is eligible for metaphysicians to mean in conducting their debates, we may conduct ontological debates in Ontologese and thereby ensure that they are substantive and not easily resolvable.

Some might have doubts already about what sense we can make of the idea of 'logical joints' of reality that 'attract' the reference of the quantifier, logical connectives, and so on. We can at least have an idea of what joints might attract the reference of predicates (say, the joint between things that are and are not red), but it is not at all clear what 'logical' joint could attract the reference of the quantifier (presumably not a joint between what things do and do not exist). I think this puzzlement is appropriate, but I will not put weight on it. For the central case to be made here is purely defensive: that the easy approach to ontology is not undermined by Sider's argument against it. Whether we can make positive sense of Sider's suggestion is another question. In defending the easy approach, I will give reason to think that Sider's idea that logical terms carve at the joints may be based on a mistake about the way logical terms function, in which case our puzzlement about what these logical joints could be (which are supposed to attract the reference of the logical terms) would be entirely appropriate. And so at the end of the day, one further attraction of the sort of easy approach I am defending is that it does not require us to make any sense of the puzzling idea of logical joints of reality. So while I will argue that an advantage of my approach is that we may be able to avoid the puzzlement, I will not make the argument that we can make no sense of Sider's notion and thus should reject his view. (To argue that no sense can be made of a notion is always a tough case to make, as the door remains open for new suggestions.)

10.2. JUST MORE METAPHYSICS?

One recurrent objection to the deflationary approach is that deflationary metaontological views like (and including) the one I have been concerned to develop turn out to be just as committed to substantive metaphysics as are those views they oppose, so that you just 'can't get away from doing real metaphysics'. In chapter 6 I discussed some of these accusations—particularly those that suggest that I am committed to first-order metaphysical views, for example, that things of various (disputed) sorts exist (Sider 2009; Sidelle 2008; and Schaffer 2009b, 155–56). I hope that I have made clear by now that taking positions on existence questions is not the issue—*of course* the deflationary approach to existence questions leads (indeed leads very easily) to answers to first-order metaphysical questions. What is more to the point is whether I must make existence claims that are *epistemically* metaphysical in Sider's sense: claims that may be answered neither by empirical nor conceptual methods (nor by these in combination).

Sider's (2011) argument develops precisely this stronger form of the objection: he argues that deflationists are committed to claims that are *epistemically metaphysical* in the above sense. He argues that those who, like I do, favor easy ontology are in fact committed to the thesis that *there are no quantificational joints of reality*: "any such metametaphysics is committed to at least this much substantive metaphysics: reality *lacks* a certain structure" (2011, vii). This, however, he takes to be a substantive metaphysical thesis about the structure of reality: that reality's structure does not include quantificational structure. That, however, is a thesis that cannot be simply established through empirical or conceptual inquiry.

Sider gives two separate arguments for the conclusion that the friend of easy ontology must reject the joint-carving quantifier.

The first is that she must do so to preserve her easy arguments. For those arguments rely on the idea that there are analytic claims, such as 'if n is Q, then n has the property of being Q, and so there is a property'. These are supposed to be definitional, in a sense (they introduce the noun term 'property'), and to entitle us to reason from, for example, 'this shirt is red' to conclude that there are properties. But what does it mean to call a sentence 'analytic'? We might (Sider suggests) try to treat analytic sentences as those that are 'definitional', where we "think of definitional constraints as messages we send to the semantic gods: 'Insofar as you can, interpret our words so that these sentences come out true, and these inferences come out truth-preserving'" (2011, 192). But definitional sentences, he argues, need not be true, nor are definitional rules guaranteed to be truth preserving. For, he argues, there may be countervailing pressures on assigning meanings. For example, there may be a conflict with other elements of use. More relevantly here, there may be 'metaphysical pressure' exerted by the reference-attracting joints of reality, which prevents meanings being assigned in such a way as to guarantee that the relevant sentences are true or that the relevant inferences are truth preserving. Thus, he proposes understanding analytic sentences as those that are definitional *and* true (2011, 193).

So once we stipulate that our terms—particularly the quantifier or the English phrase 'there is'—are to be joint-carvers, we can no longer know, just by mastering the use of the terms, whether a definitional claim is also true: "linguistic reflection can deliver at best the conclusion that [a given claim] T is definitional. And being definitional is insufficient for truth: (T)'s definitional status might be trumped by some other factor" (2011, 196). Thus if we say that analytic claims must be both definitional *and true*, we must reconsider the easy ontologist's claim that we can undertake trivial inferences leading to ontological conclusions. Take the inference above. Sider claims that linguistic reflection can at most give us the result that the linking principle ("if n is Q, then n has the property of being Q, and so there is a property'") is definitional—not that it's true (196). For if we allow that there is a joint-carving candidate meaning for the quantifier, then that meaning might be one on which the relevant inference is *not* truth preserving: there might be a more natural joint-carving candidate to be meant by 'there is' that does not make it true. But then we can't get the easy inference to an ontological conclusion. In general, if the English quantifier has a joint-carving candidate meaning, then any linking principle used in an easy argument could turn out not to be analytic. "Easy ontologists cannot, there-fore, claim merely that [the relevant linking principle] is definitional. They must also reject joint-carving quantification" (2011, 196).

To this, Sider adds a second argument: even if the deflationist is right, and ordinary English quantifiers do not (and do not aim to) carve at the joints, this will not render ontological disputes point-less. For once Ontologese is introduced, the hard ontologist can say to the easy ontologist:

> when applied to *English* quantification, [your] picture might well be correct, even if ontological realism[2] is true. But in that case, the appropriate language for conducting ontology would be Ontologese, in which the quantifiers are stipulated to carve at the joints.... Ontology in Ontologese remains hard—and better.
>
> *(2011, 197)*

That is, even if the easy ontologist is right about how our standard English quantifier works (and right about the easy inferences we can make using our English terms), hard ontology may be retained—and relocated to the metaphysics room—as long as we can shift to Ontologese and make use of a quantifier that does carve the world at its logical joints:

> we could discard [the ordinary, natural language expression] E, and enter the metaphysics room, so to speak. We could replace the ordinary expression E with an improved expression E* that we stipulate is to stand for the joint-carving meaning in the Vicinity.... This is plan B.
>
> *(2011, 74)*

---

2. Taken as the view that ontological questions are deep and substantive (2011, 168). As Nurbay Irmak has pointed out, it seems that this view would be better labeled 'meta-ontological realism'.

Thus, if the easy ontologist wants to render *all* existence disputes pointless, she must again reject the idea that there is a joint-carving use of the quantifier that we can introduce in Ontologese, in terms of which we can reframe ontological disputes and ensure that they are substantive and not answerable easily.

In each case, the key point Sider wants to press is that the easy ontologist—along with all deflationists—must reject the idea that there is a joint-carving quantifier (or that we could define one). But, he assumes, the only way to reject joint-carving quantification is to deny that there is any structure of the right sort to attract the reference of the quantifier, making the attempted introduction of the Ontologese quantifier fail: "Of course, ontological deflationists will think that the attempted introduction of Ontologese misfires, since the world lacks the necessary structure" (2011, 172). Thus he argues that deflationists are committed to the thesis that *there are no quantificational joints of reality* "any such metametaphysics is committed to at least this much substantive metaphysics: reality *lacks* a certain structure" (2012, vii).

But this in itself, he holds, is a metaphysical claim about the world: "this rejection of joint-carving is just more metaphysics" (2011, 83). Moreover, it is metaphysics in precisely the sense the deflationist claims to be suspicious of: "the assertion that quantifiers do *not* carve at the joints . . . seems to be epistemically metaphysical" as the question of its truth "resists direct empirical methods but [is] nevertheless not answerable by conceptual analysis" (2011, 187). This, Sider holds, prevents the deflationist from holding the "epistemic high ground" (2011, 187). That is, the deflationist wants to insist that an attraction of her view is that she can put to rest the old debates, and needn't rely on the idea that there are ontological questions that cannot be straightforwardly answered by conceptual and/or empirical means. But if the deflationist, too, relies on claims that are epistemically meta-physical—claims about what is and is not part of the structure of the world—she cedes the metaphysical high ground and can claim no such advantage for her view.

10.3. AVOIDING THE JOINT-CARVING QUANTIFIER

I will speak only to the sort of deflationism I have defended above: a form of deflationism that employs the easy approach to ontological questions, leading to simple realist first-order views and a form of metaontological deflationism that says something is wrong with many of the protracted debates of ontology. So, is the easy ontologist just relying on more metaphysics—of an epistemically meta-physical sort she herself should find objectionable? I will respond to this concern by arguing that the easy ontologist does *not* need to make the metaphysical claim that reality's structure does not include logical joints in order to reject the idea that there is a meaningful joint-carving quantifier in English or Ontologese. In the concluding chapter, I will show explicitly how to argue for the easy ontological position in a way that appeals to nothing more extraordinary than the empirical, conceptual, and pragmatic methods it explicitly endorses.

It is true, as Sider says, that such deflationists had better not *endorse* the idea that the world has quantificational structure tracked by our (actual English or Ontologese) quantifier. Sider's main motivation for broadening the notion of structure beyond the predicate is because the notion of structure can then be used to help distinguish which metaphysical disputes are and are not substantive—even when these do not involve predicates but rather the quantifier, tense operators, modal operators, and other parts of speech (2011,

86). Moreover, broadening the idea of joint-carving to other sorts of terms, he argues, enables us to better evaluate trades of ideology for ontology, since expanding a theory's ideology often involves adopting new terms that are not predicates (2011, 87). But the latter is only motivating for those who share the neo-Quinean methodology, while the former only motivates those looking for a way to draw the line between substantive and nonsubstantive debates in metaphysics. (This is not a task I have undertaken; I have little interest in the terminology of 'substantiveness'.)³ So the deflationist will not be moved by these motives to accept the notion of quantificational structure.

We also can easily refrain from accepting what Sider calls the 'best argument' for the view that quantifiers carve at the joints. For that 'best argument' is squarely based on (neo-)Quinean methodology: that we should accept that quantificational structure is part of the 'objective structure of the world' given its indispensability in our theories (2012, 188). But of course most deflationists reject this neo-Quinean methodology and so have no reason to be moved by an argument like this one. So it seems his arguments for extending the idea of structure beyond the predicate are preaching to the neo-Quinean choir; they presumably are not even aimed at convincing deflationists.

In short we can (and should) refrain from *endorsing* the idea that there is quantificational structure. This is of course precisely where Sider's argument comes in, as he claims that the deflationist must reject it, but is thereby making an epistemically metaphysical claim herself: the claim that reality lacks the structure needed to ground the reference of the Ontologese quantifier.

---

3. I think that ontological debates can be answered, but that the answers come as the straightforward result of conceptual and/or empirical inquiry. Does that make them nonsubstantive or substantive? I suppose that makes them substantive, but nonetheless not distinctively—or epistemically—metaphysical.

But there is more than one way to refrain from endorsing a statement. To refrain from endorsing P is not to endorse its negation; there are other attitudes one can take. One could remain neutral: one possible attitude is to refrain from endorsing the idea of quantificational structure until or unless the idea is given further clarification of a specified sort. Then, admittedly, the potential criticism of easy ontology (based on the idea that there is a quantifier meaning that may be attracted by quantificational structure in a way that trumps definitional constraints and undermines claims of analyticity) will not be blocked—but nor will the case *against* easy ontology have been made without some further clarification of the key notions it uses.

Perhaps more to the point, even if the easy ontologist wishes to go further and *reject* the claim that reality has quantificational structure, she need not do so by *endorsing* the metaphysical claim that the structure of reality is such as to lack quantificational structure. One need only look at the history of philosophical debates to see that that is not the only move available in rejecting a position. Consider Ryle's (1949) way of rejecting the claim that the mind is immaterial. It was not by embracing the contrary position that the mind is material, but rather by showing that the whole way in which the debate was set up was based on a faulty set of categories: thinking of talk of mental states as aiming to describe some special features in a substance of a particular kind (a mind) rather than thinking of it as licensing inferences. Or think of Husserl's rejection of serious forms of metaphysical realism (1933/1977, 84–88): he does not reject the realist's claim that there is a real world outside of experience by making the opposing idealist assertion (or even embracing a Kantian transcendental idealism). Instead he argues that all it can *mean* to say that something is real is given in terms of actual or possible experiences, so that both the traditional metaphysical positions of realism and idealism are without sense. A strikingly similar view was adopted by members of the Vienna Circle who, in Carnap's endorsing words, "rejected both the thesis of the reality of the external world and the thesis of its irreality as pseudo-statements" (1950/1956, p. 215). Similarly, as Carnap insists, their rejection of Platonism should not lead one to assimilate them with nominalists—instead they reject both the Platonist thesis and its negation as pseudo-statements (1950/1956). I do not mean to endorse any of these particular positions, but only to issue a reminder that one classical way of rejecting a philosophical position is not to embrace its negation, but rather to show that something is wrong with the way the position (and thus perhaps its negation too) is put: that the terms lack sense, employ the wrong set of categories, involve a mistake about the role of the terms involved, or something along those lines.

To choose an ordinary life example, imagine that you are taking a two-year-old to the zoo, and approaching the giraffes. The child says: 'Can we go see the elephant now?' You reply: 'We'll see that after'. 'The after! I want to see that after! Pick me up now so I can see the after!'. Now you need to correct the child's misunderstanding— 'No, I didn't mean to say we could see an after . . .' you begin. 'What!' the (curiously precocious) child responds. 'Are you saying that of all the creatures in the world, none are afters? Why, you're making a substantive biological claim about the kinds of creatures there are and aren't—but you're not even a biologist, and surely you haven't done the research to know that, of all the kinds of animal in the world, none are afters!' This accusation, of course, would be misguided. To correct the child's mistake, and to refrain from endorsing the idea that there are creatures that are afters, you needn't be making a substantive claim about the kinds of creature there are (and are not). Instead, you might justly say, you don't even know what it would mean for there to be an after-creature; the idea that there is an after-creature does not even make sense, given the role of the word 'after'. You need only be pointing out that a mistake has been made about the role of a term like 'after': that it is to mark an ordering of events (we'll go see the elephant *after* we see the giraffes), not a term attempting to name a sort of creature. And to point this out, we needn't be making a substantive biological claim about the sorts of creatures there are and aren't, but only about the different functions of different pieces of language.

In Charlotte Zolotow's classic story *The Bunny who Found Easter*, a lonesome bunny heads off to the East in search of Easter, after the owl tells him, "There are always rabbits at Easter". The owl, of course, (had he not dozed off) could have corrected the bunny without making substantive geographical commitments about what places did and did not lie to the East.

Perhaps an analogous diagnosis can be given of the attempt to introduce a joint-carving quantifier: a diagnosis that does not rely on any substantive metaphysical claims about what kinds of structure there are and are not.

10.4. PROBLEMATIZING THE JOINT-CARVING QUANTIFIER

The metaontological deflationist may employ a similar strategy: not saying that the structure of the world is such as to lack quantificational structure, but rather problematizing the very idea of joint-carving quantification that plays the central role in both the statement that there is quantificational structure and its negation. That idea can be problematized quite easily if we return to acknowledge a functional pluralism about language, the idea that different terms in a language serve different functions. The predicates of physics and biology, for example, might be acknowledged to have a certain kind of joint-carving function even if the quantificational apparatus of our language serves an entirely different

CAN HARD ONTOLOGICAL QUESTIONS BE REVIVED IN ONTOLOGESE?

function. The idea of terms that carve at the joints of course (as Sider fully acknowledges) was introduced to characterize natural kind terms—predicates of a particular kind. And in that context it may be well motivated. But whether it generalizes to logical terms such as the quantifier is another question.

Sider argues against the idea that quantifiers don't carve at the joints (even if some predicates do) on grounds that this is "hard to square with purity" (2011, 187)—the idea that fundamental truths involve only fundamental notions. But why accept purity? The only motivation Sider gives for it is the idea that "When God was creating the world, she was not required to think in terms of nonfundamental notions like city, smile, or candy" (2011, 106). But however compelling that may seem, it does nothing to argue for full-blown purity, in which *every notion in a fundamental truth must be fundamental*, over a restricted sort of purity of the form that every *predicate* in a fundamental truth must be fundamental. Both theses would handle the motivating examples equally well, acknowledging that God would not have to think in terms of notions like city, smile, or candy to create the world. The examples only speak to the need to state fundamental truths using fundamental *predicates*, and don't motivate thinking that the quantifier must be fundamental (joint-carving) in order for there to be fundamental truths about what there is.

Do we have any grounds to resist broadening the notion of structure in this way? I think we do. It is roughly the fourth source of resistance Sider notes to treating logical notions as joint-carving:

> It is the thought that it is appropriate to evaluate expressions for carving at the joints only when they are 'contentful'. *Predicates* are paradigmatically contentful. But logical expressions, on the other hand, are purely 'formal', so the thought goes. They do not describe features of the world . . . . Since logical expressions

are not 'worldly', it is inappropriate to speak of the world as
containing structure corresponding to those expressions.

(2011, 97)

To overcome this source of resistance, Sider suggests that it arises
from a covert attachment to conventionalism, and proceeds to
argue against conventionalism—on some old, and some new,
grounds. The old grounds include Quine's classic argument that
logic would be needed for inferring the infinite number of logical truths from more basic conventions, but Sider denies that that
gets to the heart of the problem with conventionalism (2011, 99).
Instead, he raises a critique of "the very idea of something's being
'true by convention'" (2011, 100–104). His criticisms center on
the idea that we cannot, merely by legislation, make logical truths
true: "the world must also cooperate; the world must really be as
the sentence says" (2011, 101); we cannot make sense of the idea
that adopting conventions makes the claims true (2011, 101).
Overall, Sider insists, the only sentences that may be made true
by our adopting linguistic conventions are those *about* our linguistic conventions—but logical truths clearly aren't about our
linguistic conventions. His criticisms are aimed at the following
target understanding of conventionalism: as the view that "We can
legislate-true the truths of logic" (2011, 103).[4]

But the idea that logical notions are merely *formal* by far predates
logical conventionalism. Early versions of the idea appear already
in Aristotle, and arise again among medieval philosophers such as
Duns Scotus. In its modern form, the view can be traced back at the

---

4. I have argued elsewhere (2009b) that this interpretation also misrepresents classical
conventionalism—the point of which was not to hold that logical truths are made true
by our legislating or adopting certain conventions, but rather to deny that logical truths
should be taken as attempted descriptions (in need of truthmakers) at all. But I will
leave that historical point to one side here.

very least to Kant (who was certainly no conventionalist). As we have seen in chapter 1, the idea that 'exists' does not aim to describe objects but rather plays a formal role analogous to number concepts appears also in Frege and Carnap.[5] In Kant's memorable summary at the start of the *Groundwork*:

> All philosophy insofar as it is founded on experience may be called empirical, while that which sets forth its doctrines as founded entirely on a priori principles may be called pure. The latter, when merely formal, is called logic; but when limited to determinate objects of the understanding, it is called metaphysics.
>
> *(1785/1981, 1)*

The idea that logic is—in some sense—formal or topic-neutral is, as John McFarlane (2000) makes clear, historically *central*, indeed perhaps *the* historically dominant conception of logic—and one endorsed by such diverse philosophers as Kant, Lotze, Husserl, Frege, and de Morgan. It is not to be quickly tossed aside by associations with (an uncharitable interpretation of) the conventionalism of logical positivists. The basic idea has nothing to do with logical truths being 'made true' by our adoption of certain conventions, or with the idea that we may 'legislate' certain sentences to be logically true. Thus Sider's arguments against conventionalism leave this view untouched.

So how else, apart from by embracing conventionalism, can we develop the idea that logical terms (including quantifiers) are not 'contentful', are purely 'formal', or 'do not describe features of the world'—to justify saying that, even if it may be appropriate to think

---

5. For an excellent discussion of the history of formal conceptions of logic, see McFarlane (2000).

of (many) predicates as attempting to carve the world at its joints, it is inappropriate to think of logical terms as even attempting to map structure?

We can again look to the history of treatments of logic as formal for some ideas along these lines. The basic idea behind the classical treatment of logic as formal is the idea that logic is topic-neutral, or independent of subject matter (McFarlane 2000, 51). But if logic is topic-neutral, then its topic is not the structure of the world; unlike the terminology of biology, political science, or physics, it is not attempting to map the structure of a particular part of reality. Once we have a formal/material distinction in hand, we can suggest a picture like this: some material predicates may be designed to carve the world at (certain of its) joints, to map a certain structure—for example, a structure of the world into biological or physical natural kinds.

But the distinctive feature of logical terms is that they may apply to material terms of any kind, indifferent to the distinctions among the objects and properties described, or the domains discussed. As MacFarlane puts it:

> the concept *is a thing*, the relation *is identical with*, and the quantifier *everything* do not distinguish between Lucky Feet [a horse] and the Statue of Liberty . . . . As far as they are concerned, one object is as good as another and might just as well be switched with it. Notions with this kind of indifference to the particular identities of objects might reasonably be said to abstract from specific content—to be 'formal'.
>
> *(2000, 57)*

This provides at least one way of articulating the idea that logical terms such as the quantifier are content-neutral: they may govern terms with any particular material content, many of which may aim to map different structural features of the world, but logical terms are neutral between them.

What about the idea that logical terms do not aim to describe the world, or tell us anything about the world? Kant employs a slightly different conception of formality that may express a version of the idea that logical terms abstract entirely from semantic content:

> For example, general logic treats 'all horses are mammals' simply as the unification of two concepts in a universal, affirmative, categorical, and assertoric judgment. It abstracts entirely from the content of the concepts. The way in which the concepts are united in thought is not, for Kant, a further constituent of the thought (a 'binding' concept), but a feature of the thought's *form*.
>
> (*McFarlane 2000, 61*)

To the extent that we think of semantic content as what connects our words to the world, we can then also see a way of making sense of the idea that logical terms are not 'about the world', and even that pure logical truths do not aim to describe features of the world.

I don't mean to endorse either of these conceptions of formality. They are not equivalent, and adopting either (without the other) might take us a good way towards making good on the idea that logical terms do not have a structure-mapping function. Other conceptions of formality are also available that might do the job—I have simply focused on two that most nearly match Sider's initial description.[6] Certainly I have not argued for them, but have merely sketched them. But all that is crucial here is to point out at least two ways—both of which are intuitively plausible and have played a

---

6. McFarlane (2000) identifies three separate conceptions of logic as formal, and argues that they are not equivalent.

central role in the history of philosophical thought about logic—in which we can develop the idea that logical terms are merely formal without embracing anything like the conventionalism Sider argues against.

In response, Sider has urged that logic is not topic-neutral, since it is 'about' the content of the logical constants: about conjunction, disjunction, quantification . . .⁷ Perhaps there is a merely verbal sense in which we can say that logic is 'about' conjunction, disjunction, and the rest—though even this sounds odd, and is not how the subject is typically introduced (think of the first day of logic class, in which one promises the class not that they will learn all about what conjunction really is, but rather that they will gain skills in analyzing arguments on any subject, to determine which are valid and which invalid). But even if we do say that logic is 'about' conjunction, disjunction, or quantification, given the formal conception, this should not be taken in a representationalist sense of 'about' where the terms are introduced to enable us to track and investigate what they name (as terms for species of plants and birds might be). The point of the formalist conception is that logical terms serve a very different function.

Indeed the idea that there is a distinction between the formal and material terms of our language may be adopted as part of a functional pluralist view about language: the idea (recently advocated by Huw Price [2011, 136–40] harkening back to work by Gilbert Ryle) that different parts of language (even those used in making assertions) may serve different functions.⁸ The mistake of thinking that a structure-tracking Ontologese quantifier may be defined can be thought of as arising from an implicit functional monism.

<hr/>

7. Author Meets Critics session at the American Philosophical Association (Central Division), February 2013.
8. For further details see Price (2011, 136–40).

Ryle warned against this long ago (1957/1971) in accusing Mill of assimilating far too much of language to names (thinking that their role is to name entities in the world). Thinking of the quantifier as a would-be joint-carving term seems to arise from the attempt to assimilate other parts of speech to the structure-tracking function of many of the predicates of natural science.

But if the role of logical terms such as the quantifier and connectives is not to carve the world at the joints of its 'logical' structure, what roles do such terms serve? We can gain some ideas from the above discussion (and I ventured a suggestion about the function of 'exists' in chapter 2). Even if some terms (certain predicates) aim to describe features of the world (perhaps even natural features distinguished by natural joints), other terms may serve other roles: they may instead enable us to make *use* of these predicates in *making judgments* and *reasoning with* those judgments. Terms like 'is' enable us to combine names and predicates into a judgment, as when we say "Lucky Feet *is* a horse". Other terms enable us to reason with judgments, for example 'or' enables us to infer 'Lucky Feet is a horse or Lucky Feet is a cow'. There is no need to think of these terms as aiming to map a special kind of logical structure to account for their role and importance in our thought and language: not a role in tracking structure but in enabling us to reason with concepts that do involve material (sometimes perhaps structure-tracking) content.

If our logical terms, including the quantifier, are not aiming to map structure—if they are not terms with that function at all—then we can reject the Ontologese quantifier without pronouncing on what the actual structure of the world does or does not include. This is fundamentally a thesis about the role of logical terms in our discourse, not about what sort of metaphysical structure the world has or lacks. We reject the idea that the quantifier is joint-carving on grounds of our *linguistic analysis*—that is not the sort of term it is, that is not what it is trying to do—not on metaphysical grounds of thinking that the structure of reality is such as to omit such joints. We can even deny that any term with such a material content as to be joint-carving could be a good candidate meaning for anything deserving the name 'quantifier' (just as we may reject the idea that any kind of creature could be a good candidate for the meaning of 'after'). And so we can reject both the claim that the English quantifier is joint-carving and the idea that there is a joint-carving quantifier to retreat to on Plan B—without making a new and substantive metaphysical commitment. We are not making the metaphysical claim that there are no such joints, but rather the linguistic claim that the thought that there *are* is based on a mistake about the way part of language works.

Sider admits that "all I have to offer in support of Russellian realism about logic is a critique of conventionalism; discussion of intermediate positions remains a lacuna" (2011, 98). If I am right it is an important lacuna. For the view that logical terms are formal (only sketched here, but widely held throughout the history of modern and contemporary philosophy), while associated by some with conventionalism, is merely *associated* with it in the minds of some, not tied to it. And that view is not defeated by the standard arguments against the idea that we can legislate-true the truths of logic. There are many ways—supported by some of the most dominant views in the history of philosophy of logic—of resisting the idea that there is or could be a joint-carving quantifier, without embracing conventionalism or any substantive metaphysical position about what sort of structure the world has and lacks. While I have not fully developed and defended any particular conception of logic as purely formal, I hope to have shown that Sider's arguments have not *defeated* that conception. Moreover, given the prominence of the idea of formality in thought about logic throughout the history of philosophy, the burden of proof would seem to fall on those who reject that idea and propose a different, structure-mapping, function for our logical notions.

The move to embrace an Ontologese quantifier is increasingly popular among those who wish to practice 'hard metaphysics'; Sider just gives the best-developed explication of the idea. But I have argued that the very idea of the Ontologese quantifier (at least as Sider develops it) may misrepresent the function of logical terms, based on an artificial monism about linguistic function, and this may engender new doubts about whether a move to Ontologese can save hard ontology. The attempt to introduce a term preserving the inferential role of the English quantifier but carving at joints might be like the attempt to introduce a term preserving the inferential role of "Easter" but picking out a location. And if we both abandon the idea that the English quantifier is (even intended to be) a joint-carver, and the idea that a language of Ontologese may be introduced in which it is, we may return to the suspicion that there just is no sense to 'ontological' questions in which they cannot be answered easily, by perfectly ordinary standards (*pace* Sider 2011, 166–67).

CONCLUSION

The Importance of Not Being Earnest

The neo-Quinean approach to ontology has been dominant for the last sixty years or more. It's had a good run. Part of what I have aimed to do in this volume, however, is to make clear that this approach to ontology is neither inevitable nor invulnerable. Any approach that considers metaphysics to be 'hard' in the sense that it takes existence questions to be answerable neither on straightforward empirical nor on conceptual grounds (nor on any combination of these) faces crucial challenges. Some of these have become obvious just within the debates themselves, given the spectacular failure of theories to converge and evident difficulties in adjudicating competing claims. In this sense, hard ontology seems to be a victim of its own success. Other challenges have arisen externally, for example, from defenders of quantifier variance, who argued that many core disputes were merely verbal.

What I have tried to do here is articulate a new challenge, often overlooked in debates in metaontology, which have largely focused on quantifier variance. Suppose existence questions can be answered easily—often by trivial arguments from uncontroversial premises, and always by invoking nothing more than competence with language and reasoning and straightforward empirical knowledge. That would render ontological disputes pointless in a whole new way, while remaining coherent with our everyday uses of existence questions and avoiding the epistemic mysteries of hard metaphysics. While versions of this easy approach to existence questions had previously arisen in isolated pockets, little had been done to understand it as a unified approach that presents a threat to hard 'mainstream metaphysics'. I hope to have made it clear what the unified approach is, what its consequences are (both for first-order metaphysics and for metaontology) and to have made clear that it is not easily assailed by the standard arguments leveled against views of this kind.

In this concluding chapter, I hope to make it clear, first, that the easy approach is not only a tenable view, but also an attractive one. I summarize the case that may be made for easy ontology in a way that is true to its own principles by appealing to nothing 'epistemically metaphysical'. Instead, in arguing for this view, we may appeal to empirical and conceptual factors, as well as noting the substantial pragmatic advantages we gain in accepting easy ontology over hard metaphysics.

If we adopt the easy approach to ontology, however, then we should also give up earnestly pursuing philosophical existence questions, since most of these disputed existence questions can be answered very easily.[1] So what else is there to do? Does this mean giving up metaphysics, pursuing other metaphysical questions, or doing metaphysics in a new key? In closing, I will briefly examine these questions and make some suggestions about what else we might do if we are persuaded to give up the earnest pursuit of existence questions.

---

1. This of course does not preclude there being empirically difficult existence questions—to be resolved by scientists—and difficult conceptual issues, including those that involve allegations of inconsistency in a concept or lack of clarity about the rules governing a concept and those that involve questions about how to revise a concept to better fulfill some purpose.

C.1. THE EMPIRICAL, CONCEPTUAL, AND PRAGMATIC CASE FOR DEFLATIONISM

Sider's arguments (discussed in chapter 10) that the easy approach involves 'just more metaphysics' are just one manifestation of a general suspicion that "metametaphysical critiques are metaphysical in nature" (Sider 2011, 83). More precisely, the accusation is that even the deflationist relies on 'epistemic metaphysics' by making claims that are neither empirically nor conceptually justified, forcing them to cede the epistemic high ground.

I have tried to show why the particular accusation is unfounded. Nonetheless, to fully allay this concern, I will summarize the case that has been or could be made for the easy approach to ontology, showing how one can argue for this view without relying on anything 'epistemically metaphysical'—indeed by appealing only to empirical, conceptual, and pragmatic factors.

Empirical arguments may potentially play a role in defending easy ontology. I have not generally relied on them above, since that would often require empirical work that has not yet been done. But here are some areas where empirical work could turn out to be relevant. We may be able to give empirical grounds for accepting the kind of functional pluralism about language that I have mentioned at several points above, and for which Huw Price has argued (2011). For as Price (2009, 334) suggests, the issue of what functional differences there are across the different parts of our language would seem to be one for an empirical science such as linguistics. We could use empirical arguments to justify claims, for example, about whether terms serve a tracking role or to introduce a focus effect or aid with our representations. We could also use empirical information about how terms are commonly used, what inferences are accepted, or what claims seem redundant to competent speakers in helping to justify our claims about what the rules of use for certain key terms are—for example, in trying to establish that the putative conceptual truths used in ordinary inferences really are parsed as redundant by ordinary speakers (who aren't guided in their judgment by neo-Quinean ontological qualms). While empirical information alone may not be sufficient to justify claims about the rules governing terms, it is certainly relevant, and is used by linguists all the time. One point where empirical results have already played a role in the work above is in elucidating how our ordinary sortal concept of object functions (chapter 2, drawing on Carey 2009).

Conceptual arguments have played a much greater role in the present work. The analyses I have given above of the rules of use for 'exists', 'there are', 'object' (and their interrelations), as well as the rules that are supposed to entitle us to introduce noun terms for numbers, properties, and the like are all presented as conceptual analyses: attempted explicit reconstructions of certain core rules of use, which may be grounded in extrapolation from one's own mastery, consideration of whether terms would properly apply or be refused in a variety of actual and imagined cases, consideration of combinations of statements and their redundancy, and so on. This is merely to serve as a reminder about the central role conceptual analysis has played above. (But of course it is not the same as saying exactly how conceptual analysis is to be undertaken or understood, or as justifying the claim that it can provide us with a certain kind of knowledge—those projects would have to be undertaken separately.) In certain places where the rules of use are unclear or idiosyncratic, the analyses may also be seen as having a pragmatic element, where we might think of them as implicitly suggesting: let us consider the term as governed by this core rule of use (and perhaps account for deviant uses in another manner).

Finally, with all of that in place, we may wield pragmatic arguments. Once we have identified the core formal rule of use for 'exists', its connection with rules of use for 'object', for the quantifier, and so on—why not adopt this understanding of existence questions, and jettison others? This everyday sense of 'existence' is all that we need to manage the existence questions that play a role in science and daily life—indeed anywhere, it seems, except in doing hard ontology. We also can cleanly and easily meet the challenge of allowing that ordinary existence questions and assertions are perfectly meaningful, while finding something amiss in distinctively ontological questions about existence. For those existence questions that are well formed and use the standard English terms are easy to answer. Thus those seeking a debate must be seen as doing something other than employing these terms with their standard rules of use. We also get the right answers to ordinary existence questions, for we are left with conclusions such as that dogs and tables exist, but phlogiston and witches do not. And we can give a plausible analysis of many features of discourse about numbers, fictional characters, abstracta, and so on—more plausible (I have argued) than the fictionalist can.

The deflationary metaontological approach not only gives us all we need from existence questions and claims outside of metaphysics, it also brings substantial benefits over hard ontology. Most centrally, it avoids the epistemic problems faced by hard ontology. We have a clear method for addressing existence questions and can treat all existence questions as answerable straightforwardly through conceptual and/or empirical work. We can thereby resolve and dispel many apparently interminable debates, where it was not at all clear how to move forward. We can also clarify the methodology of metaphysics, lay to rest the embarrassment of proliferating debates, and avoid the parochialism that would come from relying on merely pragmatic theoretic virtues in determining what there is (cf. Bricker, forthcoming). Moreover, we are given a straightforward account of how we can acquire knowledge of abstract entities such as numbers, properties, and even fictional characters, by way of the trivial inferences licensed by the rules of use that introduce the terms. The ability of the simple realist view that falls out of the easy approach to resolve these ancient difficulties is a very substantive advantage indeed—most particularly, an advantage over certain more traditional forms of Platonism.

We also gain advantages in being less committal in various ways than those who practice hard ontology (whether or not they accept the existence of the disputed entities). One such advantage is avoiding the difficulties and mysteries involved in finding a way to understand the special terminology that seems needed to sustain what Hofweber (2009) calls 'esoteric' metaphysics: we needn't make sense of a special metaphysical notion of REALITY or joint-carving quantification, or anything like that. We also avoid the challenges of making sense of the special 'external' sense of quantification Hofweber himself makes use of, and avoid the difficulties of saying (with the fictionalist) what *more* it would take for the ontological claim to be literally true than for its 'real content' to be true. For whether they accept or reject the disputed entities, those who engage in hard ontology are committed to the idea that there is something more at stake in resolving ontological debates—but the defensibility of easy arguments puts substantial pressure on that idea.

So, we can give a powerful pragmatic argument in favor of the easy approach to existence questions I have been defending: it does all we otherwise (apart from hard ontology) need a notion of existence to do, fits well with our ordinary familiar use, and avoids epistemological and semantic mysteries and awkward commitments. Overall, it seems like a rather plausible view that gives us hope of dissolving a great many ontological and epistemic problems, while capturing the proper use and role of existence claims in ordinary English. Unless you are committed to prolonging such debates—what's not to like?

Such, at least in outline, is a case that can be made for the easy approach to ontology making use of empirical, conceptual, and pragmatic components, but requiring nothing more.[2] One can see Sider's view as the best-developed route for defenses of hard ontology to take, the best culmination and defense of a broadly neo-Quinean approach to metaphysics. To be clear, I do not claim to have given any decisive arguments against the neo-Quinean approach in general, nor against Sider's view (though I have tried to problematize some of the key notions). But I do hope to have shown how to develop a tenable alternative, far more deflationary about the goals and methods of metaphysics—an alternative that does not rely on quantifier variance, and that had been largely lost and forgotten in the years since Carnap.

Hard ontologists, of course, have a pragmatic reason of their own to reject my approach: to be able to retain the interest in the debates to which they have devoted themselves. Where they are concerned, I can only hope to have shown that the deflationary metametaphysical approach I have developed is still standing, coherent, defensible, and distinct from the threat of quantifier variance that has attracted nearly all of their defensive attention.

But where a more neutral audience is concerned, I hope to have also shown that the alternative I have provided is, all things considered, far more appealing—on empirical, conceptual, and pragmatic grounds. In short, I hope to have shown the usefulness, indeed the importance, of not being earnest about debates in ontology.

---

2. This does not mean that I have argued for or defend the position that there is no other method for acquiring knowledge. It is only to say that I, unlike those who practice hard ontology, do not *rely* on the idea that there is.

C.2. METAPHYSICS IN A NEW KEY?

If we give up the idea that a central part of metaphysics is concerned to answer existence questions, or to formulate the best 'ontology', what is left for a metaphysician to do, once she adopts the easy approach? In part the historical overview we began with should put our minds at ease. For once we see the enthusiastic and earnest pursuit of hard ontology as a historical anomaly spawned by (misappropriation of?) Quine (see Price 2009), we can take the news that the game is over with equanimity. There was metaphysics before Quine; there will be metaphysics after his reign is over.

There is, and has always been, more to metaphysics than ontology. Beyond existence questions, metaphysics addresses a whole array of questions that are (implicitly or explicitly) modal questions: questions about essences and natures, identity and persistence conditions, existence conditions, counterfactual situations, and so on. Metaphysics also addresses relational questions: questions about how 'higher level' and 'lower level' entities are related, questions about constitution, dependence, supervenience, reduction and (most prominently in the recent literature) grounding. Some have suggested that (in light of the plausibility of easy arguments that answer many ontological questions) the project for hard ontology should be reconceived as concerned with some other question or questions along these lines. Jonathan Schaffer, for example, (2009a) endorses easy ontological arguments, accepting that debates about the existence of numbers, properties, mereological sums and the like "are *trivial, in that the entities in question obviously do exist*" (2009a, 357). But what is not trivial, he insists, is "whether [the disputed entities] are fundamental" (2009a, 357). Thus, Schaffer argues, the proper question for metaphysics does not concern what there is (the thought that it does is a confusion bred of the neo-Quinean approach), but rather what is *fundamental,* and what grounds what—indeed he argues that much of historical metaphysics is best understood as having been directed towards this question, not the neo-Quinean existence question. And indeed one possible outcome of the work in arguing for an easy approach to ontology is that it may spur a reorientation of metaphysics away from debates about existence to focus on different questions.

But here a further question arises: suppose we do shift to working on modal and/or relational questions. Will the same sorts of epistemic and methodological problems faced by hard ontology arise again there? Does answering these questions require work that is 'epistemically metaphysical'? That all depends how these questions are to be understood and answered. Can modal or grounding questions be answered through straightforward conceptual and/or empirical means, or is some 'epistemically metaphysical' work required in those areas? I have argued elsewhere (2007b, 2013a) that metaphysical modal questions can also be answered by a combination of conceptual and empirical work, but a full defense of that idea will have to be left for the sequel.[3] What about questions about various kinds of priority relations, such as "What grounds what?" Can these be understood as (to the extent that they are sensible questions) resolvable through conceptual and/or empirical work? That is not a question that can be addressed here; it must be addressed separately at the length it deserves.[4] It is worth noting here, however, that only if that and other remaining questions

3. That is, it will be spelled out in the next book manuscript, *Norms and Necessity*, in progress.
4. Thomas Hofweber (forthcoming) makes a related case that it is doubtful whether the various notions of metaphysical priority invoked to secure a distinctive domain for metaphysics are capable of being both substantial (in a way that could do the necessary work for supporting metaphysical debates) and egalitarian (rather than esoteric). Along the way he makes a compelling case that the examples commonly used to motivate a notion of priority can be understood as merely reflecting asymmetric conceptual connections.

of metaphysics can be understood as (to the extent that they are meaningful, well-formed questions at all) answerable via a conceptual and/or empirical means will we be able to claim to have fully demystified the methods of metaphysics, and avoided the need to engage in any 'epistemically metaphysical' investigations. This project is just part of a larger project that would be needed to extend the results to other areas of metaphysics than those that deal with existence questions.

But even if we do come to the conclusion that all of these questions (to the extent that they are understandable and sensible) are resolvable through conceptual and/or empirical means, there is still work to be done. Conceptual work clearly remains as territory for metaphysics. As I mentioned at the outset, the easy approach to ontology can be seen as part of a return to a view that was dominant in the century preceding Quine—that philosophy is fundamentally concerned with conceptual work rather than empirical work, giving a far more modest conception of its methods, goals, and epistemology. And there are various kinds of conceptual work that metaphysicians both do and may fruitfully engage in. This includes, of course, the work of 'conceptual analysis': work that may involve making explicit the rules of use for concepts we competently wield, their relations to other concepts, what various assertions made using them commit us to, and so on. In some cases (as in the analyses relevant to easy ontological arguments) this work may be easy. In others (working out the relations among concepts of freedom, causation, responsibility, and character; or among works of art, art world, audience, creator, object, and aesthetic value) it may be far more difficult. (Nonetheless, it may still be 'easy' in the technical sense of involving nothing epistemically metaphysical.)

Conceptual work needn't be simply explicative, however: many of our ordinary concepts may be indeterminate in various ways, and at times we may have work to do to determine how best to fill in the details of our concept of 'same person' or 'same work of art', consistent with some (ethical, aesthetic, or pragmatic) purpose. Conceptual work is also involved in determining whether tacit contradictions or incoherencies beset parts of our conceptual scheme, or whether they may be resolved or untangled in ways that vindicate our use of them.[5]

Consistently with Carnap's original picture, however, our conceptual work needn't be limited to analyzing or disentangling extant concepts. Ontologists may also be engaged in what Carnap would have called 'conceptual engineering': revising or devising systems of categories to help them better serve some practical purpose. In some cases, they may help us better express our scientific theories and reason through their consequences. So, for example, work done by Elizabeth Barnes and Robbie Williams (2011) in defending the coherence of the idea that the world may be indeterminate could turn out to be a useful way of adapting our conceptual scheme to accommodate the world as quantum mechanics presents it—much as mathematical work showing non-Euclidean geometry to be consistent proved useful in developing the theory of relativity. But the purposes for which we might need conceptual (re)construction needn't be merely scientific: social and moral purposes may also pragmatically motivate conceptual revisions. So, for example, Sally Haslanger develops constructionist conceptions of race and gender categories on grounds of "considering what categories we should employ in the quest for social justice" (2005, 10). This work she labels as 'ameliorative' conceptual analysis, quite distinct from merely descriptive or explicative analysis.

---

5. Many of the arguments against ordinary objects that I addressed (2007a) were of this nature, and resolving conceptual tangles is also one of the chief tasks in working out a philosophy of fiction (see my 1999 and 2003b).

Finally, as Huw Price has argued, there is work to do in linguistic anthropology, addressing the different functions different parts of our discourse serve. So, for example, we might begin by asking what purpose talk of existence, truth, possibility, or moral wrongness serves—why would we want to have such resources in our language? This involves approaching problems from a different angle (one emphasized in the nearly forgotten work of philosophers like Carnap and Ryle) that doesn't beginning by assuming that all discourse aims to describe, and that the metaphysician's job is to determine whether there are the entities apparently described (existence, truth, modal facts, moral properties) and what their natures are (Price 2011). As Price puts it, "issues that seem at first sight to call for a metaphysical treatment may be best addressed in another key altogether" (2011, 26). The approach may not be one distinctive to metaphysics, as it may begin from "first-order scientific inquiries into the underlying functions of language in human life" (2011, 294), but it will surely involve grounds for reassessing a great many metaphysical positions and puzzles—and that is work for metaphysics, more broadly conceived.

Much work on all of these topics remains to be done: working out whether other projects of metaphysics are meaningful and well-defined, and if so whether they may be resolved without recourse to anything 'epistemically metaphysical'; working on the idea of conceptual analysis, how it is to be done, what kind of knowledge it may provide us with, how to address various worries about it; and working out what forms conceptual work may take (purely descriptive, disentangling, constructive, ameliorative). (And this list is certainly not meant to be exhaustive, merely suggestive.) This, to me at least, is extraordinarily interesting and potentially useful work. And though it counts as 'easy' ontology in the technical sense used here (no epistemically metaphysical work is required), that is not at all to say that it's easy in the sense that it can be done without much thought on an idle Sunday afternoon.

But even where the conceptual work proves difficult, in my view, we will have made great progress if we can shift our attention to these tractable, nonmysterious issues, where we are clear about our goals and methodology, rather than remaining in the quagmire of endless (and perhaps misconceived) debates of neo-Quinean ontology. If we can come to recognize ontology as easy, perhaps we can refocus our efforts more productively.

This project, then, has largely been one of reorientation. Historically, I aimed to reorient the prevailing conception of ontology and its methods, by making it clear that the neo-Quinean approach to existence questions that has become 'mainstream metaphysics' is not inevitable, but rather a historical outlier. Then, I attempted to reorient debates in metaontology away from the exclusive focus on the threat of quantifier variance to also note the distinct challenges the easy approach to ontology presents to much work in mainstream metaphysics. Finally, and on a larger scale, to the extent that I have shown that approach to be tenable and attractive, I might hope to reorient work in metaphysics away from the misguided focus on existence questions and towards issues that may prove more tractable and clear. We might hope thereby not just to make ontology easy, but also to make metaphysics more fruitful.

BIBLIOGRAPHY

Alston, William P. (1957). "Ontological Commitments". *Philosophical Studies* NN: 8–17.

Armstrong, David M. (1978). *Universals and Scientific Realism*. Volume 2. Cambridge: Cambridge University Press.

Armstrong, David M. (1997). *A World of States of Affairs*. Cambridge: Cambridge University Press.

Armstong, David M. (2004). *Truth and Truthmakers*. Cambridge: Cambridge University Press.

Austin, J. L. (1962). *Sense and Sensibilia*. Oxford: Oxford University Press.

Ayer, A. J. (1936/1952). *Language, Truth and Logic*. New York: Dover.

Azzouni, Jody. (2004). *Deflating Existential Consequence*. New York: Oxford University Press.

Baker, Gordon. (1988). *Wittgenstein, Frege and the Vienna Circle*. Oxford: Blackwell.

Barnes, Elizabeth, and Ross Cameron. (2009). "The Open Future: Bivalence, Determinism, and Ontology". *Philosophical Studies* 146 (2): 291–309.

Barnes, Elizabeth, with Robbie Williams. (2011). "A Theory of Metaphysical Indeterminacy". *Oxford Studies in Metaphysics* (6): 103–48.

Beall, J. C. and Greg Restall (2013), "Logical Consequence". *Stanford Encyclopedia of Philosophy*. Ed. Edward N. Zalta. Winter 2013 ed, http://plato.stanford.edu/archives/win2013/entries/logical-consequence/.

Beaney, Michael, ed. (2007). *The Analytic Turn: Analysis in Early Analytic Philosophy and Phenomenology*. London: Routledge.

Benedict, Helen. (1977). "Early Lexical Development: Comprehension and Production". *Journal of Child Language* 6: 183–200.

Bennett, Karen. (2009). "Composition, Colocation, and Metaontology". In David Chalmers, Ryan Wasserman, and David Manley, eds., *Metametaphysics: New Essays on the Foundations of Ontology*. Oxford: Oxford University Press: 38–76.

Bickle, John. (2003). *Philosophy and Neuroscience: A Ruthlessly Reductive Approach*. Dordrecht: Kluwer.

Blackburn, Simon. (1993). *Essays in Quasi-Realism*. New York: Oxford University Press.

Blackburn, Simon. (2005). "Quasi-Realism No Fictionalism". In Mark Eli Kalderon, ed., *Fictionalism in Metaphysics*. Oxford: Clarendon: 322–38.

Boghossian, Paul A. 1989. "The Rule-Following Considerations". *Mind* 98 (392): 507–49.

Boghossian, Paul. 1996. "Analyticity Reconsidered". *Nous* 30 (3): 360–91.

Boghossian, Paul. 1997. "Analyticity". In Bob Hale and Crispin Wright, eds., *A Companion to the Philosophy of Language*. Oxford: Blackwell, 331–68.

Boolos, George. (1990). "The Standard Equality of Numbers." In Boolos, ed., *Meaning and Method: Essays in Honor of Hilary Putnam*. Cambridge: Cambridge University Press, 261–77.

Brandom, Robert. (1994). *Making It Explicit*. Cambridge, MA: Harvard University Press.

Brandom, Robert. (2008). *Between Saying and Doing: Towards an Analytic Pragmatism*. Oxford: Oxford University Press.

Braun, David. (1993). "Empty Names". *Nous* 27 (4): 449–69.

Brentano, Franz. (1874/1995). *Psychology from an Empirical Standpoint*. Ed. Oskar Kraus, trans. Antos C. Rancurello, D. B. Terrel, and Linda L. McAlister. London: Routledge.

Brentano, Franz. (1982/1995). *Descriptive Psychology*. Ed. and trans. Benito Müller. London: Routledge.

Bricker, Phillip. (Forthcoming). "Realism without Parochialism". *Modal Matters: Essays in Metaphysics*. Oxford: Oxford University Press.

Bueno, Otavio. (2005). "Dirac and the Dispensability of Mathematics". *Studies in History and Philosophy of Modern Physics* 36: 465–90.

Button, Tim. (2013). *The Limits of Realism*. Oxford: Oxford University Press.

Cameron, Ross. (2008). "Truthmakers and Ontological Commitment: Or How to Deal with Complex Objects and Mathematical Ontology without Getting into Trouble". *Philosophical Studies* 140 (1): 1–18.

Cameron, Ross. (2010). "Quantification, Naturalness and Ontology". In Allan Hazlett, ed., *New Waves in Metaphysics*. New York: Palgrave Macmillan, 8–26.

Carey, Susan. (2009). *The Origin of Concepts*. Oxford: Oxford University Press.

Carnap, Rudolf. (1937/2002). *The Logical Syntax of Language*. Trans. Amethe Smeaton. Chicago: Open Court.

Carnap, Rudolf. (1947/1956). *Meaning and Necessity: A Study in Semantics and Modal Logic*. 2nd ed. Chicago: University of Chicago Press.

Carnap, Rudolph. (1950/1956). "Empiricism, Semantics, and Ontology". In *Meaning and Necessity*, 2nd ed. Chicago: University of Chicago Press.

Chalmers, David. (2009). "Ontological Anti-Realism". In David Chalmers, Ryan Wasserman, and David Manley, eds., *Metametaphysics: New Essays on the Foundations of Ontology*. Oxford: Oxford University Press, 77–129.

Chalmers, David. (2011). "Revisability and Conceptual Change in Two Dogmas". *Journal of Philosophy* 108 (8): 387–415.

Chalmers, David, Ryan Wasserman, and David Manley, eds. (2009). *Metametaphysics: New Essays on the Foundations of Ontology*. Oxford: Oxford University Press.

Cohen, Ted. (1990). "There Are No Ties at First Base". *Yale Review* 79 (2): 314–22.

Creath, Richard. 2004. "Quine on the Intelligibility and Relevance of Analyticity". In Roger F. Gibson, ed., *The Cambridge Companion to Quine*. Cambridge: Cambridge University Press, 47–64.

Creath, Richard 2009. "The Gentle Strength of Tolerance: How the Logical Syntax of Language Produced a Positive Philosophic Program". In Pierre Wagner, ed., *Carnap and the Logical Syntax of Language*. New York: Palgrave Macmillan, 203–16.

Devitt, Michael, and Kim Sterelny. (1987/1999). *Language and Reality*. 2nd ed. Cambridge, MA: MIT Press.

Dorr, Cian. (2005). "What We Disagree about When We Disagree about Ontology". In Mark Eli Kalderon, ed., *Fictionalism in Metaphysics*. Oxford: Clarendon, 234–86.

Dummett, Michael. 1959. "Wittgenstein's Philosophy of Mathematics". *Philosophical Review* 68 (3): 324–48.

Dummett, Michael. (1976). "What Is a Theory of Meaning (II)". In Gareth Evans and John McDowell, eds., *Truth and Meaning: Essays in Semantics*. Oxford: Clarendon, 67–137.

Dyke, Heather. (2008). *Metaphysics and the Representational Fallacy*. New York: Routledge.

Eklund, Matti. (2009a). "Bad Company and Neo-Fregean Philosophy". *Synthese* 170 (3): 393–414.

Eklund, Matti. (2009b). "Carnap and Ontological Pluralism." In David Chalmers, Ryan Wasserman, and David Manley, eds., *Metametaphysics: New Essays on the Foundations of Ontology*. Oxford: Oxford University Press, 130–56.

Eklund, Matti. (2006a). "Neo-Fregean Ontology". *Philosophical Perspectives* 20: 95–121.

Eklund, Matti. (2006b). "Metaontology". *Philosophy Compass* 1 (3): 317–34.

Elder, Crawford. (1989). "Realism, Naturalism and Culturally Generated Kinds". *Philosophical Quarterly* 39: 425–44.

Elder, Crawford. (2004). *Real Natures and Familiar Objects*. Cambridge, MA: MIT Press.

Evnine, Simon. (Forthcoming). "Much Ado about Something-from-Nothing". In Sandra LaPointe and Stephan Blatti, eds., *Ontology after Carnap*. Oxford: Oxford University Press.

Field, Hartry. (1980). *Science without Numbers*. Princeton, NJ: Princeton University Press.

Field, Hartry. (1984). "Critical Notice of Wright's *Frege's Conception of Numbers as Objects*". *Canadian Journal of Philosophy* 14: 637–62.

Fine, Kit. (2009). "The Question of Ontology". In David Chalmers, Ryan Wasserman, and David Manley, eds., *Metametaphysics: New Essays on the Foundations of Ontology*. Oxford: Oxford University Press, 157–77.

Frege, Gottlob. (1884/1974). *The Foundations of Arithmetic: A Logico-Mathematical Enquiry into the Concept of Number*. Trans. J. L. Austin. 2nd ed. Oxford: Blackwell.

Gabriel, Gottfried. (2007). "Carnap and Frege". In *Cambridge Companion to Carnap*, ed. Michael Friedman and Richard Creath. Cambridge: Cambridge University Press, 65–80.

Gallois, André. (1998). "Does Ontology Rest on a Mistake?". *Aristotelian Society Supplement* 72 (1): 263–83.

Goodman, Nelson, and W. V. O. Quine. (1947). "Steps towards a Constructive Nominalism". *Journal of Symbolic Logic* 12 (4): 105–22.

Grover, Drorothy. (1992). *A Prosententialist Theory of Truth*. Princeton, NJ: Princeton University Press.

Grover, Dorothy, Joseph L. Camp Jr., and Nuel D. Belnap Jr. (1975). "A Prosentential Theory of Truth". *Philosophical Studies* 27: 73–124.

Hacker, P. M. S. (1996). *Wittgenstein's Place in Twentieth-Century Analytic Philosophy*. Oxford: Blackwell.

Hale, Bob. (1988). *Abstract Objects*. Oxford: Blackwell.

Hale, Bob. (2010). "The Bearable Lightness of Being". *Axiomathes* 20: 399–422.

Hale, Bob, and Crispin Wright. (2001). *The Reason's Proper Study: Essays towards a Neo-Fregean Philosophy of Mathematics*. Oxford: Clarendon.

Hale, Bob, and Crispin Wright. (2009). "The Metaontology of Abstraction". In David Chalmers, Ryan Wasserman, and David Manley, eds., *Metametaphysics: New Essays on the Foundations of Ontology*. Oxford: Oxford University Press, 178–212.

Harman, Gilbert. (1999). "The Death of Meaning". In *Reasoning, Meaning and Mind*. Oxford: Clarendon Press, 119–137.

Haslanger, Sally. (2005). "What Are We Talking About? The Semantics and Politics of Social Kinds." *Hypatia* 20 (4): 10–26.

Hawley, Katherine. (2007). "NeoFregeanism and Quantifier Variance". *Proceedings of the Aristotelian Society*, supplementary volume, 81: 233–34.

Hawthorne, John. (2009). "Superficialism in Ontology". In David Chalmers, Ryan Wasserman, and David Manley, eds., *Metametaphysics: New Essays on the Foundations of Ontology*. Oxford: Oxford University Press, 213–30.

Hawthorne, John, and Andrew Cortens. (1995). "Towards Ontological Nihilism". *Philosophical Studies* 79: 143–65.

Heck, Richard. (1992). "On the Consistency of Second-Order Contextual Definitions". *Nous* 26: 491–95.

Heil, John. (2003). *From an Ontological Point of View*. Oxford: Oxford University Press.

Hilpinen, Risto. (1996). "On Some Formulatons of Realism, or How Many Objects Are There in the World?" In R. S. Cohen, Risto Hilpinen, and Qui Renzong, eds., *Realism and Anti-realism in the Philosophy of Science*. Netherlands: Kluwer, 1–10.

Hirsch, Eli. (2002a). "Quantifier Variance and Realism". In Ernest Sosa and Enrique Villanueva, eds., *Realism and Relativism*. Philosophical Issues 12. Oxford: Blackwell, 51–73.

Hirsch, Eli. (2002b). "Against Revisionary Ontology". *Philosophical Topics* 30: 103–27.

Hirsch, Eli. (2007). "Ontological Arguments: Interpretive Charity and Quantifier Variance". In Theodore Sider, John Hawthorne, and Dean W. Zimmerman, eds., *Contemporary Debates in Metaphysics*. Malden, MA: Blackwell, 367–81.

Hirsch, Eli. (2009). "Ontology and Alternative Languages". In David Chalmers, Ryan Wasserman, and David Manley, eds., *Metametaphysics: New Essays on the Foundations of Ontology*. Oxford: Oxford University Press, 231–59.

Hirsch, Eli. (2011). *Quantifier Variance and Realism*. New York: Oxford University Press.

Hirsch, Eli. (Forthcoming). "Three Degrees of Carnapian Tolerance". In Sandra LaPointe and Stephan Blatti, eds., *Ontology after Carnap*. Oxford: Oxford University Press.

Hofweber, Thomas. (2005a). "A Puzzle about Ontology". *Nous* 39 (2): 256–83.

Hofweber, Thomas. (2005b). "Number Determiners, Numbers, and Arithmetic". *Philosophical Review* 114 (2): 179–225.

Hofweber, Thomas. (2006). "Inexpressible Properties and Propositions". In *Oxford Studies in Metaphysics*, vol. 2, ed. Dean W. Zimmerman. Oxford: Oxford University Press, 155–206.

Hofweber, Thomas. (2007). "Innocent Statements and Their Metaphysically Loaded Counterparts". *Philosophers' Imprint* 7 (1): 1–33.

Hofweber, Thomas. (2009). "Ambitious, yet Modest, Metaphysics". In David Chalmers, Ryan Wasserman, and David Manley, eds., *Metametaphysics: New Essays on the Foundations of Ontology*. Oxford: Oxford University Press, 260–89.

Hofweber, Thomas. (Forthcoming). *Ontology and the Ambitions of Metaphysics*.

Horgan, Terence, and Matjaž Potrč. (2000). "Blobjectivism and Indirect Correspondence". *Facta Philosophica* 2: 249–70.

Horwich, Paul. (1998). *Truth*. 2nd ed. New York: Oxford University Press.

Horwich, Paul. (1999). *Meaning*. New York: Oxford University Press.

Horwich, Paul. (2004). *From a Deflationary Point of View*. Oxford: Clarendon.

Horwich, Paul. (2010). *Truth-Meaning-Reality*. Oxford: Clarendon Press.

Hume, David. (1739/1985). *A Treatise of Human Nature*. London: Penguin.

Hume, David. (1777/1977). *An Enquiry Concerning Human Understanding*. Indianapolis: Hackett.

Husserl, Edmund. (1900/2000). *Logical Investigations*. Trans. J. N. Findlay. New York: Humanity Books.

Husserl, Edmund. (1933/1977). *Cartesian Meditations*. Trans. Dorian Cairns. Dordrecht: Kluwer.

Husserl, Edmund. (1970). *The Crisis of the European Sciences*. Trans. David Carr. Evanston, IL: Northwestern University Press.

Husserl, Edmund. (1989). *Ideas Pertaining to a Pure Phenomenology and to a Phenomenological Philosophy: Second Book*. Trans. R. Rojcewicz and A. Schuwer. Dordrecht: Kluwer.

Johnston, Mark. (1988). "The End of the Theory of Meaning". *Mind and Language* 3 (1): 28–63.

Kalderon, Mark Eli. (2005). *Fictionalism in Metaphysics*. Oxford: Clarendon.

Kant, Immanuel. (1785/1981). *Grounding for the Metaphysics of Morals*. Trans. James W. Ellington. Indianapolis: Hackett.

Kaplan, David. (1989b). "Afterthoughts". In J. Almog, J. Perry, and H. Wettstein, eds., *Themes from Kaplan*. New York: Oxford University Press, 565–624.

Kim, Jaegwon. (1993). *Supervenience and Mind*. Cambridge: Cambridge University Press.

Kriegel, Uriah. (2013). "The Epistemological Challenge of Revisionary Metaphysics". *Philosopher's Imprint* 13 (12): 1–30.

Lakoff, George. (1987). *Women, Fire and Dangerous Things*. Chicago: University of Chicago Press.

Lewis, David K. (1983). "New Work for a Theory of Universals". *Australasian Journal of Philosophy* 61: 343–77.

Lewis, David K. (1984). "Putnam's Paradox". *Australasian Journal of Philosophy* 62: 221–36.

Lewis, David K. (1986). *On the Plurality of Worlds*. Oxford: Blackwell.

Lewis, Peter. (2006). "GRW: A Case Study in Quantum Ontology". *Philosophy Compass* 1: 224–44.

Linnebo, Oystein. (2009a). "Introduction". *Synthese* 170 (3): 321–29.

Linnebo, Oystein. (2009b). "Bad Company Tamed". *Synthese* 170 (3): 371–91.

Linnebo, Oystein, ed. (2009c). *The Bad Company Problem*. Special issue of *Synthese* 170 (3).

Lowe, E. J. (1989). *Kinds of Being: A Study of Individuation, Identity and the Logic of Sortal Terms*. Oxford: Blackwell.

Manley, David. (2009). "Introduction: A Guided Tour of Metametaphysics". In David Chalmers, Ryan Wasserman, and David Manley, eds., *Metametaphysics: New Essays on the Foundations of Ontology*. Oxford: Oxford University Press, 1–37.

McFarlane, John. (2000). "What Does It *Mean* to Say That Logic Is Formal?" Ph.D. dissertation, University of Pittsburgh.

McGinn, Colin. (2011). *Truth by Analysis: Names, Games and Philosophy*. Oxford: Oxford University Press.

Merricks, Trenton. (2001). *Objects and Persons*. Oxford: Clarendon.

Miller, Barry. (2002). "Existence". *Stanford Encyclopedia of Philosophy*. Ed. Edward N. Zalta. Fall 2009 ed. http://plato.stanford.edu/archives/fall2009/entries/existence/.

Oddie, Graham. (1982). "Armstrong on the Eleatic Principle and Abstract Entities". *Philosophical Studies* 41: 285–95.

Pettit, Philip. (2002). *Rules, Reasons and Norms*. Oxford: Clarendon.

Price, Huw. (2009). "Metaphysics after Carnap: The Ghost Who Walks?". In David Chalmers, Ryan Wasserman, and David Manley, eds., *Metametaphysics: New Essays on the Foundations of Ontology*. Oxford: Oxford University Press, 320–46.

Price, Huw. (2011). "Expressivism for Two Voices". In J. Knowles and H. Rydenfelt, eds., *Pragmatism, Science and Naturalism*. Zürich: Peter Lang. 87–113.

Price, Huw. (2011). *Naturalism without Mirrors*. Oxford: Oxford University Press.

Putnam, Hilary. (1987). *The Many Faces of Realism*. La Salle, IL: Open Court.

Putnam, Hilary. (1990). *Realism with a Human Face*. Cambridge, MA: Harvard University Press.

Quine, W. V. O. (1935/1976). "Truth by Convention". In *The Ways of Paradox and Other Essays*. Rev. ed. Cambridge, MA: Harvard University Press.

Quine, W. V. O. (1948/1953). "On What There Is". In *From a Logical Point of View*. Cambridge, MA: Harvard University Press.

Quine, W. V. O. (1951/1976). "On Carnap's Views on Ontology". In *The Ways of Paradox and Other Essays*. Rev. ed. Cambridge, MA: Harvard University Press, 203–11.

Quine, W. V. O. (1951/1953). "Two Dogmas of Empiricism". In *From a Logical Point of View*. Cambridge, MA: Harvard University Press.

Quine, W. V. O. (1966/1976). *The Ways of Paradox and Other Essays*. 2nd ed. Cambridge, MA: Harvard University Press.

Quine, W. V. O. (1991). "Two Dogmas in Retrospect". *Canadian Journal of Philosophy* 21: 265–74.

Rayo, Augustin. (2013). *The Construction of Logical Space*. Oxford: Oxford University Press.

Ripley, David. (2013). "Paradox and Failures of Cut". *Australasian Journal of Philosophy* 91 (1): 139–64.

Russell, Gillian. (2008). *Truth in Virtue of Meaning: A Defence of the Analytic/Synthetic Distinction*. Oxford: Oxford University Press.

Ryle, Gilbert. (1949). *The Concept of Mind*. London: Hutchinson.

Ryle, Gilbert. (1950/1971). "'If', 'So', and 'Because'". In *Collected Papers*, vol. 2. London: Hutchison.

Ryle, Gilbert. (1957/1971). "The Theory of Meaning". In *Collected Papers*, vol. 2. London: Hutchison.

Ryle, Gilbert. (1962/1971). "Phenomeology versus the Concept of Mind". In *Collected Papers*, vol. 1. London: Hutchison.

Ryle, Gilbert. (1970). "Autobiographical". In Oscar Wood and George Pitcher, eds., *Ryle*. New York: Doubleday, 1–15.

Schaffer, Jonathan. (2009a). "On What Grounds What". In David Chalmers, Ryan Wasserman, and David Manley, eds., *Metametaphysics: New Essays on the Foundations of Ontology*. Oxford: Oxford University Press, 347–83.

Schaffer, Jonathan. (2009b). "The Deflationary Meta-ontology of Thomasson's *Ordinary Objects*". *Philosophical Books* 50 (3): 142–57.

Schiffer, Stephen. (1994). "A Paradox of Meaning". *Nous* 28: 279–324.

Schiffer, Stephen. (1996). "Language-Created Language-Independent Entities". *Philosophical Topics* 24 (1) 149–67.

Schiffer, Stephen. (2003). *The Things We Mean*. Oxford: Oxford University Press.

Searle, John. (1969). *Speech Acts*. Cambridge: Cambridge University Press.

Searle, John. (1995). *The Construction of Social Reality*. New York: Free Press.

Sidelle, Alan. (2008). Review of Amie L. Thomasson *Ordinary Objects*. *Philosophical Quarterly* 58 (230): 172–76.

Sider, Theodore. (2001). *Four-Dimensionalism*. Oxford: Oxford University Press.

Sider, Theodore. (2007). "Neo-Fregeanism and Quantifier Variance". *Aristotelian Society*, supplementary volume, 81: 201–32.

Sider, Theodore. (2009). "Ontological Realism". In David Chalmers, Ryan Wasserman, and David Manley, eds., *Metametaphysics: New Essays on the Foundations of Ontology*. Oxford: Oxford University Press, 384–423.

Sider, Theodore. (2011). *Writing the Book of the World*. Oxford: Oxford University Press.

Spelke, Elizabeth. (1990). "Principles of Object Perception". *Cognitive Science* 14: 29–36.

Stoljar, Daniel, and Nic Damnjanovic. (2010). "The Deflationary Theory of Truth". *Stanford Encyclopedia of Philosophy*. Ed. Edward N. Zalta. Winter 2010 ed. http://plato.stanford.edu/archives/win2010/entries/truth-deflationary/.

Strawson, P. F. (1949). "Truth". *Analysis* 9: 83–97.

Strawson, P. F. and H. P. Grice. 1956. "In Defense of a Dogma". *Philosophical Review* 65 (2): 141–58.

Thomasson, Amie L. (1999). *Fiction and Metaphysics*. Cambridge: Cambridge University Press.

Thomasson, Amie L. (2001). "Ontological Minimalism". *American Philosophical Quarterly* 38 (4): 319–31.

Thomasson, Amie L. (2002). "Phenomenology and the Development of Analytic Philosophy". *Southern Journal of Philosophy* 40, supplement (Proceedings of the 2001 Spindel Conference "Origins: The Common Sources of the Analytic and Phenomenological Traditions"): 115–42.

Thomasson, Amie L. (2003a). "Foundations for a Social Ontology". *Protosociology* 18–19 (Understanding the Social II: Philosophy of Sociality): 269–90.

Thomasson, Amie L. (2003b). "Speaking of Fictional Characters". *Dialectica* 57 (2): 207–26.

Thomasson, Amie L. (2007a). *Ordinary Objects*. New York: Oxford University Press.

Thomasson, Amie L. (2007b). "Modal Normativism and the Methods of Metaphysics". *Philosophical Topics*, 35 (1–2): 135–60.

Thomasson, Amie L. (2007c). "Conceptual Analysis in Phenomenology and Ordinary Language Philosophy." In Michael Beaney, ed., *The Analytic Turn: Essays in Early Analytic Philosophy and Phenomenology*. London: Routledge, 270–84.

Thomasson, Amie L. (2008). "Existence Questions". *Philosophical Studies* 141: 63–78.

Thomasson, Amie L. (2009a). "Answerable and Unanswerable Questions". In David Chalmers, Ryan Wasserman, and David Manley, eds., *Metametaphysics: New Essays on the Foundations of Ontology*. Oxford: Oxford University Press, 444–71.

Thomasson, Amie L. (2009b). "The Easy Approach to Ontology". *Axiomathes* 19 (1): 1–15.

Thomasson, Amie L. (2010). "Fiction, Existence, and Indeterminacy". In John Woods, ed., *Fictions and Models: New Essays*. Munich: Philosophia Verlag: 109–48.

Thomasson, Amie L. (2012). "Experimental Philosophy and the Methods of Ontology". *Monist* 95 (2): 175–99.

Thomasson, Amie L. (2013a). "2012 Nancy D. Simco Lecture: Norms and Necessity". *Southern Journal of Philosophy* 51 (2): 143–60.

Thomasson, Amie L. (2013b). "The Ontological Significance of Constitution". *Monist* 96 (1): 54–72.

Van Inwagen, Peter. (1990). *Material Beings*. Ithaca, NY: Cornell University Press.

Van Inwagen, Peter. (1998). "Metaontology". *Erkenntnis* 48: 233–50.

Van Inwagen, Peter. (2009). "Being, Existence and Ontological Commitment". In David Chalmers, Ryan Wasserman, and David Manley, eds., *Metametaphysics: New Essays on the Foundations of Ontology*. Oxford: Oxford University Press, 472–506.

Walton, Kendall. (1990). *Mimesis as Make-Believe*. Cambridge, MA: Harvard University Press.

Williamson, Timothy. (2003). "Blind Reasoning". *Aristotelian Society Supplementary Volume* 77 (1): 249–93.

Williamson, Timothy. (2007). *The Philosophy of Philosophy*. Oxford: Blackwell.

Williamson, Timothy. (2011). "Reply to Boghossian". *Philosophy and Phenomenological Research* 82 (2): 498–506.

Wittgenstein, Ludwig. (1922/1933). *Tractatus Logico-Philosophicus*. Trans. C. K. Ogden. London: Routledge.

Wittgenstein, Ludwig. (1953/2001). *Philosophical Investigations*. Trans. G. E. M. Anscombe. 3rd ed. Oxford: Blackwell.

Wittgenstein, Ludwig. 1958. *The Blue and Brown Books*. Oxford: Blackwell.

Wright, Crispin. (1980). *Wittgenstein on the Foundations of Mathematics*. London: Duckworth.

Wright, Crispin. (1983). *Frege's Conception of Numbers as Objects*. Aberdeen: Aberdeen University Press.

Xu, F. (1999). "Object Individuation and Object Identity in Infancy: The Role of Spatiotemporal Information, Object Property Information, and Language". *Acta Psychologica*, special issue, "Visual Object Perception", 102 (2–3): 113–36.

Yablo, Stephen. (1998). "Does Ontology rest on a Mistake?". In *Proceedings of the Aristotelian Society*, supplementary volume 72: 229–61.

Yablo, Stephen. (2000a). "A Paradox of Existence". In Anthony Everett and Thomas Hofweber, eds., *Empty Names, Fiction, and the Puzzles of Non-existence*. Palo Alto: CSLI Publications, 275–312.

Yablo, Stephen. (2000b). "A Priority and Existence". In Paul Boghossian and Christopher Peacocke, eds., *New Essays on the A Priori*. Oxford: Oxford University Press, 197–228.

Yablo, Stephen. (2001). "Go Figure: A Path through Fictionalism". *Midwest Studies in Philosophy* 25: 72–102.

Yablo, Stephen. (2005). "The Myth of the Seven". In Mark Eli Kalderon, ed., *Fictionalism in Metaphysics*. Oxford: Oxford University Press, 88–115.

Yablo, Stephen. (2009). "Must Existence Questions have Answers?" In David Chalmers, Ryan Wasserman, and David Manley, eds., *Metametaphysics: New Essays on the Foundations of Ontology*. Oxford: Oxford University Press, 507–26.

Zalta, Edward N. (2008). "Gottlob Frege". *Stanford Encyclopedia of Philosophy*. Ed. Edward N. Zalta. Spring 2014 ed. http://plato.stanford.edu/archives/spr2014/entries/frege/.

Zalta, Edward N. (2014). "Frege's Theorem and Foundations for Arithmetic". *Stanford Encyclopedia of Philosophy*. Ed. Edward N. Zalta. Summer 2014 ed. forthcoming. http://plato.stanford.edu/archives/sum2014/entries/frege-theorem/.

INDEX